Void and

Without Form

The R's of Creation

by **THE LAYMAN**

 www.trafford.com

North America & international
toll-free: 1 888 232 4444 (USA & Canada)
phone: 250 383 6864 ♦ fax: 812 355 4082

CONTENTS

INTRODUCTION

It is not the purpose of this work to persuade you into changing your beliefs in anything. That may sound rather strange giving all the works now in publication which aver their direct insight into our God's will, but I do not lay claim to such privileges.

I have over the years, read the Old Testament, Flavius Josephus, Arthur W. Pink, J. Vernon McGee, and G. H. Pember's works on Genesis; As well as selected parts of the Bishop's Bible and just about anything else I could find.

With Genesis, there has never been, for me anyway, that fulfilling, answer as to why things just don't seem to fit. To look at Gen 1 without understanding Gen 2, is like trying to understand Revelation without Ezekiel, Daniel, or Jeremiah to fill in the obvious holes.

I hear theologians proclaim the Scriptures as "God Breathed," and with my whole heart, I am saturated with that truth; however, they then try to explain that the first of Genesis is in question as to its translation because it is broken down in such and such a manner. So am I to believe after reading all past brethren, that God started the Genesis Scriptures out in rough draft, then edited it, then gave up and picked up the genealogy of Adam in the fifth chapter when He finally got it right? I am proud to say that my Father does not do this.

I don't know the number of books I have purchased that the author begins explaining each little Scripture detail, only to skip over the very thing I wish to know; he then goes on to something that is a couple of verses beyond, and which is as clear as the morning sun. I find my mind doing the same thing in Scripture. Find something hard to understand, and our mind makes this "buzz" and looks to the next statement hoping to understand it. Even the one who holds the highest respect in my heart, A. W. Pink, who I quote most often, gets up to the fourth day of creation and skips to chapter 2.

In the creation story as presented from pulpits today, I have trouble seeing my God, who is perfect in every aspect, creating something that is nothing but a hunk of junk, and then He sets out to "picture puzzle" it all together. Whether it be the composition of Scripture, created, tangible, physical, adamant or in-adamant, I would have to believe what I will not believe; He is a trial and error God. Stop and think. Here is our God of wisdom who designed the entire universe in all its majesty, complexity, and upon the Lord's confession,

1

(John 14:2); full of many other abiding places and God creates a hunk of junk here. I am sorry, but I cannot swallow that, and there is an audience on both sides of "Jordan" who feel the same.

I have listened to a "radio" pastor who is otherwise very sound in doctrine, give several lectures on Genesis and it was so evident that he did not know what to do with the first chapter in relation to the second chapter, that one wondered why he didn't just shut up and let the choir sing. He went into finite detail about the "Ten, Lets of Creation"(There are fourteen "lets" in the first chapter, ten are creative, and the other four are what I call instructive.): He then proceeds to compare the second chapter, to a parallel of the first, and I have to admit that he sure chased a lot of squirrels. Know something? He also described the Hebrew words for "living creatures," and "creeping things" of Gen: 1, but I waited in vain for him to tell about the dinosaur. He just pretended that the enormous skeletal remains in a large hall of the Smithsonian Institute in Washington D.C. are not really there.

I have heard theologians sing praises on the construction of Genesis, but not one of them tell where the dinosaur was, or when it was created, or when it died out. I mean there were Stegosaurs, Sauropods, Sauroposiedons (at 60 feet tall), Ankylosaurs, Ornithopods, Pachycephalosaurs, Pterosaurus (with a wingspan of 36 feet), Ceratopsians, Mamenchisaurus (with a 36 foot long neck), Tyrannosauruses, Gigantoraptors, Parasaurolophuses, Erketu', Velociraptors, sinosauropteryxes, Tuojiangosauruses, Mononykuses, styracosauruses, Paralititans, Spinosauruses, Afrovenators, Nigersauruses, Majungasauruses, Masiakasuauruses, Leaellysasauras, Carnotauruses, Amargasauruses, Carchadodontosauruses, to name but a few. Think of it, they varied in size from less than an ounce to one of the largest, the Argentinosaurus which stood 70 feet tall, and measured 115 feet in length. This creature weighed as much as 100 tons.

How about what paleontologist calls the bipeds; Are we to say that these creatures are only figments of our imagination, and the bony remains are but a myth? I will concede that perhaps dinosaurs were not the ferocious beast that we are told. Perhaps they were just enormous cows and four footed buzzards which God's Scripture chooses to ignore, and for good reason I might add. Do not leave me now: We must here, address the un-addressable. God made dinosaurs and bipeds that existed, on this earth, where we now live, millions of years ago. We will cover more on this subject later.

There is a fundamental fact:

One: There were God created dinosaurs and bipeds on this earth, or some God created alien used our earth for a burial ground. These early creatures were not the type which would be socially acceptable within the average community. We find bones on every continent on earth. I ask, "Please tell me chapter and verse of the Scripture where I might find them," of course none of us can. I know that God discussed a fire breathing thing with Job. Job seemed to know what He was talking about, but that does not indicate to me that the dinosaur was on earth during that time. I mean God could have discussed these creatures (If in fact this is not a representation of Satan.) with Job at an earlier date.

Two: There was a creature on this earth which paleontologists have tried to call a "The Cave Man." He was a different species, or genetic line. His DNA **was not** that of any other present day creature, he somewhat looked like a man, he walked much the same as man. He was a hunter/gatherer, and scientists say they had a crude family life. Was this a living, breathing, God created being? If this creature was created the same time as Adam, his DNA would show a genetic match; it does not. We will cover this subject later, but suffice to say at this point, this creature was not Homo sapien. I am just saying that even though it has absolutely **nothing** to do with our salvation, I just want to know a little more of my Fathers work and I hope that is what I am presenting to all.

I see fossils of myriad sea life on my ranch (if I can call 25 acres a ranch) in Central Texas, and around the world as I traveled with the Army; some way up upon mountain tops. Are we to suppose that in the one year of the flood they lived, died, and deposited themselves in solid rock to be left in plain sight on top of a mountain in West Texas, and around the world?

I ask myself what time was there between creation, the seventh day when God "Rested", Adam, and the end of the flood? Have we ever stopped and asked ourselves about when it said "God ended his work which he had made; and he rested..." how long did He rest? Don't we think it significant that He told us the fact that He "rested?" Don't we ever stop and ask ourselves these questions? Now precious follower, I am not saying that God rested as we do when we are tired.

3

The Layman

Haven't we all completed certain projects, and just stepped back and enjoyed the results of our labor for a while?

Do we **really** believe that all creation happened in short spans of time; I mean really believe it, or just pass it by, so not to give the impression that we are an evolutionists? I hear preachers pound the podium and scream that a person is an infidel if they believe other than the six days of creation. Well I have to agree to disagree with them, but that still does not answer my first question, does it?

I cringe when I hear someone so intent on debunking evolution that they grope for non existent straws, and make themselves twice the fool-hearted as the evolutionist. I feel we are prone to fall into the same sea of ignorance that evolutionist drown in, when we attempt to gloss over some hard things to understand. There are undisputable facts that creatures have occupied this old earth for, possibly a hundred millions years. Each family group was destroyed in sequence by volcanic activity, ice ages, or meteor activity: only to have **entirely different creatures miraculously appear** who are fully formed with no discernable evidence of their origin.

Here is the wall that we must face: we must either resign within our hearts that our God put them here for a purpose we may never fully understand, or we have to believe in evolution.

The Holy Scriptures must be taken, and absorbed within our very souls. It is the unerring, infallible, God Breathed, Word of God, and I believe it with all my heart. I can not explain His works, but I can marvel in them and search for answers as to why something is, as it is, and that is the thrust of this work.

I was pleasantly delighted when monitoring a class at **Liberty Baptist College** one morning. I would do the professor honor, but could not tell anyone his name if my life was depended upon it, but perhaps, if he should read this, he will allow his soul to smile.

A student asked, "If Christ knew, knows and has the wisdom to fashion the future even before the foundation of the earth, then why did He curse the fig tree outside Jerusalem because it had no fruit?"(Mark 11:13 *And seeing a fig tree afar off having leaves, he came, if haply he might find any thing thereon: and when he came to it, he found nothing but leaves; for the time of figs was not yet.*) (Emphasis is mine)

The professor smiled and said "I honestly don't know:" How utterly refreshing. That man can not even start to imagine the respect he gained from that class of future preacher boys and me as well, when he said that. I was at first amazed that this professor had said that he

4

didn't know, because I had what I thought was a very good explanation. I sure am glad he didn't call on me for my infant (No! I didn't misspell infinite) wisdom that day, because he then continued to give three beautiful possibilities for the Lord's action, and I am ashamed to admit that only one of them fit what I was thinking, at all.

I have attended classes at Georgia Tech., Texas Western University, and while in the service, some classes with the University of Maryland, and I have never heard one professor tell me that they didn't know everything.

I have made a conscious effort in this work, to have everyone understand, one thing, "I do not know everything." When I think there is a hard thing to understand, I have tried to call attention to such. I honor the few who do the same. When we teach Scripture, we should not skip over what we do not understand and proceed several scriptures ahead to what we can live with. We should cover the Scripture and readily admit that we have, or have not been enlightened on such and such, before continuing.

It is most important that we make it perfectly clear to the younger generation, that there were animals, birds, fish and a creature which **resembled** a human being on this earth, millions of years ago, and being that they existed, and are no longer here, one would be most foolish not to know **that God made them and put them here**. We may never understand it all, but that does not mean that it didn't happen. It was ordained by and for His good pleasure and to bring honor to Him. He started saving grace in motion possibly a hundred billion years ago. Every thing in its time, and in its order; known, fully, only by Him.

I do not limit my God, nor do I try to ease Him out of a tight situation. My friend, He just doesn't need us to mess things up any more than we already have. I am totally enthralled over the wisdom which He teaches me, **by what He does not say** in His word. I am not one who romanticizes Scripture to make it go down easier, nor do I make excuses for that which is beyond my infant knowledge, faith and belief. I am so embarrassed to hear a "preacher" rejoice over the fact that science has found something "which proves the Bible correct." If anyone feels that way, perhaps they should not read this work. Precious Christian, the Scriptures are correct, and **they verify** that what science has finally stubbed their toe upon is, to that point, correct.

5

The Layman

As human, we first try to bring God down to our own level which is incomprehensible. Somehow, we then feel that we can obtain sufficient perfection to elevate ourselves up to His level, which is even more incomprehensible. Having failed to do either we try to misinterpret scripture to fit our lives or even worse, we find excuses for why we have failed, and it is never our fault, but most assuredly, must be His.

It is only when we fully acknowledge that He is sovereign, but became man, unmovable in perfection, but forgiving my imperfection, and totally unreachable, save through the blood of His Son, my Savior, who He allowed to be sacrificed: it is only then, that we can even start to realize there are two standards; One is His, the other is the one He places upon His creation. We should not try to put ourselves where we cannot stand.

I say this in humility, now do not misunderstand me here, we have a Holy God; however, one of His facets is pride, in that everything is made by Him, for Him, and for His honor and pleasure. Pride brought Lucifer crashing down and can easily bring us down to the pit as well, but pride is a shining star in His crown. We must realize that Christ died to first bring honor to God the Father, and secondly to bring salvation to us; we need not forget that. We are to bring honor to Christ which in turn brings honor to our Father. Everything in this universe is to be pointed directly toward Him for His honor and glory.

That is the way a King is.

I sometimes get so jealous of that, but now,

I just think He is so great.

There is a God we want
and then there is a God who is
but, They are not the same.

BEFORE TIME

"In the beginning God:"

What a monumental introduction to His Word. How could any work start with more power, grace, or authority than those four words? It is God's stamp of approval to the entire Scriptures. His Word starts with "In the beginning God" and ends with, our Lord's "Surely I come quickly. Amen."

Sandwiched between those two all encompassing statements lay the hope or doom of all creation.

Gen 1:1 ¶In the beginning:

In the beginning; what beginning one might ask? The one which is signified by "The", of course: it was that beginning. God does not say "At" the beginning for that would place a significant time upon it. God does not state "During" the beginning for that would just not do. A beginning is a beginning and it either starts or it doesn't, but for some reason, He doesn't want to put quite a handle upon it: Know why? It is because; God could not explain this beginning. "Whoa!" one would say. "God can do everything." Well He couldn't here brethren for the simple reason He would have to explain it to us and that would be impossible because "time" has not yet been created. Try to explain when something happened and don't use time. We cannot hold a decent conversation without relating to time. If I were to tell someone to try it! I would have already put a time on it by implying as of yet they had not, and that they should now, or in the future do so. See we cannot even explain what it isn't, without getting confusing. We anchor our lives on a base of time.

The beginning that we now approach is not our Lord God's beginning; of course we know that was first in sequence, but we are now address the beginning of our little spot in space, time and continuum.

THE SEQUENCE BEFORE TIME

Sequence one:

God is timeless and even though we age, He does not, for He is the same today, as yesterday, and the same tomorrow. But even a beginning has a beginning. Re 3:14 *"And unto the angel of the church of the Laodiceans write; These things saith the* **Amen**, *the faithful and true witness,* **the beginning of the creation of God**;*"* (Emphasis is mine) Well how about that? There was a "Whatever" at Gen 1:1, but we cannot say it was a time, we cannot say it was even before; we can say it was **first in sequence**. Sequence is order of events, and is not time, but it borders within our minds a vagueness of time. To even say "When" signifies a time. I delight in the wisdom of our God. I do not know of any other way to start Genesis than the way He does. Anyway; the **Amen** was the first thing in sequence that God created, no matter, when. "Whoa! Christ is eternal," one would rightly say. "True! However, if Christ was created in eternity, He **is** eternal at that point, and in eternity there is no beginning or end, for in eternity, there is no time; therefore, He is and has always been eternal."

Wait there's more of this sequence. How about? Col 1:15 *"Who is the image of the invisible God,* **the firstborn of every creature**: *16. For* **by him were all things created**, *that are in heaven, and that are in earth, visible and invisible, whether they be thrones, or dominions, or principalities, or powers:"*

And again Joh 17:5 *"And now, O Father, glorify thou me with thine own self with the glory which I had with thee* **before the world was**.*"*(Emphasis is mine) This had to be *"In the beginning God created heaven..........***Then**....*"* *the earth.*

It is important that we observe scripture, for that is what our whole discussion is about, and here is another one of reflective support; In the book of Hebrews we have, Heb 1:1 *" God, who at sundry times and in divers manners spake in time past unto the fathers by the prophets,* Heb 1:2 *Hath in these last days spoken unto us by his Son, whom he hath appointed heir of all things, by whom also he made the worlds;"* (Emphasis is mine) Now remember the explanation, "**made the worlds**." We will develop this statement a little later. (Emphasis on the above are mine)

Sequence two:

Job 38:7 "When the **morning stars** *sang together, and* **all the sons of God** *shouted for joy."* This speaks of the heaven and the world at Gen 1:1, *"When the morning stars sang together."* There was a time when

8

morning stars sang together. One was, I feel, the Lord, and I feel one was Lucifer. Now I know no one has ever taught this; however let's look at Scripture and I feel we can be justified in this assumption. Scripture defines star, as used here;

First:
Concerning our Lord:
    1. 2 Peter 1:19 *We have also a more sure word of prophecy; whereunto ye do well that ye take heed, as unto a light that shineth in a dark place, until the day dawn, and* **the day star** *arise in your hearts:*
    2. Revelation 2:28 *And I will give him the* **morning star.**
    3. Revelation 22:16 *I Jesus have sent mine angel to testify unto you these things in the churches. I am the root and the offspring of David, and the bright and* **morning star.**
    4. 2Pe 1:19 *"We have also a more sure word of prophecy; whereunto ye do well that ye take heed, as unto a light that shineth in a dark place, until the day dawn, and* **the day star** *arise in your hearts:"*
    5. One final Scripture I will give: Nu 24:17 *"I shall see him, but not now: I shall behold him, but not nigh: there shall come a* **Star out of Jacob,** *and a Sceptre shall rise out of Israel, and shall smite the corners of Moab, and destroy all the children of Sheth."* (Emphasis in the above is mine)

"The Bright and Morning Star" is with the Father, and will remain forever. It is to Him that all authority will finally be placed. It is to Him that the Father will fashion that which follows.

Second:
Concerning Satan:
    1. Isaiah 14:12 *How art thou fallen from heaven, O Lucifer,* **son of the morning***! how art thou cut down to the ground, which didst weaken the nations!*
    James-Faucet-Brown commentary says this about Isaiah 14:12 *"The Jews address him as a* **fallen, once—bright star."**
    I understand "**son of the morning**" is also translated the same as **morning star**. I too, would have used the separate meaning when writing the text. The truth is we find a duality throughout Scripture; our Lord/Lucifer, Adam/Woman, Able/Cain, Isaac/Essau to name but a few. We have two bright stars here in the heavenlies, but one begins to dim. As Cain rebelled, so did Lucifer and was no longer called Lucifer outside of this one verse. Elsewhere he is known as

Satan, serpent, murderer, liar, Beelzebub, devil and that old dragon. Perfection still reigns, Lucifer is expelled, and is no longer in the choir.

2. Re 8:10-*11 And the third angel sounded, and there fell **a great star** from heaven, burning as it were a lamp, and it fell upon the third part of the rivers, and upon the fountains of waters; And **the name of the star** is called Wormwood: and the third part of the waters became wormwood; and many men died of the waters, because they were made bitter.*

3. Re 9:1 *And the fifth angel sounded, and I saw a **star fall from heaven** unto the earth: and to him was given **the key of the bottomless pit.*** (Again emphases in the above Scriptures are mine.)

I have no proof that Lucifer was one of the Morning stars. From what is given and knowing that he was one of the most beautiful creations in heaven, I honestly feel that as there is up, down, left, right, positive, negative, good and evil. Our Lord was and will always be the good. I feel that Lucifer was the opposite, and represents the evil opposite of our Lord. I will have to leave it there, study the Scriptures given and come to your own understanding.

I will point out that the only two deities that I can find in Scripture who are addressed in this manner are our Lord and when speaking of Lucifer, in Isaiah, and later as Satan he is noted as a star in Revelation. 8:10, 11 and Revelation 9:1

A star of God, in Scripture holds a few meanings. One is that it defines a prince, another is found in Revelation 1:20 where it is given as "The **seven stars** are the angels of the seven churches." Though there are other meanings, another means a fiery orb we call a star. I invite everyone to see the different meanings elsewhere in Scripture, but it is never used the same as we discussed here.

Now for the rest:

"The sons of God shouted for joy." These are the angels of heaven. How many? I cannot tell. I do know that from this point on there will be fewer voices "shouting for joy" with each sequence of events. There will of course, remain the faithful to the LORD God, but there will be a number which Scripture only allude to: Legion, upwards of from three to six thousand to fill one man, there are those who will invade earth and procreate with mankind, and be bound in chains of darkness forever.

Re 12:4 tells us of one third of the stars of heaven having being drawn to Satan. Then we have the number of angels as recorded in Dan 7:10 and Rev 5:11 "*...the number of them was ten thousand times ten thousand, and thousands of thousands;*" both represent to me an innumerable count. We must understand that the fallen were 1/3 of an innumerable number, and would, therefore also be innumerable.

When were the angels created?

There is one more event which we need to explore: <u>when were the angels created</u>? Scripture does not define an exact moment; however, if one feels that the world<u>s</u> were both created in seven days, then it is anyone's guess. If, however, we take the world<u>s</u> as separate creative/restored events it is quite clear that the angels were created before or at the beginning of the first world when Scripture says, *"God created **heaven** and (Then) the **earth.***

Now consider; the angels are noted as "<u>the sons of God</u>," and in Job, it is told us that they were joyously shouting. Job 38:7 *"When the morning stars sang together, and **all** the sons of God shouted for joy?"* We should take this to mean before the fall of Lucifer, because it says "**all**", not most of, the sons of God. Later, there will be fewer and this could not then be said.

If this is the all inclusive "7 day creation" may I kindly say I do not know what the sons of God had to cheer about when looking at a hunk of junk, "Void and Without Form earth."

However, if this is the first, original creation, with the earth pristine in presentation, covered with foliage beyond description, and created life in perfect order, then, I can see shouts of victorious joy.

I will emphasize this time and again, if the reader is locked in on a 24/7 re-creative act, none of this makes logical sense, and it might be best to omit the first chapter of Genesis altogether because **there will never be harmony between Gen 1 and Gen 2**. To delete the first chapter would be to state that the Father didn't say what He meant: **precious we know better.**

For some reason, almost as if hypnotized, Christian scholars are blindly affixed on a 24-7 hour day of creation, and totally, as if mentally blind to a prior world that certainly **did** exist. We know it is not spelled out in scripture; however, if one remembers all the Bipeds, dinosaurs, ice ages, meteor destructions and volcanic destruction, how can some of us as born again Christians, in our minds deny it all existed: Yet some enjoy visiting museums and <u>view the very thing</u> which is denied. It is as if we have a planet in duality, the scientist has one, and we are comfortable with ours. Are we both become as a Pharisee in our understanding?

11

The Layman

The argument will arise, "My God can do anything." My answer is "Why should He?" He established His natural laws in eternity. Why would He not observe them in action no matter the span it took? Our Father is bound by His established laws and statues. He will not break them with the exception that for a time, or moment to advance our faith, and/or the advancement of the Kingdom, as it is necessary. By that statement may I inject; the flood, Jonah, parting of the sea, fiery furnace, the 10° movement of the sun, our Lord healing the sick, and raising the dead to name but a few.

When one feels this is wrong, let me describe a picture I have that haunts me. There is a small dying black child, crouched on the ground with a hungry vulture standing behind it. Its little legs look as if it has been sitting there, crying for help. Fever and the scorching sun has caused it to wilt forward, but rising up on one elbow it cries fruitlessly for mothers help.

We think this is heartless of the city to abandon this little thing to eventual death; however, we do not understand that they have no medicines to cure this child's communicable disease, which would most probably cause havoc with them all.

Why does God not heal this sick little innocent thing, no one would know but Him? Why? Because He told us the penalties of sin, and this is only another example of what it brings.

Two famous astronomers presented separate findings to the scientific world, proving that the world was not the center of the universe. Both were openly chided by the "church" and at the risk of imprisonment, each recanted their findings.

Today we face exactly the same obscured thinking as that "church", no, it has long been shown that our galaxy is only a small part of a universe and we along with our galaxy are but a speck on its outer extremity. However, **we are faced with clergy that cannot explain Gen 1: when comparing it to Gen 2:** so they dogmatically hop, skip and omit most of it, and charge, if one will excuse the expression, blindly ahead leaving both themselves and the congregation in bewilderment and wonder, when absolutely no one denies the pre-existence of what they see in museums or what they observe frozen in time, in the rocks that many find in their back yard.

On the other hand, we have scientist that do not have a clue as to how anything was created, who dogmatically cling to the antiquated theory of evolution when there has never been, nor will there ever be one shred of evidence to even make a caricature in its support.

Well back to the subject:

If the angelic realm was not created at the first of Gen 1: I cannot explain when, and I am convinced no one else can either.

HEAVENLY BEINGS:

0. **The Alpha and Omega**. Re 1:8 *"I am Alpha and Omega, the beginning and the ending, saith the Lord, which is, and which was, and which is to come,* **the Almighty.***"*

1. The **Amen** is created. Re 3:14 *"And unto the angel of the church of the Laodiceans write; These things saith the Amen, the faithful and true witness,* **the beginning of the creation of God;***"* Again we have, Col. 1:16 *"For* **by him were all things created***, that are in heaven, and that are in earth,* **visible** *and* **invisible***, whether they be* **thrones***, or* **dominions***, or* **principalities***, or* **powers***:"*(Emphasis is mine) We have the <u>Architect</u> who is **God the Father**, and the <u>Builder</u> who is **God the Son**, and in a few lines we will have the whole of the <u>Trinity</u> in **God the Spirit** as it moves upon the waters.

2. The **Archangels** (as I am led to believe) **Michael, and Gabriel** who are the chief princes of the Angels; However, it is Michael who is Israel's Prince, and it seems Gabriel has more to do with the ushering in of the Messiah. Good news bad news: If Michael shows up, one should watch out; however, if Gabriel shows up, it seems always to hold good tidings.

3. What we fail to realize it that Michael has angels assigned to him; **Revelation 12:7** *"And there was war in heaven: Michael and his angels fought against the dragon; and the dragon fought and his angels,"*

4. Then so too does Gabriel have a host assigned to him: **Luke 2:13** **"***And suddenly there was with the angel a multitude of the heavenly host praising God, and saying,"*

5. There is also:

Mt 13:41 *"The <u>Son of man</u> shall send forth <u>his angels</u>,"*

Mt 18:10 *"Take heed that ye despise not one of these <u>little ones</u>; for I say unto you, That in heaven <u>their angels</u> do always behold the face of my Father which is in heaven."*

Mt 25:31 *"When the Son of man shall come in his glory, and <u>all the holy angels with him</u>,"*

6. Mt 26:53 *"Thinkest thou that I cannot now pray to my Father, and he shall presently give me more than twelve legions of angels?* (Emphasis is mine)

As we noted before the Legion varied in size, but was from three thousand to six thousand, plus many charioteers and the like. That means our Lord was saying that He could call more than 36,000 to 72,000 angels if He were mindful to do so.

Heb 13:2 *"Be not forgetful to entertain strangers: for thereby some have entertained angels unawares."*(Emphasis is mine)

7. The **Angels which stayed loyal to God**. In Revelation it describes, Re 5:11 *"And I beheld, and I heard the voice of many angels round about the throne and the beasts and the elders: and the number of them was ten thousand times ten thousand, and thousands of thousands;"* this is really signifying a number beyond our imagination, because our Lord has already said He could call a legion, of 72,000 not the whole army.

8 Then **Lucifer** his self, Isa 14:12 *"How art thou fallen from heaven, O Lucifer, son of the morning! how art thou cut down to the ground, which didst weaken the nations!"*

I want to call attention, that there is not a (?) at the end of either statement? It rather seems a statement to him, I would think.

9. In Daniel we read of the **Angels who fell with Lucifer**. Of the Prince of Persia, the Prince of Grecia, we read, Da 10:12 *"Then said he unto me, Fear not, Daniel: for from the first day that thou didst set thine heart to understand, and to chasten thyself before thy God, thy words were heard, and I am come for thy words.* Da 10:13 *But the prince of the kingdom of Persia withstood me one and twenty days: but, lo, Michael, one of the chief princes, came to help me; and I remained there with the kings of Persia."* Da 10:20 *"Then said he, Knowest thou wherefore I come unto thee? and now will I return to fight with the prince of Persia: and when I am gone forth, lo, the prince of Grecia shall come."*

How about the Legion? Mr 5:9 *"And he asked him, What is thy name? And he answered, saying, My name is Legion: for we are many."* If Lucifer can spare up to 6,000 to possess one man, think of just how many he has. Also, Jude 1:6 *"And the angels which kept not their first estate, but left their own habitation, he hath reserved in everlasting chains under darkness unto the judgment of the great day."*

10. His Books: I do not know exactly when, but I know sometime before the world began, there were at least three books created.

In one book was written every name, in, and under heaven. It is the book of life. How do we know this existed? Read, Eph 1:4 *"According as **he hath chosen us in him before the***

14

foundation of the world, *that we should be holy and without blame before him in love:"* (Emphasis is mine) OK! But that just shows that He foreknew some, but not that everyone is in that book of life. Look at:

Re 17:8 *"The beast that thou sawest was, and is not; and shall ascend out of the bottomless pit, and go into perdition: and they that dwell on the earth shall wonder, whose names were not written in* **the book of life from the foundation of the world***, when they behold the beast that was, and is not, and yet is."*

Re 3:5 *"He that over cometh, the same shall be clothed in white raiment;* and **I will not blot out his name out of the book of life***, but I will confess his name before my Father, and before his angels."* To be blotted out, it had to be put in at some time.

One other passage in which the LORD tells us sinners are in that book until they are blotted out Ex 32:31 *"And Moses returned unto the LORD, and said, Oh, this people have sinned a great sin, and have made them gods of gold. 32. Yet now, if thou wilt forgive their sin--; and if not, <u>blot me, I pray thee, out of thy book</u>* **which thou hast written***. 33 And the LORD said unto Moses,* **Whosoever hath sinned against me,** <u>*him will I blot out of*</u> <u>**my book**</u>*."*(Emphasis is mine*)*.

Since the LORD is perfect, and will not make mistakes, He would not have anyone in Hell say, "I was scheduled for Heaven, but someone forgot to put my name in that book." My friend, that book contains every name of every being which ever existed in time past, present, and time future, into eternity. When one fails to accept the "free gift," **they blot their own name out**, so to speak, at their last defiant breath.

The book of works that have been done, let's look at: **Re** 20:12 *"And I saw the dead, small and great, stand before God; and the books were opened: and another book was opened, which is the book of life: and the dead were judged out of those things which were written in the books, according to their works."*

Re 20:13 *"And the sea gave up the dead which were in it; and death and hell delivered up the dead which were in them: and they were judged every man according to their works."* They will be rewarded for all their deeds, good or otherwise. **Re** 22:12 *"And, behold, I come quickly; and my reward is with me, to give every man* **according as his work** *shall be."* We will see all the opportunities missed, and all the good works accomplished.

The book of every idle word; Mat 12:36 **"***But I say unto you, That every idle word that men shall speak, they shall give account thereof in the day of judgment."*

The Layman

I do not think we have even approached the magnitude of the creative acts of my God at this point. Perhaps, someday, He will allow me to take joy in seeing these myriad of events. Keep in mind, we haven't even begun.

Sequence three:

I could only venture a guess as to when there was the first division of the heavenly posers. I am led t

not find that event in Genesis, but **I do find** his influence over the serpent <u>already</u> in the garden.

It is well noted that in Isaiah 14:12 Isaiah is speaking about the king of Babylon, however; it is a direct parallel to the true and mirrored image of Lucifer who he is using as an example. He describes why Lucifer fell, and comparing it to the king. Scriptures like this are what I call "Dualities;" That is, part of it applies here and another part applies at another time. It explains Lucifer's fall, and is used here to reinforce the destruction of the Babylonian king due to his character in similarity.

Sequence four:

I think this sequence starts at Genesis 1:1, and carries all the way through Scripture until the Lord, in Re 10:6 states *"...that there should be time no longer:"* We now have a war that is beyond our feeble minds to comprehend.

Paul stated Eph 6:12 *"For we wrestle not against flesh and blood, but against principalities, against powers, against the rulers of the darkness of this world, against spiritual wickedness in high places."*

Paul stated that, 2Co 10:3 *"For though we walk in the flesh, we do not war after the flesh:"*
2Co 10:4 *"(For the weapons of our warfare are not carnal, but mighty through God to the pulling down of strong holds;)"*

Peter warned, 1Pe 5:8 *"Be sober, be vigilant; because your adversary the devil, as a roaring lion, walketh about, seeking whom he may devour:"*

In warfare, Elisha brings the battle to reality when his servant was frightened when seeing the opposing force, but Elisha knew: 2Ki 6:16 *"And he answered, Fear not: for they that be with us are more than they that be with them.* Then, 2Ki 6:17 *And Elisha prayed, and said, LORD, I pray thee, open his eyes, that he may see. And the LORD opened the eyes of the young man; and he saw: and, behold, the mountain was full of horses and chariots of fire round about Elisha. "*

Further warfare is in Jg 5:20 *"They fought from heaven; the stars in their courses fought against Sisera."*

I am convinced that if we saw the forces, both good and evil, which surround us daily, it would completely overpower our human mind to the point that we would be as babbling idiots.

I am always amazed at the world romanticizing Scripture. Has the world ever depicted an angle that wasn't a woman with long lustrous hair flowing over her shoulders, or a cute little girl with Shirley Temple curly hair, rosy cheeks and tiny little wings? Friend we need to stop romanticizing God's words. I promise one thing, neither Gabriel nor Michael **is ever seen as women or cute little girls**, no reflection on the ladies, but these are God's angelic **men of war**. I don't know why the world has to romanticize everything.

THE THEN WORLD:

The first world was destroyed (I add that in my opinion) either by God's Divine Judgment, or Lucifer's hate. One has to remember that no matter which way it went, God is never taken by surprise, and **nothing happens without His action and/or approval**. I must inject this; if we do not believe that there was a world before Gen 1:2, then we are again faced with the problem of a perfect God making perfect junk.

Do the same opposing forces influence us today? Well I ask one to examine the religions of the world. If they have the time and are interested, there are several good references with which one can gain insight into the following subjects:

Hinduism with man **saving himself** by perfecting through repeated reincarnations.

Confucianism is a system of **man's morality**, and having no aspect of God.

Buddhism is the outgrowth of Gautama Buddha (563-483 BC) when he concluded that the cause of suffering is a craving due to ignorance, and proclaimed a way for this removal through **mental discipline and right living.**

Taoism founded traditionally, by Laotse in the sixth century B.C., **is folk-faith** of the Chinese. Taoism features a multiplicity of gods, occultism, and superstitions, including geomancy, fortune-telling, divination, magic, and the use of charms.

Shintoism (Spiritual Way) The soul of the sun god when he was on earth, supposedly founded the reigning house of the Japanese emperor, and then the Japanese emperor was worshipped as divine, well until the end of World War II. Now it has gone to ancestral **veneration and sacrifice to departed heroes.**

Islam is a religion established by the "prophet" Mohammed (A.D. 570?-632). Mohammedans believe in God, but reduce Christ to a good teacher somewhat lower in importance to Mohammed himself. Islam means **"Submission, Surrender"**, but even this, after the World Trade Center disaster seems only a demonic delusion. It rejects the

Person and redemptive work of Christ. They have a fanatical movement today, as one of the "Christian" religions did in the past, in that these fanatics demand obedience or, to put it bluntly, "you believe what we believe or you will taste the sword," or as other "religions" have done, to be tortured and burnt at the stake.

Judaism must be sadly included in this group. Scripture clearly states that one must believe that Christ is the son of God or we are to reject it as false. The Jews believe in the same God as Christians.(When in this work I use the term Christians, I am using it as those who are "Christ like" sinners saved by grace and not as the Roman Catholic's have tried to coin the thought for themselves.) The Jew does not believe that Christ was more than a great prophet, teacher, and moral leader of His day. Sadly for them, Jesus said Joh 14:6 *"Jesus saith unto him, I am the* **way,** *the* **truth,** *and the* **life:** ***no man cometh unto the Father, but by me."***

Catholicism is truly **an amalgamation of both pagan and Christianity.** One can find the Mother/Child dating back to Ezra where we learn, Eze 8:14 *"Then he brought me to the door of the gate of the LORD'S house which was toward the north; and, behold, there sat women weeping for Tammuz."* Tammuz's mother, Simerous, was supposedly born in a miraculous way by sun rays sent from the sun god. Tammuz was supposedly immaculately conceived because Simerous, according to legend, was impregnated by Nimrod. So it was declared that Tammuz was immaculately conceived.

When Tammuz became a man, he was killed by a wild boar, and his death was mourned by the women for 40 days (Lent) after which he was miraculously resurrected.

I want to caveat the above by saying there are so many interpretations of those two that it is, for me, an impossibility to exactly pin down which is correct. The above is repeated the most and is presented.

Hyslop, in his book, The **Two Babylons** has this to say of the mother and child. *"In Papal Italy, as travelers universally admit (except where the Gospel has recently entered), all appearance of worshipping the King Eternal and Invisible is almost extinct, while the Mother and the Child are the grand objects of worship."* He continues: *"From Babylon, this worship to the Mother spread to the ends of the earth. In Egypt the Mother and Child are worshipped under the names of Isis and Osiris. In India, even to this day, as Isi and Iswara; in Asia as Cyybele and Deoius; in Pagan Rome as Fortuna and Jupiter; in Greece as Ceres... or Irene, the goddess of peace and the boy Plutus in her arms; even in Itbet,* *in China, and Japan, the Jesuit missionaries were astonished to fine the counterpart of Madonna and her child as devoutly worshipped as Papal Rome itself"*

There are five references to the queen of heaven. Jeremiah 7:18, 44:17, 18, And 19, And 25: I use only one.

Jer 44:25 *"Thus saith the LORD of hosts, the God of Israel, saying; Ye and your wives have both spoken with your mouths, and fulfilled with your hand, saying, We will surely perform our vows that we have vowed, to burn incense **to the queen of heaven**, and to pour out drink offerings unto her: ye will surely accomplish your vows, and surely perform your vows."*

Jer 44:26 *"**Therefore hear ye the word of the LORD, all Judah that dwell in the land of Egypt; Behold, I have sworn by my great name, saith the LORD, that my name shall no more be named in the mouth of any man of Judah in all the land of Egypt, saying, The Lord GOD liveth.**"*(Emphasis is mine)

The "Holy War" where Dr. Jeremiah says, "50 million Saints of the LORD, were killed in the name of Christ." I cannot understand where any organization can claim to have the power of "Excommunicating" which supposes to put nonconformists out of the "church" and if remaining there they are doomed to a Devil's Hell. I do not know who could think, or even consider that Jehovah God would give His Christ to die on the cross and then turn the decision in the judgment of souls over to just any cranky, got up on the wrong side of the bed, mortal man?

I am <u>not</u> Catholic bashing, and don't think I am. I know there are good men of the "cloth" who really do not follow any but Jesus. I have good friends in the Roman Catholic Church who are far better Christians than I will ever be. They do not pray to a woman and baby for help and forgiveness. They do not believe that the pope or any man wearing a long skirt and white collar resembling Darth Vader© has anything whatsoever to do with the salvation of their souls. In fact most of them cannot say why they attend a meeting at all.

If further study need be made on the subject, one would be wise in obtaining "**Demons in the World Today**- Merrill F. Unger; Tyndale Publishing." I always recommend "**Fox's Book of Martyrs**" to see where a religion can sink when relying upon man's judgments. There is "**Fifty Years in the Church of Rome**, by Father Chiniquy, Baker Publishing, for those who would see the legalistic side of such, from a former Roman Catholic priest. One of the most condemning, fact filled works I have ever read and as excerpts from the same has already been used, of this Popish system is "**The Two Babylon's,**" by Rev. Alexander Hislop, Published by Loizeaux Brothers. This work has 260 original sources of facts in its support of Catholicism amalgamating paganism into its church cannons.

Don't get me wrong, I pray for brethren within this organization. I truly feel that the Roman Catholic Clergy are very wrong and scripturally unsound. I am not their judge that is not my call. I take care of the one I see in the mirror and try to help those I see from my window; however, our brethren must always remember, Joh 14:6 "Jesus saith unto him, **I** am the **way**, the **truth**, and the **life: no man cometh unto the Father, but by me.**" Heb 7:25 "*Wherefore **he** (Jesus)is able also to **save** them (you and me) to the uttermost that **come unto God** (Our Father) by **him**(Jesus), seeing **he** (Jesus)ever liveth to **make intercession**(forgiveness)for them(you and me).*" (Emphasis is mine) That is pretty clear…

Look at **Baptist today;** where are they headed when they start injecting, rejecting, and misinterpreting the Bible to be "Politically Correct."

Here in Central Texas, I was discussing a scripture with a college professor in the church I was attending when the "liberal" pastor approached. I made a statement of such to the professor and the pastor interjected, "I like to think myself as a moderate." I laughed and asked him to define "moderate." Surprisingly enough, after interjecting a number of flowery statements, he couldn't, other than that moderates went along with the crowd. I told him that I was a fundamentalist, and as far as I was concerned there were fundamentalist, and liberals. I told him that it was easy to define a fundamentalist, he was one that believes the Bible from cover to cover, as written and disclosed by the Holy Ghost, and liberals interpret Scripture to suit the way they or their congregations are living. He again protests that moderates were really not either, but held mutual ground.

I thought later that I should have brought my military sword to Church. I would have the professor to hold one end, I would hold the other and we would let him straddle it; whatever remained on the edge of the sword after we raised it above our heads, I would consider a moderate. I would then quoted, Heb 4:12 "*For the **word of God** is quick, and powerful, and sharper than any two-edged sword, piercing even to the dividing asunder of soul and spirit, and of the joints and marrow, and is a discerner of the thoughts and intents of the heart.*"

Today, because of "Political Correctness" the Baptist, along with several other "Faith's" allow women as pastors when Scripture says 1 Cor 13:45 "***It is a shame for a woman to speak in the Church***"(Emphasis is mine) I know that will cause some to recoil; however, I am telling what the Bible says. Should some precious ones be offended, talk to the one who gave us the Scriptures: I am only quoting them.

Genesis 3:16 "*....and thy desire shall be to thy husband, and he shall rule over thee.*" When was the last time, during a Baptist wedding ceremony that we have heard the bride say "I do" when asked the part about "**love, honor and obey**"?

Scripture tells us in 2 Timothy that 2Ti 4:3 *"For the time will come when **they will not endure sound doctrine**; but after their own lusts shall they heap to themselves **teachers**, having itching ears; 2Ti 4:4 And **they shall turn away their ears from the truth, and shall be turned unto fables.**"* (Emphasis is mine). There is an old "saw" quoted about sin which says: "***First is to hate; then tolerate, and then embrace.***"

Then: Sodom and Gomorrah were both destroyed because of homosexuality. Now: "churches" allow the same to pastor its flock.

Today: few Ministers of any denomination will dare preach the demands of the Scriptures for fear of loosing their position. Sad as it is, money, power, recognition and prestige have all replaced "Hell-Fire-and-Brimstone" awareness. They tell of gallant conquest of the patriarchs, fire of the furnace, or of the faith of others with no challenge today for standing for the faith of those before us. Look at our Nation as an example of complacency. Isn't that the reason the Pharisee's rejected our Lord, was it not for fear of loosing their prestigious position?

Other religions in general: Neither time, nor printed space would allow covering the different Protestant beliefs. They cover the gauntlet of understanding. Are each sincere in their following? I pray so, but that in itself does not excuse any of us from searching the "Holy Script" for the real truth for ourselves.

There is not one "religion" today that Satan hasn't shoehorned the world into, nor can one easily be found, which truly stands upon the Holy Bible as the Infallible, Unerring Word of God. If there is such a one, it will be chided by all others as "radicals, and fundamentalist." Someone somewhere will start quoting what they know of Greek or the Hebrew languages to impress everyone that they know more than the men of old.

It is interesting that in the news that they are calling the Taliban movement of "Osama Bin Laden", **a fundamentalist** movement of Muslims? It is sometimes very hard not believe that some people really came from monkeys, but <u>I wouldn't tell a good monkey that if he could reach them.</u>

Should one think I am a little harsh by saying we are losing our fundamentalism, I would bring this to everyone's attention; during the news the other night, it was quoted that some Roman Catholic priest averred that we should start calling God, Allah so as not to offend the Muslims.

Allow me to tell that fellow something. As far as I am concerned, Allah is not my God, and if Muslims want to learn of my God I will be glad to teach them, when they stop calling Allah, Allah, and start calling on my God. When it comes to my faith, I do not care if it offends every Muslim, Buddha, Roman Catholic, Mormon, sun worshiper or any other of the numerous religions that have ever existed. **I do not tread on their faith, nor kill them because of it**; they can keep their faith, but do not tread upon mine. Dr. J Vernon McGee used to say, "Your rights end where my nose begins." I will say this: **one of us is going to hell; think on that.**

Now I pose the question, what is man's fate given the present course of the world? Is it, Could it be the same as "In the beginning God created heaven and earth, and the earth was (became) Void and Without Form?" The Book of Revelation clearly states this world's fate. Re 21:1 *"And I saw a <u>new heaven and a new earth</u>: for the first heaven and the first earth were passed away; and there was no more sea."* (Emphasis is mine). Why a new heaven? Well I think, as the first earth and this one we are on now, has been changed by sin, so was the first heaven, and God will make all things new--again, but war now rages.

The Layman

PHASE I CREATION I: WORLD I

Before I begin, let me let me explain the title. We are at this point about to cover the original creation of the earth. I realize the title is somewhat different; however, stay with me, and I will be able to make it clear a little later on.

I want to inject one statement as we begin. This work is not a verse by verse rendering of Scripture. We will cover those Scriptures which favor us, and also those which do not. Lets begin:

We will begin with Gen 1:1 *"In the beginning God created (Bara Eth) the heaven and the earth."* This term "Bara Eth" means, "Bara" (to create), "Eth" (personally). Bara is used 46 times, and Eth 18 times in Scripture; however they are used only here side by side. To me, and again I am no linguist, it means God personally created the heaven and being used with the term earth, means He personally created the earth.

There is quite an argument over the use of the term "Bara." Bara, and I am not a linguist and am not attempting to tell anyone what I know of such and such a word; However, I am told, that (Bara), as used here, means to make something from nothing, and not to fashion something with what someone already has, such as a potter does with clay. The word "Bara" is the only word the Hebrew writers had, or have to express this type of creation. There was not, and as far as I know, there still is not, a Hebrew word for making something from nothing. No one ever heard of, or had need of such a word until God said it. So why have words that no one knows its meaning? People don't make up words in reserve for meanings to be attached later. People make statues to unknown gods, but not words to unknown meanings. I do not readily know a single English word when used alone, would express to make something from nothing. I am sure there are those who might read this that will be most anxious to correct me if such does exist, and that is ok with me.

This word, Bara is like a "Logo" in Genesis. If the Scriptures had been written by man, for man, man would not dream up some nonexistent, otherwise impossible thing, and then not have anyway of telling what it was, because he did not have words to describe it. This is not the only logo we have in scripture. We will cover another such

24

word when we get to the creation of man. There are so many hidden keys in His word that puts His stamp of approval upon it.

That the Hebrews did not have such a word is in fact verified by one Rabbi Nackman. Quoting Rabbi Nackman in his discourse on the word "Bara" from, PP. 22 of **Earth's Earliest Ages**, states *"There is no other word to express production out of nothing."*

Do I find that hard to believe? Not really. Write a letter to someone who is coming to visit and tell them, "Oh! Please bring me a cap." May I ask if they would know if it were a bottle cap, cap for the head, maybe one for the toy gun? Many words have double meaning out of necessity until one is invented to separate them into one idea, or until applied correctly to a thought: This happens to be one of them.

GOD MADE SOMETHING FROM NOTHING

Let's look at scripture which says that is exactly what He did, Heb. 11:3 *"Through faith we understand that the **worlds** were framed by the word of God, so <u>that things which are seen were</u> **not made of things which do appear.**"*(Emphasis is mine)

As early as the eighteen hundreds, scientist made the statement that <u>nothing could come from nothing</u>. In the nineteenth century we were told that <u>matter can neither be created, nor destroyed</u>. Today "good science" will attest that all matter has a "Half Life." **Matter, as we know it is not eternal**. Our sun will someday go out; every star in the heavens will fade; atoms will decay. (When I use the term Good Science, or "Science", I am only indicating that good scientist use accepted techniques, and other scientists, I assume use (S.W.A.G.).

Another most interesting thing is that in 1929, **Dr. Hubble** determined that the farther a galaxy is from Earth, the faster it appears to move away. That would mean the orderly expanding universe is not slowing down, as was originally predicted, which supported the "Big Bang Theory" where our "scientist" described the expansion, collapse, bang, expansion, collapse , but is in fact speeding up its expansion which means there is no collapse. There went another wild theory with a Bang!

There was a team who measured the Hubble Constant to be 70 km/sec/mpc, with an uncertainty of 10 percent. This means, in terms I can understand, that a galaxy appears to be moving 160,000 miles per hour faster for every 3.3 million light-years away from Earth.

The Layman

Today scientist has determined this phenomenon is caused by **"Dark Matter."** This matter, I am told, does not have the properties of known matter in that it does not have gravity as we know it, but exhibits the properties of repulsion. And of course the poor little professor will say that according to his calculations this was suspected all along. Well they have even come up with the new speed of the universe's expansion. I am pleased to learn that we have many better scientists than I first realized. I do not know the exact velocity, I have read of several, so for those who want to figure it out for themselves, I present the following accepted formula instead.

$$v = Ho\ r$$

v = recessional velocity
Ho = Hubble constant
r = distance

I give the formulas for those who want to know, however it is beyond my discipline. Good science is putting evolutionist in a corner daily.

If there is up and down; if there is light and darkness; if there is positive and negative; and if there is always equal and opposite in every thing we know, why should it be so amazing that there is matter and antimatter, gravity and antigravity. When God pulled NOTHING apart, He made matter and antimatter. Bring the two together and one has pure energy release and nothing again. It may be a surprise to many, but scientist creates antimatter today in atomic accelerators in their study of the atomic structure of Gods building blocks.

Physicists at **Lawrence Livermore National Laboratory** have developed an economical way of producing large amounts of antimatter. They shoot short, powerful laser bursts at a target of gold. This produces "Positrons" which is opposite of electrons, or "Antimatter."

If I can close my eyes and bring to life past events, if I can remember scenes which are vivid to my imagination, if I can recall the emotion of those moments in my finite mind so real that my heart begins to beat with the afore excitement, how dare I to think that God could not only do the same, not only that but also put matter in an otherwise void, by architecting creation with His mind alone! The first world was brought into existence by God the architect and the LORD God the builder. How long it stood before its destruction I can not even venture a guess; perhaps billions of years. One thing we know is that our LORD God would not start with a lump of clay and start molding, with an occasional, No! That isn't right. No! I think I will try this. Only the ignorant and complete air headed evolutionist would ever think God would be as unorganized as they.

There was a time when in the field of Electronics, I could close my eyes and design a circuit. I would describe it while my associate would put it on paper. Some circuits were digital and required exact synchronization with its sister circuits. I could take this from my mind to paper, to bread board, to reality. How could we ever doubt the genius of our God's ability to materialize perfection with only a thought? That is the most amazing thing to me about my LORD God on the cross. How He kept from taking this universe out of existence while under such demonic ridicule is completely beyond my comprehension. I can't even drive the freeways without wishing I had a Sherman tank to show old so and so how to drive.

Suppose for a moment that God told us exactly how, when, how long it took, and in what order He created everything, and then left little clues for our scientists to find: the truth of the matter is He already has. Suppose they then stubbed their toe on clues and then declared "The Bible is marvelously and precisely accurate, a book of science of the highest order, full of as yet unraveled mysteries." Right! That will happen right after they **find Noah's Ark**. God tells us of its existence, even the very mountain on which it is docked, and we still can't find it. Know why we can't find it? No! I know that some are thinking that God won't let us. I do not believe that, my Father never hides the truth. I believe we won't find it because those who could **don't want to find it**. If they found that Ark sitting on one of the tallest mountains in Turkey, they would have to admit to the world being covered, Gen 7:20 *"Fifteen cubits upward did the waters prevail; and the mountains were covered."* They would have to acknowledge that there isn't that much water in the atmosphere which would lend itself to only one conclusion. They would have to acknowledge that there is a true God and when He created the world He was smarter than they are, and my friend, **their pride will keep them in that sea of ignorance until our LORD returns to this earth.** Some will keep searching for evidence that there is no God even when they are on their way to Hell, and the flames lick their souls.

We Christians today need to get off of milk and get into the meat of Scriptures. Satan has his way with the news, science, and even our educators. "Oh." one says, "Everyone on earth is only in search for the knowledge of truth." I whole heartedly agree that science is, day by day closing the doors on speculation and guess work; however, let's use the example of Noah's Ark. Suppose Scripture said that within that Ark, there was the largest diamond the world had ever imagined, and it was surrounded in a protective encasement of three feet of pure platinum, studded with every jewel imaginable? Do I need to finish my question?

If we all only knew that the love of the LORD God is far more valuable than earthly riches? Perhaps religion has forced **good scientist** and **our clergy** as well, out of valid acceptance by refusing to admit what is most evident; man was not the first creatures; or possibly civilizations, on this old planet, and life did not just happen by accident.

The more important the decision you are facing,
The greater care you should take in choosing
Your counselors.

David Jeremiah

VOID AND WITHOUT FORM

We now direct our attention to Gen 1:1, where we see the term God **"created,"** and then the term **"Void and Without Form."** These two terms just do not somehow complement each other. How could a perfect God, and He is perfect in the Triune form or separate, create anything which was "Void, and Without Form?" I do not now, nor will I be convinced that a perfect, triune God could ever bring Himself to spend time making something "tohu" and "bohu."

So if God made the earth from nothing (bara), He would not make it void (tohu) and without form (bohu) because in Isaiah 45 we read, Isa 45:18 *"For thus saith the LORD that created the heavens; God himself that formed the earth and made it; he hath established it,* **he created it not in vain (tohu), he formed it to be inhabited (not bohu):** *I am the LORD; and there is none else."* (Emphasis is mine) Again, I am not a linguist. I am told that "tohu" signifies that which is desolate, and "bohu" signifies that which is empty.

I am really postulating here because this is not only found in my thinking, but in the head of G.H. Pember, Arthur W. Pink, and Dr. Chalmer to name just a few. It was Dr. Chalmer who in the 1800's pointed out that the word **"was"** in Gen 1:2 should be translated as **"became"**. In other words to read Gen 1:2 in that manner one would read it, *"And the earth* (**became**) *without form, and void; and darkness was upon the face of the deep. And the Spirit of God moved upon the face of the waters.* (Emphasis is mine)

For those of who know grammar, I will quote G.H. Pember, **"Earth's Earliest Ages**; PP 25. *"Now the "and," according to Hebrew usage- as well as that of most other languages-proves that the first verse in not a compendium of what follows, but a statement of the first event in the record. For if it were a mere summary, the second verse would be the actual commencement of the history, and certainly would not begin with a copulative. We have, therefore, in the second verse of Genesis no first detail of a general statement in the preceding sentence, but the record of an altogether distinct and subsequent event..."*

One further comment upon the transition of the word "and" to the word "became." If one has opportunity to read **"Earths Earliest Ages,"** by G.H. Pember, he has a good grasp on things. I will let Dr. Pember explanation stand for itself. He states that the use of this word is elsewhere recorded in Gen 19:26 when in reference to Lots wife and here the word is translated "became". Quoting Dr. Pember now, on PP. 27; *"An instance of this may be found in the history of Lot's wife, of whom we are told, that "she **became** a pillar of salt." Such a meaning is by far the best for our context; we may therefore adopt it, and render, "And the earth became desolate and void; and darkness was upon the face of the deep."* (Emphasis is mine)

Dr. Scofield's comment in relation to these verses: 1. *Jer 4:23-27 "I beheld the earth, and, lo, it was without form, and void; and the heavens, and they had no light."* 2. *Isa 45: "For thus saith the LORD that created the heavens; God himself that formed the earth and made it; he hath established it, he created it not in vain, he formed it to be inhabited: I am the LORD; and there is none else." Clearly indicate that the earth had undergone a cataclysmic change as the result of divine judgment. The face of the earth bears everywhere the marks of such a catastrophe. There are not wanting imitations which connect it with a previous testing and fall of angels."*

Scofield, 1917, says on creation; *"The first creative act refers to the **dateless past, and gives scope for all the geologic ages."*** (Emphasis is mine)

Darby's commentary says *"In the beginning God created the heavens and the earth." What may have taken place between that time and the moment when the earth (for it only is then spoken of) was without form and void, is left in entire obscurity."*

James-Fausset-Brown commentary *"In the beginning--a period of remote and unknown antiquity, hid in the depths of eternal ages; and so the phrase is used in **Pr** 8:22-23."*

It was after *"When the morning stars sang together, and **all** the sons of God shouted for joy."* There is no joy in what we are viewing now. What joy would the sons of God have to shout about? Why would the morning stars sing over a "Void and Without Form" world?

I again quote the part in Hebrews, Heb 1:2 *"Hath in these last days spoken unto us by his Son, whom he hath appointed heir of all things, by whom also **he made the worlds;"*** There is another scripture, and in fact it is the second and only other scripture in the Bible which says "worlds", Heb 11:3 *"Through faith we understand that the **worlds** were framed by the word of God, so that things which are seen were not made of things which do appear."* (Emphasis is mine) This is a hang-up for evolutionists.

This Scripture says that God made the world from nothing. It is most important that we keep asking, would God make something from nothing, and create a "Void and Without Form" nothing? I will acknowledge that the world was void of life at the very beginning. Life appeared on earth **at the hand of God** when the world was ready to support it. Life was created by God; it did not creep from between the toes.

LAND BEFORE TIME

The heaven-the earth:

God made a world and it fell apart. "WHOA! One would say, God **don't make no junk**." Well a few moments ago, some were willing to believe He made a world which was **a hunk of junk**. There is one thing which we must make perfectly clear about God and creation; a perfect God cannot make perfect junk. Anything God does is in order, and perfect.

Quoting A. W. Pink; from his book, '**Gleanings in Genesis**': "*In the beginning God created the heaven and the earth.*" "*As we have already observed, the original condition of this primary creation was vastly different from the state in which we view it in the next verse. Coming fresh from the hands of their Creator, the heaven and the earth must have presented a scene of unequalled freshness and beauty...*" "*And the earth became without form and void; and darkness was upon the face of the deep.*" "*Some fearful catastrophe must have occurred. Sin had dared to raise its horrid head against God, and with sin came death and all its attendant evils.*"

F. W. Grant had this to say. "*There was, then, a primary creation, afterward a fall; first, 'heaven and earth', in due order, then earth without a heaven-in darkness, and buried under a 'deep' of salt and barren and restless waters. What a picture of man's condition, as fallen away from God! How complete the confusion! How profound the darkness! How deep the restless waves of passion roll over the wreck of what was once so fair! The wicked are like the troubled sea, when it cannot rest, whose waters cast up mire and dirt.*'"

J. V. McGee: **Through the Bible Commentary, Book 1,** pp13. "*Although this view has been discredited by many in the past few years, I believe that a great catastrophe took place between verses 1 and 2. As far as I can see, there is an abundance of evidence for it. I believe that the entire universe came* *under this great catastrophe. What was the catastrophe? We can only suggest that there was some pre-Adamic creature that was on this earth. And it seems that all of this is connected with the fall of Lucifer, son of the morning, who became Satan, the devil, as we know him today. I think all of this is involved here, but God has not given us details. Apparently, this vast universe we live in had been here for billions of years, but something happened to the earth and to a great deal of the creation."*

Clarence Larkin, Rightly Dividing the Word. "**The Original or Pre-Adamite Earth**"

"This creation was in the dateless past. The six days' work as described in Gen. 1:3-31 was the restoration of the earth to its original condition before it was made "formless and void" and submerged in water and darkness. Peter speaks of it as the "World that **then was,** *that* **being overflowed with water,** *perished." 2Pe.3:5-7.*

The Three Stages of the Earth: The manner of the creation of the "Pre-Adamite Earth" is not revealed in the Scriptures. They simply declare that "In the **beginning** *God* **CREATED** *the heaven and the earth." And in that statement we have all the Millenniums of time that science may require for the formation of the earth as a planet."(Emphasis is mine)*

We who are followers of our Heavenly Father have in so many ways shot ourselves in the foot, maybe both feet. For a pastor, or professor in our great universities to stand before believers and aver that the world is only six-thousand or so years old is shameful. God, nowhere in Scripture even alludes to the age of the earth, or the universe. When we look at the ages given in the margins of our Bibles, we need to recognize that these are only **predictions** based upon the genetic ages of those who followed Adam, and one predicting that Adam was a certain age at an estimated time, so to have a base line.

I know full well there are brethren who are jumping up and down when I say the above; however, they have a fundamental reason to do so. Evolutionist has pressed this time issue to support their hypothesis that they need to enforce the farce of evolution. Stay with me here; I will state firmly that this time was not a 24/7 time period, and no matter if it represented a million years for each phase, no evolution has ever occurred on this earth, and good science verifies that.

Precious believer please understand that genuine artifacts have been found, and these artifacts are ancient. Now **science** should not aver accurate dates for them, nor the many skeletal remains found all around this planet; however, neither should our **clergy** be as error prone as **to say that they are only six-thousand years old.**

I cover this elsewhere, but <u>we do not even know how old Adam was before the LORD God cloned Woman</u>. Now please do not jump at Adam's age when Seth was born. We are told that he was one-hundred-thirty-years-old **at that point**, but that was his age **after** he had sinned by disobeying the LORD God. We do not know how many years he spent on this earth before he and Woman sinned. Don't freeze up on me here. Examine this: if Adam was eternal, **which he was** before he sinned, then he was not any older when he sinned, than he was when the LORD God formed him from the dust of the earth. We do not know what time passed between these events. Now I am not saying millions of years here. Adam was not in the Garden when the LORD God **planted it**. We should ask ourselves, where was Adam and how long was he there? I don't know exactly where Adam was because it is not told us; however, I think I have a pretty good idea and we will cover that later. Adam was later put in the Garden to dress and keep it. How much later **until it became a garden**, we just do not know.

Before Adam, there was the "Void and Without Form" earth and God created **dinosaurs** were on this earth before it became "Void and Without Form". There was **God created** dinosaurs that lived on this earth **for hundreds of millions of years**. There was **God created bipeds** on this earth for years, if one calls them a "cave-man" they are without sound evidence at this time.

Later in this work, we cover many things that just could not have happened in six-thousand-years. I know there are "pious people" who will read this and say "God can do anything." May I respectfully ask why He should when He is having fun with His creations? Why not let it "perk" **within His already established laws**; the same laws that govern the earth and the universe even today.

Now some might say that they don't see the need for a division between a first earth, that is to say the one before Gen 1:2, and the six days of Creation I have termed Phase II. Well let's discuss some things which are not explained without it.

CRITTERS STUCK IN ROCKS:

In my North pasture, in Central Texas, I have a rock which I look at on occasion; it is among other rocks and among Johnston grass. In that limestone rock, which is about twenty four inches on a side and about four inches thick, are about two or three thousand little critters that have been frozen in time. I know how bad some want to say that all that happened in six thousand years, and some hearts pounds at even the idea of agreeing, but in my opinion, it just didn't. I do not make excuses for God; I have experience that He can stand on His own without my help.

On my little Ranch, I have found fossilized Ammonite shells that are larger than a small tire. For those who immediately pictured a roller skate wheel, lets say the same as a wheelbarrow's tire. On a ranch next to where our former president has his Texas ranch, these Ammonite shells were so plentiful that people used them as door stops for their chicken coops. I have a clam like shell that was dug up when I built a fence that has both the top and bottom still together. I look at it and wonder what the little feller inside looked like. Probably like that skunk's face just before I hit it with the Dodge the other day.

While stationed at Ft. Bliss, Texas, the family and I used to enjoy climbing the surrounding mountains to the east and snoop into the Indian religious cave. One day we were on top of this one mountain which is a few miles North of Waco Tanks, my son and I noticed in the crevice of the rocks were these small little shells; we picked them up by the hand full. Looking at them, I was amazed at what I found. They were these small shells like the ones seen in the movie that some islander blows into the end of, which makes this weird sound. These shells were all the same configuration, but of a smaller size. I still have several, and they are less than one quarter of an inch long and probably three sixteenths of an inch across at the widest part. I am told that they were salt water marine life, and that the desert area around El Paso, was all a sea bed at one time. That makes sense, in, that animal life from the sea needs sea water. El Paso is 4300 feet above sea level, and that mountain was a lot higher than back there in town.

"Well!" Some will say. "That could have just happened during the flood." The flood was upon the earth, one year-ten days, when Noah stepped forth from the ark. I will not dispute anyone in the fact that the flood waters could have deposited a lot of things there, but there were many more of the little fellers still stuck in the hard rock which formed that mountain.

34

POSSIBLE HOLE:

I said that I would not jump over a hard Scripture, and I don't aim to. In the account of the flood it tells of the animals which were destroyed. We will discuss the dinosaur later, but I want to put in the fore front of everyone's mind Gen 7:21, 22; **21.** *"And all flesh died that moved upon the earth, both of fowl, and of cattle, and of beast, and of every creeping thing that creepeth upon the earth, and every man:*
22. *All in whose nostrils was the breath of life, of all that was in the dry land, died."* **It does not say that the fish died**.

This is most interesting because if man ever gets a better handle on DNA, they will see a similar genetic squeeze on all animals upon the earth which occurred at the time of the flood, but they will see that some of the aquatic's do, and some do not have the similar "squeeze."

We leave many good scientist outside our circle when events like the following occur, which is quoted in part from the "**Genome Research**". "The 5-foot, 130-pound fish in question, called the "Coelacanth," ekes out an existence in cool, deep-water caves off the Comoro Islands in the Indian Ocean and northern Indonesia. Its lobed fins, skeleton structure and large, round scales are **practically unchanged from its fossilized ancestors**." Though I cannot prove this, I do not doubt for a second that this fish and many other reptilians came through the "Void and Without Form" of Gen 1. I say that because when speaking of the original earth, Scripture says the "earth" was void; Scripture does not say that about the sea. I know that is weak, but the above shows some survived, or our LORD God made the same, old ones, in Ge 2:19.

WHAT WAS THE FIRST BEGINNING

Looking in 2 Peter 3:5 *"For this they willingly are ignorant of, that by the word of God the heavens were of old, and the earth standing out of the water and in the water:"*

Jmaieson-Fausset-Brown has this to say: *"Standing out of the water and in the water; rather, consisting out of water and by water. The reference is to the chaotic watery mass out of which the earth was formed, Ge 1:2. At the command of God it rose out of this, and took its form of dry land; so that it consisted out of water, and by means of water."*

35

The Layman

Matthew Henry has this to say: *"This was done by the word of his power, and it was also done according to the word of his promise; God had said that he would destroy man, even all flesh, and that he would do it by bringing a flood of waters upon the earth, Ge 6:7,13,17.* **This was the change which God had before brought upon the world,** *and which these scoffers had overlooked; and now we are to consider...,"* (Emphasis is mine)

Now the "heavens were of old" (heavens, plural) does not to me indicate that Peter was meaning the present heaven, because the heaven which God formed during Gen 1:6 *"And God said, Let there be a firmament in the midst of the waters, and let it divide the waters from the waters.",* was a part of the six day creation. I feel, as many commentators do also, Peter is talking about the original heaven when he says "of old"; the one existing before that of Genesis 1:2. Notice that he says, in relation to the earth **"Standing out of the water and in the water."** If he were talking about the flood here, he would have said *"in the water and out of the water"* as his last statement. For anyone to deny that there was an existence before Gen 1:2 would be in my mind, untenable.

God, in the beginning, created the Heaven and the Earth, and it was a beautiful place. It was a lush garden of foliage unimaginable, animals that defy description, and a prior race of bipeds, pre-Adamic, if you please. If there were a sun or not is a mute point because God's presence is sufficient to sustain what He has created. If the people who, **science calls** "Cave Man" existed, is for now, totally unproven. There is ample evidence that bipeds and dinosaurs did exist, and the undeniable fact is that we do know we can find their bony remains, so they **did exist**. We also know that this **was not** during the second creation, or as I have expressed, "Phase II Creation II," because when these creatures were here, **there were carnivore animals** back then. God did not give those of the Phase II (Gen 1:29, 30) meat to eat. It was after the flood that God gave man meat to eat, so it was He who changed or better still, allowed graminivorous people to become carnivorous.

One could envision the earth with vegetation of such profusion that would stagger the imagination. Animals which have yet to be discovered roamed this old planet: Pterodactyls soared in the skies, and hungry Rexes looked for a meal. There must have been far more than we have found, and someday, God willing, we will find more in our oceans than we ever dreamed. It is indisputable that our dry land was once an ocean floor, and it conversely follows that what is now ocean

36

floor was once dry land. We today, know more of the solar system than we know of our oceans.

Let's look at "Cave Man:"

In the recent past there have been two paleontologists' finds that have captured the news.

The first was "**Lucy**" found in the north east African area of the Hadar region of Ethiopia, and was of the category, Australopithecus afarensis that was dated as living between 4-2.7 million, BC (of course these paleontologist's use the politically correct BCE) The name Lucy indicates the skeleton was that of a female. Lucy was supposed to be "**The missing link**", and was tooted as the evolutionist's inroad to debunk Bible believers. This find was later confirmed to be of the ape family, even though it appeared that Lucy walked in a bipedalism (one who walks erect) manner.

The second was the discovery of **ARDI** by Tim White, Gen Suwa and Berhane Asfaw. ARDI was found in the Middle Awash region, west of the Awash River in Ethiopia. The find was of the category of **Ardi**pithecus ramidus, or ARDI for short; this was also a female. Well ARDI was supposed to have lived between 5-4.5 million years BC, which placed it as the earliest find of this classification, to date.

At first this was a find that could not be classified as any existing animal. It was later determined that ARDI was of the ape family, the skull was only a plaster representation, but the arms were of the same proportion as that of a chimp. A chimp's arms are of a ratio of 95% of the upper leg, whereas human ratio is around 70%.

ARDI has the long arms of a Chimp; however the hands, though much longer than human, lacked the signature of a knuckle walker of the chimp, which at first gave speculation that it might be more human than all else found. Later evidence has shown that ARDI was an entirely different species, but not Homo.The real signature was the discovery that ARDI's feet had opposing big toes: A tree climber.

From: ("**Myths and Methods in Anatomy," Journal of the Royal College of Surgeons, Edinburgh, vol., 11, pp.87-114, 92.**) I quote Lord Solly Zuckerman, **one of the most eminent anatomists of the twentieth century**: It was Zuckerman's considered opinion *"That all classes of Australopithecines, from the Taung child all the way to Lucy, were nothing more than apes, virtually identical to the pigmy chimpanzee, known as the Bonobo. So Lucy wasn't so unique after all."* Oxnard along with others

37

have said the same thing, Australopithecines were simply apes that walked upright at times." (Emphasis are my insertions)

The pigmy chimpanzee known as Bonobo was unique in that it did not walk in the knuckle fashion of other chimps, but in fact walked upright in the bipedalism fashion, or it was what I call a biped.

The term HOMINIDAE relates to apes. In my opinion, the study of Hominidae today represents a collection of evolutionist who are still trying to achieve one goal, to bind all bipeds in creation under the auspice of Homo related. I present the following time table for information only. The times given are questionable even by their colleagues.

Here are the estimated Hominidae time lines:
1, Australopithecus ramidus------5 to 4 million years BC.
2. Australopithecus afarensis-----4 to 2.7 million years BC.
3. Australopithecus africanus-----3.0 to 2.0 million years BC.
4. Australopithecus robustus------2.2 to 1.0 million years BC.
5. Homo habilis--------------------2.2 to 1.6 million years BC.
6. Homo sapiens-------------------400,000 to 200,000 BC.
7. Homo sapiens neandertalensis-200,000 to 30,000 BC.
8. Homo sapiens sapiens-----------130,000 BC to present.

I inject here again that these dates are paleontologists' estimated dates, and reflect mostly, an evolutionary slant. I have read, and state later that the date for the Neanderthal as given here at 200,000 to 30,000 has been determined to be in line and co-existing with the Cro-Magnon, who is suspected to have lived until about the time of the flood.

Oh! One would say; Science is out for evidence and has no ax to grind. Well let us look at the Piltdown man? The Piltdown man is one of **the most famous frauds in the history of science.** In 1912 Charles Dawson discovered the first of two skulls found in the Piltdown quarry in Sussex, England, <u>skulls of an apparent primitive hominid, an ancestor of man.</u> The Piltdown man, or Eoanthropus dawsoni, to use his scientific name, was a sensation. He was the much expected **"missing link"** a mixture of human and ape with the noble brow of Homo sapiens and a primitive jaw. "<u>Best of all</u>," one has said "<u>he was British!</u>

The Piltdown man was a creature without a place in the human family tree. Finally in 1953, the truth cam out, the Piltdown man was a fabricated hoax, and these most ancient of people tooted by science, were those, who never existed. Someone had filed the canines and made the teeth to look as humans.

To equate how evolution scientist describes data is much the same as a blind man describing the beauty of his surroundings: though true to them both, they are but fabrications of their minds and do not exist in reality.

THE WORLD BEFORE GEN 1:2

There are possibly several scenarios, and my friend, I am only, with God's patience, and long suffering, **subjectively guessing.**

Firstly: There could have been divine judgment: some disobedience to God's rules having occurred, and God took the only action He could under the circumstances. God has shown us in our history what He does when things get out of hand. Look at the Flood, Tower of Babel, Sodom and Gomorrah, the destruction of Jerusalem, and the destruction of Pompeii, and next **if I may prophesy**, the destruction of **Sodom America**, the tribulation, millennium and, then the end as told us in Revelation.

Let's look at such a judgment already described in His word. Jer. 4:23 "*I beheld the earth, and, lo, it was without form, and void; and the heavens, and they had no light. Jer. 4:24 I beheld the mountains, and, lo, they trembled, and all the hills moved lightly. Jer. 4:25 I beheld, and, lo, there was no man, and all the birds of the heavens were fled. Jer. 4:26 I beheld, and, lo, the fruitful place was a wilderness, and all the cities thereof were broken down at the presence of the LORD, and by his fierce anger. Jer. 4:27 For thus hath the LORD said, The whole land shall be desolate;* yet will I not make a full end. Jer. 4:28 For this shall the earth mourn, and the heavens above be black: because I have spoken it, I have purposed it, and will not repent, neither will I turn back from it.*"(Emphasis is mine)

Did the LORD God pronounce a **similar** divine judgment upon the first world? It could well have been. The Bible commentators all agree, that the state of Israel reminded them of the chaotic condition of the "Void and Without Form" world.

Now before some hit the ceiling **I am not** trying to squeeze this Scripture into my topic. I have not used this Scripture to plug up one of the many holes. I give it as an example of what **will happen**, and what **could have similarly happened** when whatever crossed the threshold that God had established, and He must, have taken action.

The Layman

When we read prophesy, I feel it important to view it as having a past, present, and future meaning. Again, **I am not saying that this Scripture** tells us of the past earth. I say if it is going to happen to this earth, it may well hold a clue as to what happened to the earlier. Ec 1:10 *"Is there any thing whereof it may be said, See, this is new? it hath been already of old time, which was before us."*

Could a similar scenario have happened to those of the first occupants of this earth? I honestly do not know; however something happened and these are only presented as possibilities

We cover this later; there are many scientists who feel a large asteroid or small planet struck the earth, which propelled debris of sufficient quantity to later form the moon. It could have caused the catastrophe we are discussing. I do not think it is soul saving important or God would have told us, and perhaps He doesn't want us speculating about what I am writing. He is my Father and the one I serve and want to please, and none other.

Secondly: Of all hypotheses, **this is the one I would vote for.** Lucifer could have destroyed the world out of hate, or what may be called his super ego. Lucifer, when he was dethroned, Isa 14:12 *"How art thou fallen from heaven, Oh Lucifer, son of the morning! how art thou cut down to the ground, which didst weaken the nations!"*(Emphasis is mine) and knowing that God loved, loves, and will always love His creation could have made it "Void and Without Form". Imagine if possible, all the hate Lucifer held towards God when he thought he was powerful enough to assert himself above God, and then he suffered total humiliation by being kicked out of heaven. I have no problem seeing him lashing out at whatever he knew our Father loved, loves, and will always love; His creation. Revenge is such a blinding, unrewarding force.

How Lucifer did it is beyond me. Perhaps it was with a large meteor or small planet as we discussed earlier, that would certainly do it.

BEFORE PHASE II CREATION II

If the earth, which is speculated to have started its formation around 4.5 billion years ago, progressed as God wanted, and each phase supported the next, there is no real dilemma here, but we don't really know.

40

What our theology fails to consider is that in earth's early state, **magma has to cool**, rocks have to form, and air and water must be provided by His same natural processes in order for erosion to occur. God forms simple plant life, providing food for more and more complex plants, all the way to where He planned it to be in the first place.

If one has plants, they must have something for the plants to eat, then they must have something besides solid rock for roots to grow in, then there must be water to carry the food to the roots that are in the soil that was formed by erosion. Erosion takes time to make soil from solid rock. It must have rained in the world that existed then, for soil to form. I know in my heart that God started with simple algae, and then as each decomposes at the end of life's cycle, that leaves fertilizer for ever increasing complex plant life to draw from. That is His plan and **has nothing to do with an evolutionary act**. It continues today, but **the algae are still algae**.

Now after this has been established there can be plant eating animals, and later other creatures progressing up and down the food chain.

Please, do not try and put our Father on a time table. Eternity is something none of us on this planet has the slightest idea about. Do not loose sight of the fact that our Father was looking at each of us today, our kids and grandkids for tomorrow, when He did those things eons ago. He knew, knows and will always know what <u>must</u> transpire for His plan to be carried out. He set laws in motion which He allowed to progress accordingly. Let me pose a question; **how long did God wait in His existence before He even started all this anyway**?

If one has food then we can support what I think was the ugliest dinosaurs one can imagine, possibly as told us by Job one of them was **Leviathan**. Job 41:1-34 *"Canst thou draw out leviathan with an hook? or his **tongue** with a cord which thou lettest down? Canst thou put an hook into his **nose**? or bore his **jaw** through with a thorn? Will he make many supplications unto thee? will he speak soft words unto thee? Will he make a covenant with thee? wilt thou take him for a servant for ever? Wilt thou play with him as with a bird? or wilt thou bind him for thy maidens? Shall the companions make a banquet of him? shall they part him among the merchants? Canst thou fill his **skin** with barbed irons? or his **head** with fish spears? Lay thine hand upon him, remember the battle, do no more. Behold, the hope of him is in vain: shall not one be cast down even at the sight of him? None is so fierce that dare stir him up: who then is able to stand before me? Who hath prevented me, that I should repay*

41

him? whatsoever is under the whole heaven is mine. I will not conceal his parts, nor his power, nor his comely proportion. Who can discover the face of his garment? or who can come to him with his double bridle? Who can open the **doors of his face?** *his* **teeth** *are terrible round about. His* **scales** *are his pride, shut up together as with a close seal. One is so near to another, that no air can come between them. They are joined one to another, they stick together, that they cannot be sundered. By his* **neesings***(breath) a light doth shine, and his* **eyes** *are like the eyelids of the morning. Out of his* **mouth** *go burning lamps, and sparks of fire leap out. Out of his* **nostrils** *goeth smoke, as out of a seething pot or caldron. His* **breath** *kindleth coals, and a flame goeth out of his* **mouth***. In his* **neck** *remaineth strength, and sorrow is turned into joy before him. The flakes of his* **flesh** *are joined together: they are firm in themselves; they cannot be moved. His* **heart** *is as firm as a stone; yea, as hard as a piece of the nether millstone. When he raiseth up himself, the mighty are afraid: by reason of breakings they purify themselves. The sword of him that layeth at him cannot hold: the spear, the dart, nor the habergeon. He esteemeth iron as straw, and brass as rotten wood. The arrow cannot make him flee: slingstones are turned with him into stubble. Darts are counted as stubble: he laugheth at the shaking of a spear. Sharp stones are under him: he spreadeth sharp pointed things upon the mire. He maketh the deep to boil like a pot: he maketh the sea like a pot of ointment. He maketh a path to shine after him; one would think the deep to be hoary. Upon earth there is not his like, who is made without fear. He beholdeth all high things: he is a king over all the children of pride.*"(Emphasis is mine)

Notice that it is recorded, "he is a king over all the children of pride." **This could as well speak of that old dragon Satan. One must agree that he is described in perfect detail here.** I cannot fight him, and friend no one else can either. The LORD God just told us to; *"Submit ourselves therefore to God.* **Resist the devil** *and he will flee from you."* Jas 4:7 (Emphasis is mine)

Let's look further in other possibilities. Most reputable commentators all agree that this was an animal. The Syrid, Abaric languages as well as the Septuagint all agree on the term, "Dragon." We just do not really know how to define this beast.

In reference to the Scripture in Job: Job did not ask God what He was talking about. I would have! A fire breathing thing that was so horrible that one couldn't even look upon him? <u>I would have asked God what He was talking about</u>, that is, if I had not already known. God indicates that He is able alone to control and lead him away.

As a point of repetitiveness, I want to make this comment. If we turn to explanatory text of our believing brethren, we will find some, once again making excuses for scripture. Some say this is a whale. How many whales has one seen that belch fire and smoke, or a spear would not kill? Again some say this is a Crocodile. Well I have never seen a Crocodile with a tongue which one could catch him by. I never saw one that when I looked at him would make me tremble and become weak. In fact if he came at me, I would show him how fast I could run, but I certainly have never seen one that belched fire. I have read one author who at length tried to convince the reader that this was a rhino. Will we ever stop making excuses for what God gave us, so it can be digested by the world? These unfounded examples, given by illiterates are so the skeptic will be comfortable. Child of God, He is telling us that it is a **monstrous fire belching creature** which we have no knowledge of. <u>God does not make up fairy tales to amuse us</u>. How can we learn if we don't take what He says as what He means, and quit trying to make excuses for what our ignorance cannot understand? This is one of many scriptures that I do not fully understand. I know this creature was real; Job knew it also.

"Aw come on! **A fire breathing dragon,** that's stuff that stories are made of, like Sir Lancelot and all. You don't really mean that you believe a live animal could belch fire do you?" I like what Dr. W. A. Criswell said to someone who asked him, *"You don't really believe that Jonah was swallowed by a whale and stayed there for three days, do you?"* Dr. Criswell answered, *"Sir. God never said that Jonah was swallowed by a whale, He said He prepared a 'big fish', and I will tell you if the Bible said Jonah was in the belly of that fish* **watching television,** <u>*I would believe it with all my heart.*</u>"(Emphasis is mine) Amen! Amen! Brother.

Little Dragon:
It may come as a shock to know that there is **a beetle living on this earth today that spits steam**. I was corrected in my usage of the term "spit". I was told by a "learned Entomologist" it was <u>squirt</u>. I am not learned, so I use spit, squirt, and eject. Well I have to admit that snakes, people, camels and the like "spit" and if it comes out any other orifice it is "squirt." Webster says it is "ejected" that is what I shall use when talking **to such intelligent people**
Now if God makes beetles that ejects steam, (I would like to see evolutionists explain that one.), I am here to give assurance—He truthfully has made a beetle that ejects steamy acid---then He made an animal that belched fire from his nostrils. I can only tell everyone of

the one that I know of, and here is the explanation, which I have been given of this amazing little Bombardier beetle.

The **Bombardier beetles** include those ground beetles in the four tribes Brachinini, Paussini, Ozaenini, and Metriini. Now I furnish those names for those who are Entomologist', but I have no idea what they mean. Here is what I found on this little critter.

The components making up the beetle's effective chemical warfare have been analyzed by chemists and biologists down to the molecular level with some trying to prove evolution, and of course those scientists who know who the architect is. When the beetle senses danger, it secretes two chemicals, <u>hydrogen peroxide</u> and <u>hydroquinone</u>, that end up in a storage chamber inside its body. By tensing certain muscles, it moves the chemicals to still another chamber, called the **explosion chamber,** where <u>catalytic enzymes</u> are present.

Boy what a rejected bunch of beetles there must have been back when evolution was trying to work all this out. I mean, carrying around the world's first case of "Acid-Reflux" until a catalyst can be formed. That isn't half of the story, when the catalyst is finally formed, millions of beetles exploded until an opening can be made through millions of years of evolution to eject it. Isn't evolution great? Think of those little beetle parts laying around for all the birds to eat. I guess that is the reason that early "evolutionizing" birds didn't starve.

Enough barb throwing. I will get back to what is found by science. Inside the beetle's body, the two chemicals are injected into the explosion chamber where now the three chemicals are present. These reactions release free oxygen and generate enough heat to **bring the mixture to the boiling point and vaporize about a fifth of it.** As a result, a boiling hot and toxic liquid is **squirted out of the beetle's rear** toward the threatening predator's face. Notice that I used the term "squirted"? See I can learn.

What is equally amazing is that this process is repeated with the mixing of all the chemicals at the rate of 500 ejections in less than a second.

I ask myself; just how many beetles blew up before "natural selection" was able to provide three chambers to be filled with three separate chemicals and an anal hole to release the explosion? It was probably called **a "Suicide Bomber"** beetle before it perfected the system. One can image that when a predator tried to eat it, the

Bombardier Beetle would charge forward and wrap itself around the predator and self destruct. They learned that from man, I suppose.

<u>All three chemical elements and chambers</u> have to exist for this powerful defense system to work. How could such a complex system evolve by gradual steps? With only the two chemicals mixing, nothing happens. But, when the catalyst is added in the proper amount and at the right time, the beetle is then equipped with an amazing chemical cannon. Could all these components appear by a gradual, step-by-step process? Only an evolutionist could be so naive.

I have heard the sound made when the beetle ejects this steamy liquid: It sounds like a cap pistol. I also saw the man who excited the little feller, pull his finger away in considerable pain.

When I was doing research on this subject, I contacted an "expert" who gave the impression he was an Entomologist, and had a web site on critters. His site had one of those catchy phrases like "May peace and prosperity be with you…etc." I queried him about a beetle that spit steam. He told me of a family of the Beetles called **"Bomadier (sp) beetles,"** only after informing me that, "I **don't know of a beetle that spits** steam." He impressed me by further stating that **snakes "spit"** and **beetles "squirt."** Well I couldn't find anything on such a critter and reinitiated contact. It turned out that he had misspelled **Bombardier** and seemed quite upset that I wasn't smart enough to know that. He also invited me to "stop bothering him," when I couldn't find his "**bomadier beetles**".

Isn't science wonderful? I found six or more references which affirmed that the liquid reached 212° or as some said 100C and since that is the **boiling point** the beetle in fact does eject 20% of the liquid as steam. I started to give that other fellow the references, but I remembered that I wasn't to bother him so I didn't. **I also found an expert that knew how to spell Bombardier** and so I didn't need to "bother" him again. Why wake up a **sleeping** giant?

My friends; when God tells us something that is hard to believe, He is telling us a special secret which the world will never come to grips with. He is telling us a secret; one which is just for our ears only. There was a fire "ejecting" animal. If a little exoskeleton with an explosion chamber can produce steam, God has already shown us that an animal, He is referencing to, ejected fire and embers.

WHAT WAS HERE

I want to pause here for a moment and maybe provide an insight into why I am dedicated to this work. When our young people attend Church, they are bombarded with **well meaning,** pious pastors who are **in sincerity** stressing the abilities of our God to marvelously create the impossible in a week. Could He do that? Of course He ultimately has the capability if He saw the need; however, with all my heart I say that I honestly believe He <u>would not</u>. If He did, He would violate every natural law He Himself established for His creation in the first place; **why should He hurry?**

We wonder why our young adults drop out of organized religion when they leave home and enter colleges. It is **not** that they are finally out from under the heavy hand of the parents. It is **not** the sins of the world that at first dissuades them.

The young people enter college and began to study techniques which define:

1. **There were dinosaurs** and many other species on the earth.

2. They can now use techniques, though not exact, still define the ages of these creatures, and each discovery **screams millions upon millions of years.**

3. They discuss these findings with their pastor who shakes a bony finger in your face and **demands a 24/7 creation,** and tells them, they are a heathen if they think any different.

They are now in a quagmire, and the only solution is, in most cases, **forget it all.**

Listen to me, I may be old enough to be your parent's grandfather, but I went through the same thing. By the will of God **I tell YOU-- YOU are right, and WE have been wrong!**

The sad part is that many clergy are not going to change because they are **"the authority of Scriptures"** no matter what **everyone else says.** Remember the Pharisees?

I say to all that read this, stop and think. We each have had it pounded into our heads that **this world and all the universe** was

46

created in seven, twenty-four-hour days. We have taught our children to believe this, and on field trips that I have made, and I am sure many have also, we go to a museum and there stands the skeletal remains of **a grotesque dinosaur, and we know** from all evidence we have that **they did not live from Genesis 1:2 to Revelation 22:21**.

We have all seen little critters embedded in limestone, and limestone is made up of decayed little critters. We have seen pictures taken of leaf images on lumps of coal. I have a piece of petrified wood **that the Smithsonian Institute dated at over fifty million years old**, which was dug up by my father's construction corporation in the District of Columbia during the construction of I-95. **I do not state** that the dating of this wood by science is **definitively accurate**, but for me to try and cram billions of years of His creative work in seven days is so very, very wrong. Am I to say then that evolution existed for billions of years, then God found this "Void and Without Form" planet which He redid in seven creative days; NO! Does that make sense? **It does not** when considering the creativeness of our Father.

Our Father sets up laws that He will not disobey: Could He? In most cases no. There are cases where He does, temporarily, for a divine purpose; however, can we reason why He should create a world in 24/7, then hide fake critters in rocks, oceans, strata layers of the earth and caves? Could we trust our Father, if He were trying to bewilder us? Precious, **God imposes higher standards upon Himself, than He would ever impose upon us**.

I want to take time to present another example of someone making a wrong guess, and later being accepted as a fact. I can remember a score of prominent researchers publishing all sorts of evidence to support their notion that dinosaurs were "Cold Blooded Creatures;" Over grown lizards, if you please. One went so far as to describe how he had measured the capacity of the mouth and throat, (Now how he did that when all they had were skeletal remains, I do not know.) and it was his **professional** conclusion that the dinosaur could not convey sufficient food down this passage even if it were continuously fed, to keep it alive, if it were anything but cold blooded.

It was interesting that they later found a petrified dinosaur, and know what they found in the chest? Yep! Everyone probably guessed it. It was the heart of a mammal, because it had an "Aorta" which carries the blood from the left ventricle of mammals to the rest of the body. This, if all have not already surmised it, shows the dinosaur was a warm blooded animal, not a lizard.

47

The Layman

A new finding debunks the theory that grasses did not emerge until long after the dinosaurs died off. Recent discovered fossilized dung seems to tell a different story: The most prominent plant-eating dinosaurs <u>were digesting different varieties of grass between 65 million and 71 million years ago</u>. This came as a surprise to scientists who never thought to look at the dinosaur's digestive system.

With reference to dinosaur ecology, Dolores Piperno and Hans-Dieter Sues of the **Smithsonian Institution's National Museum of Natural History**, made the following observation: *"These remarkable results will force reconsideration of many long-standing assumptions."*

I bet that little professor would like to retract his remarks about the lizard.

We must turn our hearts towards our maker and say "If God said it; <u>I believe it no matter what</u>."

This reminds me of this preacher who was eating pancakes for breakfast while putting the final touches on his sermon for that morning. Well when Church started and it was time for him to read the introductory Scripture, he proceeded Ok, until he reached the part about Noah's wife. "And Noah's wife" he exclaimed as he quickly turned the syrup stained page of his bible, "shall be three hundred cubits, the breadth of it fifty cubits, and the height of it thirty cubits." Wide eyed, he again read, "Shall be three hundred cubits, the breadth of it fifty cubits, and the height of it thirty cubits. Well!" He exclaimed, "That was certainly some woman, but if the bible says it, I believe it."

Precious brother, the point is that **He never said that he made this earth in seven days**: not the first time and not the second. In fact the opposite is true. There is profound evidence all over this globe that has been left to clearly show that this world has gone through catastrophic events, and our Father approved it all.

Now back to the sequence before Gen 1:2

Facts of findings attest the ugliest dinosaurs one can imagine, roamed and roared with attention getting sounds upon the earth. They were carnivores and God didn't allow that until after the flood. I think what has been termed by evolutionist as the "Cave Man" (Which may have been a chimp) wandered around just as paleontologists, have found. The earliest date for the dinosaur has been pegged at 251 million years.

I believe that from the original creation told us by Gen 1:1 until Gen 1:2, when the Phase II Creation started, there was a tremendous expanse in time, and though time, as we know it may not have been invented, I have no other way of expressing this sequence of events, so forgive me for using the term, "time."

I am not versed on how many cataclysmic events this earth has undergone, but I am not so blind as to turn my reasoning off: after each event occurs and **all living species were wiped out, that there is a group of species that "<u>suddenly</u>" appear, which differ from the previous groups that were here before**. No scientist will dare admit what is fact that, **complete extinction** occurred many of these times. Do we know why they will not admit this extinction? To do so would force their mind to admit what they have already reasoned out: without a Creator, it could not be so.

I ask the reader to understand that I am not trying to convince anyone of anything. I am saying these or similar things happened. What science, and our religious leaders must never forget, **God caused, allowed, and/or directed <u>every bit of it</u>. Nothing happened on this planet, or in the entire cosmos, without His intervention or nod of approval.**

WHY AN EXPANSE OF TIME

Well consider the following:
  1. OIL:
  Some say if the first creation had vegetation, it **could well have been a flotilla**, and could have sunk. The movements of the earth's crust and vast quantities of sediment during the chaotic era between Gen 1:1 and Gen 1:2 could have covered it, the magma could have perked it, and it could have given the whole world what we now call petroleum.

This would not in itself explain the myriads of oil thousands of feet beneath the surface of a seabed which is in itself thousands of feet beneath the surface of the sea. That is but one reason I do not think that this was the sequence.

Then consider: **The world was a lush garden** of vegetation, and myriads of life. Allowing that God let things "perk" as they should, and when the world became "Void and Without Form", and the waters covered the earth, there would be upheavals unimaginable. Could this be the time petroleum was "perked" after being deposited in its own oven? Well that would be closer, but to answer the question for the vast quantities we know of today, I just can not imagine the numerous "mountain tall" piles of vegetation it would take.

The Layman

Next we would have to consider the quantity of oil, and later coal, it has taken to run this world. Look at any freeway today and remember that it is full of trucks and cars twenty four hours every day of the year. I read in a recent work that OPEC produces one third of the world's need for oil, and that they ship over twenty-eight thousand barrels of oil each day. That would equal a world need of eighty-five million barrels of oil each day of each week, of each month, of each year. That quantity of oil equals over thirty-one million barrels of oil each year. (I am not positive of these numbers since different documents have varying accounts. It is a huge quantity of oil, no matter the amount.)

Can we even stretch our mind to fathom the tremendous growth of vegetation it would have taken to make even a million barrels of oil, just how many thousands upon thousands, of feet high, the vegetation had to be, to produce this quantity of oil? I have not found the expert who could tell me how many pounds of vegetation it would take to make one quart of crude. Then one would have to figure out how to pile it upon itself so fermentation could start, but we are still left with how one takes tons of anything and get it thousands of feet beneath the surface which is thousands of feet beneath our oceans. I mean, last time I checked, oil floats on water.

More and more learned persons are today discounting the idea that even given billions of years, there could be enough organic matter to produce the world's need, let alone store it at such unbelievable locations.

Up to this point, I sound like I am a petroleum expert; something like my little professor: well **I am not an expert**. Perhaps my know it all attitude is better explained from the following.

Here is something to think about and to reinforce the fact that we just do not know all of our Lord's ways. I am not belittling our geologists, I am saying that science in most cases does the very best that they can with what they have to work with. I sometimes wonder if our Father doesn't have a greater sense of humor than we give Him credit for. Well let's read the following and start to forget all we thought we knew about oil.

I read an article which described a wonder occurring off the cost of Louisiana. There is an oil field which was discovered about thirty years ago. After seismic evaluation it was estimated to have approximately 60-million barrels of crude. This was seemingly verified in that the wells produced 15000 barrels a day, then as predicted began to deplete down to around 3000 to 4000 barrels a day.

Now here is the amazing part. The field began to increase its production capacity to 13000 barrels a day, and new seismic evaluation estimates that it has grown from the original 60-million barrel capacity, to a capacity of 400-million barrels, which means that the original basin is refilling itself, but for how long and how much is anyone's guess.

There is another rather puzzling finding. Scientist who drew samples from this well say that the crude coming from the well is of an entirely different age and quite different from what was first discovered.

This is not as surprising, as that found in the Middle East' world reserves. The world has, for more than half a century, drawn from this reserve, and in spite of extensive exploration, little has been found to add to the resources there. Now, I have not found what the original reserve was calculated at, but to the astonishment of scientist, the reserve has more than **doubled** itself in the past twenty years.

Thomas gold, a respected astronomer and professor emeritus at **Cornell University, Ithaca, N.Y.** has been quoted as saying for years that *"oil is actually a renewable primordial syrup which is continually manufactured by the Earth while under an extremely hot environment. As it is produced, it migrates from internal pressures toward the surface where it is infused with bacteria, which give the substance the appearance of being of ancient origin."*

While many scientists discount Professor Gold's theory as unproved, *"It made a believer out of me,"* Robert Hefner, chairman of **Seven Seas Petroleum Inc.**, which specializes in ultra deep drilling, is quoted as saying.

"This is a completely new twist to our original thinking, but allows a much needed explanation in discovering the vast quantities of this substance we have and are still consuming every day. It eases my mind on the vast flotilla of foliage needed to even approximate its existence."

2. COAL: Again this could have happened with the same "time" frame; however, it is seriously doubted that coal is a natural geological process as explained by Professor Gold since we find imprints of leaves on some lumps. There are coal mines in the Eastern United States, which exceed hundreds of feet down inside the earth, and are in seams over twenty feet in depth, with an estimated five-hundred-thousand square mile reserve. Coal deposits are now found buried beneath layers of sandstone, limestone and shale all over the world. **These are sediment layers found under seas**, which could easily have formed before, or during the "Void and Without Form."

If one is eternal as our Father is, why should they hurry to do anything? God knew, God knows, and God will always know what He is doing to make His will complete. I cannot impress that thought upon the reader enough.

I used to build and fly model airplanes. I could either buy, what today is called a "fast-build" kit or the regular one. I always chose the regular one because I loved to take my time and know every part of it to completion. I see my Father doing much the same. I could have taken the short cut, but I had before me plans, these plans if followed would result in a finished product, and I took my time, and enjoyed every stick of balsa that I glued together. My Father did the same with His creation, I just know He did.

3. FOSSILS: Fossils are uncovered which were, by time lines, buried millions of years before the flood. We know that strata are a fool's game of estimation, but when one finds fossils which are embedded in solid rock, we have to question the six thousand to ten thousand time period.

4. DNA: When examining species: These genetic codes are so different from life today that we just cannot bury our head in the sand. The biped had no genetic characteristics of the Neanderthal, Cro-Magnon, monkey, ape, dog, cat, or "Modern Man." These are fragments of the past which lack genetic trails and without these genetic trails, they are otherwise unexplained, but we will discuss one other thing that is most impressive, later.

I must pause here and emphasize that there **were** ancient animals, plants and a creature that **resembled man,** which some scientist still call a "cave man;" however, good science still sees them as a biped, or chimp. The point I want to emphasize it that they were all here, **God created them** for whatever His purpose was: **never** loose sight of that fact.

5. THE TIME LINE: I prefer to call it a sequence of events; Why? Are the dates correct? No! Now I want to add that there are equally good comments by many which have their own theory as to the time it took to form each of the above animate, inanimate and resources. Are they wrong? Only our Father really knows, I don't, but they should be considered before making final judgment.

6. ESTIMATING TIME: There are several loose ends which must be tied together before we begin to discuss the sequence of events which are to follow. We must establish what we believe and separate that from what we want to believe. There is only one time line and that is God's. Man, as we will disclose, hasn't perfected his abilities here, but new techniques give promise.

Any respected scientist will tell us that they are just doing their very professional best while using the present day data and techniques, which they have at their disposal to establish ancient time. No one knows the past **radiation** level, the **carbon dioxide** level, the **ozone** level, nor do they know anything before mankind could detect or record such.

I know they sample ice flow, rocks and the like to get a real good idea, but peaks of an event will not be so recorded, and it is obvious that the present assumption is that the same level of activity was global, when only a local event may have occurred.

Science proves the miracles of the Bible: Let say something about a magazine which recently published this article. They were in reference to 2 Kings 20:11 *"And Isaiah the prophet cried unto the LORD: and he brought the shadow ten degrees backward, by which it had gone down in the dial of Ahaz".* There was this explanation by some fellow that if, while someone was viewing a sundial, a cloud covers the sun, and the shadow of the dial will change by going backwards.

Now in the first place, the fellow did not prove the miracle of the Bible, because the shadow will not go back a full 10°, he kind of failed to mention that:

1. The shadow would go forward, or backward depending upon the position of the blown cloud, the sun and the sun dial.

2. If one observed this actually occurring, it would become obvious that the most that the shadow would appear to go in either direction would not equal ten degrees. He kind of failed to mention that fact too.

3. Anyone, especially those who ever used a sun dial to tell time would know they were looking at a diffused shadowing on the dial and would wait for the sun to give its full strength before trying to tell the time. One hast to remember that the people mentioned in Scripture did not have wrist watches, they used the sundial and would not fall for such a ploy. The Scriptures are not "smoke and mirrors."

4. If the Lord said that He would make the shadow go back 10°, it was not diffused, but a solid shadow, and **it went back exactly 10°**, plus or minus nothing.

To demonstrate what that fellow was saying, put a ceiling fan on the medium or the lowest speed. If one has a light under the blades as I do, look at the shadow as it passes a point on the ceiling. On my ceiling, which is a rough, cork-blown one, every time the shadow crosses one of the little peaks, I can see the shadow actually move back and forth, and gets more exaggerated the further away from the fan one looks. One can hold a straw against the ceiling and watch the same effect if they have a smooth ceiling. I know this is **not** exactly the same as that fellow presented, but will present a similarity.

LET'S LOOK AT TIME

Allow me to elaborate further on this determination of "**time**." These scientists found a dead seal in the Antarctic. They cut flesh samples and froze them, sent them to a number of labs for dating. With the specimens there was the explanation that this was a suspected specimen from an earlier period and they needed verification for weight of finding, in order to publish their discovery in such-and-such a paper. Well what were the results? The earliest date that they received was that the specimen was over 4000 years old? I must ask myself, if a mistake is made of this magnitude, what creditability could I place on other examples?

I read an article where the author was discussing the questionable validity of establishing a time for items found. He stated that "**Bones, found in the same dig**, belonging to **the same animal**, when subjected to the same **accepted test** to determine their age, they were determined to be "**tens-of-thousands-of-years-apart**." Now I don't know about anyone else, but that gives me confidence.

It is my understanding; the people who have been doing this confirm that with any sample given, there are multiple dates which could be used. They simply select the one they honestly think "**fits**" and use that one. I was further informed that they will no longer give a date to you until you provide them your estimate of the date. Now that seems good. I give them a date that I want it to be and they tell me it fits close to one of the many numbers I gave: I then have an old-old find.

When some **rock paintings were found in South Africa** in 1991, they were sent to Oxford University's radiocarbon accelerator. Upon computing the date of this find, the unit **dated them as being around 1200 years old**. This would mean they were the oldest "Bushman" paintings found in open country. It seems that everyone was going around slapping one another on the back and preparing publications lauding their achievement. I can see my little unknown professor stating to the press, "My studies have lead me to believe this was highly possible for some time now."

Well, the advertised news of all this finally reached one **Mrs. Joan Ahrens, an art teacher and Cape Town resident**. She immediately recognized the rock paintings as being the <u>work of her art class</u>! It seems thieves had stolen them from her garden. If she had not come forward to claim them, everyone would have accepted the very wrong radiocarbon date. They now were faced with only two choices;

1. Mrs. Ahrens was 1200 years old, or

2 The date was wrong.

Scientists have found animals living which were killed, then dated by carbon 14, which were found to be thousands of years old; how can this be if they were still living and freshly killed? It cannot be and we know it; sadly scientists know also, yet they still use it as fact, rather than to admit that it is **suspected** to be, **not factually so.**

Shells of mollusks that were still living have been dated as having died, 2300 years ago!

Seals that had just been killed gave an age of 1300 years in one case and as discussed earlier, over 4000 years.

An **English castle** that had been built 785 years ago gave an age of over 7000 years when it was dated.

Mummified seals that had been dead about 30 years were dated at an age of 4600 years.

Making a positive statement about how old something is just iffy. For someone to say billions of years old, would I guess, be more accurate than several thousand, but the times should be given as "estimates" not fact. I know that "Nuclear Accelerators" are supposed to give a truer date. Well, so they thought about carbon 14 dating.

Good Science, and there are **many good scientist**, will tell us that is the best technology we have right now. I appreciate they are doing the very best that they can, and most would not try and misrepresent anything to gain prominence, but it would help if it were explained that it is only an educated guess.

There are those who hold to the **stratified layer theory** of time. As I understand it, one should use extreme caution here to access time. There was this interesting article about a professor who was conducting a dig, and was "tooting" this stratifying theory as the only true means of dating a thing. Well it is amazing that this fellow was elaborating on this, and pointing out to some who were members of his dig, the accuracy of it all, when a part of the dig collapsed. Wouldn't we know it? There was a tree bole which stood there penetrating several thousand years of time.

I have seen pictures of a mummified foot, still in a **modern** boot, so I don't think mummification holds any real clue to age either. I do <u>not</u> suppose that these dates are misrepresentations. Everyone makes mistakes even under the greatest care. I just do not think these dates are anything but within "the ball park, and should be presented as estimated times; **not fact**

LET'S LOOK AT LIGHT

What about the billions of years that light has been traveling to earth? Science has said the universe is 12 to 15 billion years old because they see light that is coming from galaxies billions upon billions of light years from earth. Is it really billions of light years away? This is one of the most commonly asked questions I have heard people ask when discussing time, and deserves our honest analysis. There are three things one needs to consider when answering the question concerning "Star Light."

1. Scientists cannot mathematically measure distances to stars beyond 100 light years and I seriously question even 10 light years, accurately.

2. We do not even know what light is, let alone if it always travels at the same speed throughout all time, space and matter. Have they ever studied the prism? I would ask, "Ever see the rainbow of colors it makes? Ever ask why?"

Look at sound which used to be the referenced speed. Matter and its density greatly effects sound's speed, and amplitude retention. I mean, stand on one side of a pond, or swimming pool and have someone click two rocks together while one of your ears is under water, and the other out. Even that short distance is discernable that the ear in the water hears the sound much sooner that the one out of the water. Who knows anything about space? When we sent the first "Space Probe" to our own planets, know what happened? They rewrote the books about our Solar System. **It sometimes seems someone can say anything, that someone else cannot disprove, and it will become accepted "Fact."** However, let someone present accepted thought of the Creator, and it will be dismissed as naïve dogma.

3. Creation was finished and matured according to divine laws when God made it. When the LORD God made Adam, I suppose, though I do not know, he was full grown. When God said "Let there be light" that was **His light.** When the stars were made we do not know if they even emitted light or not. When God "**Created**" light, He did not tell us that He did, or did not make it to shine <u>everywhere at once</u>. In other words, Adam was, as far as I can tell, a mature man at one second old. Light was mature at one second old. Please excuse my use of time, but this is the way we have of relating events. I know that Adam was one second old, one second after he violated the LORD God's law, but by the same axiom, light was fully mature, and could have shined throughout the entire universe, everywhere, all at once.

4. With the introduction of black holes, and the recognition of dark matter, there is now an entirely different outlook on light. There are some who feel that the universe may by its nature form prisms, lenses, and have areas where light doesn't have the same definitions it has within our realm.

LET'S LOOK AT DISTANCE

No one can measure star distance accurately. Let's look at the first attempts at mathematically measuring star distance. The nearest accurate distance man can measure is 10 light years, and with a little tongue in cheek 20 light years (some textbooks say up to 100), **not several billion light years**.

1. Man first measured star distances using parallax trigonometry. By choosing two measurable observation points and making an imaginary triangle to a third point, and using simple trigonometry, man calculates the distance to the third point. The most distant observation points available are the positions of the earth in solar orbit six months apart, plus the distance of an orbiting satellite, let's say June and December. This would be a **base for our imaginary**

triangle of 186,000,000 miles or 16 light minutes. (93 million miles+ 93 million miles divided by 186,000 miles which light travels per second =1000 seconds divided by 60 seconds = 16.6666 minutes). Now I do not know what the distance is to the satellite which they now use, so will go with only the orbit of the earth to the sun as reference. There are 525,948 minutes in a year. Even if the nearest star were **only one light year away** (and it isn't), the angle at **the third point measures .017 min.** Well there are some who will read this that certainly understand that a whole lot better than I do.

To keep it in simpler terms, let's use the same distances, but now use triangulation to solve for the unknown angle. (For those who are familiar with this, please allow that I have **not** included the radius of the sun, the diameter of the earth or the satellite orbit to present this simplified approach.)

If I were to look at a distant object which was only one light year (ly) away, I would have one angle which we know is 90°, and the distance is (186000X60X60X24X365.25= 5869713600000miles away.) This means that we would have an angle of 89.9782°. Or a difference of 0.0218°

I will not bore anyone with the rest of the calculations, but here are the figures, which when subtracted from 90° would be the resulting angle to find the desired distance. I did not do this with any but the last one to show the foolishness of such an approach.

1 ly= 89.9782

10 ly= 89.99872

100 ly= 89.999782

1mil ly= 89.9999999782 or an angle of 0.0000000218°

Want to try and express "Billions" of light years away? Oh, but listen; **these distances were taught over the years as fact in every educational institution on earth.** For a while, I must sadly say, it was truly "The blind leading the blind."

The stars may be that far away and further, but modern man has no way of measuring those great distances **by triangulation**. We are valid in our assessment that, using this method, "No one can state definitively the distance to the stars."

I know that they do not use this method any longer. There are several reasons for this; one reason for this is that in 1919, a scientist by the name of Eddington selected two sites to photographically monitor a solar eclipse. One was from Brazil and the other was from Principe Island. The eclipse pictures showed an offset in the positions of stars due to solar gravitational bending of light that confirmed Einstein's theory. This bending is called "**Gravitational Lensing**." If black holes were to similarly represent stars in different locations, one could certainly not tell where they really were.

Several other methods such as Hubble's "standard candle" and "red shift" are employed to try to approximate at greater distances. All such methods, though red shift for me holds <u>far better accuracy</u>, have serious <u>problems and assumptions</u> involved.

I have, as best I could, studied Hubble's formula, if I may condense it to that simple of a term: It is far beyond my discipline. I do not ridicule the "Red" shift approach. I do, however, say that <u>all things do not remain constant, traveling through non-constants</u>. Red shift seems the best science we have, and it should be used, but **not** presented as fact.

For a more complex and slightly different answer to the star light question from a Christian perspective, see the book "**Starlight and Time** by Russell Humphry available from **The Institute for Creation Research**." The reader would be surprised at what is presented. Another Christian reference I give as interesting is titled, "**Scientific Approach to Christianity**," by Robert W. Faid. Yet another I **have not,** as yet read, is "**God Verses Science**," by Albert Einstein, 1921.

2. We do not know what light is. Science calls it a "photon," but no one can explain what a photon really is. **Webster's Dictionary** states the following. *"Photon:" "The quantum of <u>electromagnetic energy</u>, generally regarded as a <u>discrete particle</u> having <u>zero mass</u>, <u>no electric charge</u> and an indefinitely long lifetime."* Now that is the closest that anyone will ever get Webster people, to say, 'I don't know.' It is "a particle," yet having "no mass," yet is "electromagnetic energy," which has "no charge," and it has "an indefinitely long lifetime." In other words we see by it, it is going to last forever, but it doesn't exist, whatever it is, or isn't.

The speed of light may not be a constant. Recent observations have concluded that it does vary in different mediums. We observe that in the rainbow effect of light going through a prism. It is a theory that light in fact may vary in speed and possibly spectra shift in different places in space. The entire idea behind the black hole theory is that light can be attracted by gravity (yet light has no mass or electric charge) and be unable to escape the great pull of the Black Holes. Of course no one knows what the density of the black hole is or the gravitational pull of it. No one knows what light is let alone that its velocity has been the same all through time and space until it reaches earth. Black Holes may in fact refocus or reflect or refract the light.

Since atomic clocks use the wavelength of the Cesium 133 atom as a standard of time, if the speed of light is decaying, the clock would be changing at the same rate and therefore not be noticed. Much as the experiment of placing a frog in a pan of cold water and slowly raising the temperature until it boils him without his ever knowing a change has been occurring.

Just when science thinks it has, it all figured out, up jumps one professor Lene Hou, of the **Roland Institute for Science**, who has been able to slow light down by a factor of 20 million fold. The end result was a light photon that traveled at 28 miles an hour. To top that, she later, stopped it completely before turning it loose to resume its 186,282 mph journey.

3. The creation account states that God made light before He made the sun. *Ps 74:16 "The day is thine, the night also is thine: thou hast prepared the light and the sun."* Again remember that I sometimes put "**Then**" in place of "**And**". "Thou hast prepared the **light then the sun.**"

Star's were made but light may have been at the time God chose for each. The God of our universe, whom we worship, is not limited by anything involving time, space or matter since He created it all.

A tour was proceeding through one of the country's better museums of ancient history, when they paused at a fossil specimen. "How old is this specimen?" Queried one of the tour.

"One-hundred-thousand-ten-years-three-months, and ten days," Replied the tour guide.

"WOW! How on earth can you be sure with such accuracy?" The person asked.

"Well" The guide replied, "When I started working here, I was told that it was one hundred thousand years old, and I have been working here ten-years-three-months, and ten days."

Think on This:

I have to remind myself that this universe is not what we really think it is. I am not sure that the whole realm of that which we see outside our reach is nothing but a presented **hologram**. We sometimes do not read, what we read. I find that when my mind comes upon something that it cannot put into a neat cubby hole, so to speak, it just does that familiar" buzz" over it.

Let me give two examples:

Isa 34:4 *"And all the host of heaven shall be dissolved, and the **heavens shall be rolled together as a scroll***: *and all their host shall fall down, as the leaf falleth off from the vine, and as a falling fig from the fig tree."*(Emphasis is mine)

Re 6:14 *"And the heaven departed **as a scroll** when it is **rolled together,** and every mountain and island were moved out of their places."*(Emphasis is mine)

I hope and pray that I fully understand those scriptures someday.

I love scripture; it is so exact, in what it says, and what is between the lines. It was Dr. Einstein who said *"It would not surprise me that we and the whole known universe were but a speck of dust on the sleeve of a parading soldier's uniform."*

If we could understand everything in our Bible, and universe it just wouldn't be much of a challenge; would it? I would love to see the face of the astronomer who is quietly viewing images from the Hubble telescope and suddenly a corner of the night sky begins to peel back, and he sees an eye looking right back at him, and he looks outside only to see what he deemed far distant stellar objects falling like figs.

From the discussion thus far, we should agree, at least in part, that **neither science nor theologians**, really have the total answer here. Time; Distance; Space: No one knows what is real but the God we worship, and He muses over our "mud pie" approach. I marvel over "Good Scientist's, they marvel, they ponder, they poke and prod, but they never loose sight of, our LORD God, the builder.

BACK TO BEFORE TIME

Now back to the inhabitants of the earth **before** Gen 1:2. We have said before that we do not for even a moment contemplate that the biped had a "living soul." I think they were what science has found, but **I am not sure they have found it all**. There is a place in Texas that the owner has shown a foot print resembling a human's: It is found on the same strata as the foot print of a dinosaur. That is as far as I will go with that now. That print does not appear to be of a chimp, but I am not qualified to say it was of a Homo sapien either. All that can be said is there is a footprint that looks like a Homo sapiens who lived at the time of the dinosaur. He is presented to us, by scientist, as a primitive being and it may well have been those on the earth just before the "Void and Without Form" destruction.

There was a recent article that I would like to paraphrase here, which disputes the accepted chain of "evolutionary" events.

Let me set the stage:

There has been extensive discussion over recent findings in relation to the extinction of the dinosaur when the area north of what is now the Yucatan Peninsula was struck by a giant object from space, about 65-million years ago.

It has been taught in schools that **most all** animal life was brought to extinction at that time. Then it was supposed that all life that remained were then allowed to procreate freely without being eaten by the larger dinosaurs. These animals were supposed to be those including modern day mammals:

Wrong!

Some scientists conducted a broad and massive DNA family tree and found that no such prolific burst of modern day animals actually occurred, only those animals of ancestral creation that survived showed some increase, but again not of the expected numbers thought.

I was given a quote by one Ross MacPhee, who is curator of vertebrate Zoology at the **American Museum of Natural History** in N.Y., which said, *"I was flabbergasted; at the time of the dinosaur demise, mammals were small, about the size of shrews and cats. The long-standing idea has been that, once the dinosaurs were gone, mammals were suddenly free to exploit new food sources and habitats and as a result, produce a burst of new species."*

"This new study says that happened to some extent, but that the new species largely led to evolutionary dead ends. In contrast, no such explosion of species was found among the ancestors of modern-day mammals like rodents, cats, horses elephants and people."(Emphasis is mine) I will not cover this here in detail; however, remember this statement, and I will expand on it when we get to the creation of animals and male and female on page 103.

As more scientists employ the use of DNA they will discover that, aside from a few fish and possibly reptilians, **everything on the present day world is <u>new</u>**. DNA has unlocked so many doors that threaten the very foundation of the evolutionist. Good research, with good researchers, has clearly shown that every genius on the planet has suddenly appeared: was totally developed; evolved from nothing, and/or into nothing new. Past life either died from lack of procreation, or was destroyed by climate, meteor impact, volcano activity and finally the cataclysmic "Void and Without Form." **This is an excepted fact, then why isn't it taught in our schools?**

Don't leave me now. Let us take a closer look at the last of these events, the "Void and Without Form". Look at, Isa 24:1 *"Behold, the LORD maketh the earth empty (all life removed), and maketh it* **waste** *("Void and Without Form"), and turneth it upside down, and scattereth abroad the inhabitants thereof..."* (Emphasis is mine) It is so tempting to use this Scripture to define the first destruction, and it certainly pertains to the end of our present world. I do think that this parallels the destruction of **the first world,** if our Father destroyed it because of existing sin.

EVOLUTION

Ps 14:1 *"The fool hath said in his heart, There is no God."*(Emphasis is mine) I want to make it absolutely clear that **I do not** entertain even for one moment that God used evolution to do, or make anything. It has been tooted that "All the fossils found from the early era would fit in a shoe box, or at most on a pool table. That statement was made <u>years ago</u> when the "Theory" of evolution emerged. Today millions and millions of fossils have been unearthed on every continent. New species are discovered, and old ones have been added: so complete are the findings as to build a skeleton which aids in interpreting patterns of a species' habit, rather than fabricate, what one thought might be there. I know that some within the scientific community will take a tooth and make it into a family, and another will tell us what it ate as its primary diet from the grinding patterns, and another will build a whole body and if not careful, a complete family structure.

The problem I have with what appears to be a scientific community, is that things are taught, documented, and accepted as fundamental truth, with little or no supporting proof. It appears that rogue scientist can say anything, and as long as we cannot prove it wrong, it will be accepted fact. This then means that we are accepting scientist theory, as fact, by default. The evolutionist comes back with the same axiom, "Show me proof of your God."

The Layman

The easiest way to prove that something exists is one's failure to **prove it does not exist**. Ps 139:14 *"I will praise thee; for I am fearfully [and] wonderfully made: marvellous [are] thy works; and [that] my soul knoweth right well."* Allow me to give an example of proof:

There are approximately ten-trillion cells in the human body (I have read where there are over 50-trillion); however, let's use 10-trillion. If the DNA that is in a <u>dual</u> helix of one inch, were uncoiled and attached end to end, they would then be 2 inches in length. Let's see how long that would be if stretched out. We would have: 10trillion, times 2" would equal 20 trillion inches; 20 trillion inches divided by 12 would equal 1.67 trillion feet; and 1.67 trillion feet divided by 5280 would equal 315,656,565 miles, or 613 trips to the moon and back.

Looking further one will find that there are approximately ten-thousand miles of arteries, veins, and capillaries in the human body that feed every one of these ten-trillion cells.

If someone reads this, they have the ability to think, remember, and logically decipher it in total, or in part. **There is no random number generator in God's creation.**

I accept the existence of God by faith, plus the fact that with the obvious complexity of all my surroundings, I would be a lunatic to think it could have existed without intelligence. **NO! I do not** accept intelligent design. **I accept only that my God, the Father of my Lord, designed it, and the LORD God built it, and set it all in motion.** The term "Intelligent design" is, to me, a cop out, an embarrassing statement to gain possible acceptance of the scientific illiterate, and I will not be compromised to accommodate them.

What is Evolution

There are within the "Theory of Evolution" actually two dogmatically <u>surviving</u> theories;

1. There is a theory which states that many living animals can be observed over the course of time to undergo changes so that a new species is formed. This is called "**Special Theory of Evolution.**"

This theory, which, in my opinion, has been coined when evolution could not be shown to be valid, and has tried to hide behind what is a God given adaptation within a species, called "Natural Selection."

2. There is a theory which states that all forms of living in the world have arisen from a single source which itself came from an inorganic form. This is called the "**General Theory of Evolution,**" and <u>is disregarded</u> today **by all but the most naïve**, yet they do still exist.

One confirmed evolutionist, a Swedish botanist, Dr. Heribert Nilsson, wrote *"My attempts to demonstrate evolution by experiment carried on for more than forty years, have completely failed... At least I should hardly be accused of having started from a preconceived antievolutionary standpoint... It may be firmly maintained that it is not even possible to make a caricature out of pale biological facts. <u>The fossil material is now **so complete** that it has been possible to construct new classes</u> and the lack of transitional series cannot be explained as due to the scarcity of material. Deficiencies are real. They will never be filled... **The idea of an evolution rests on pure belief.**"*(Emphasis is mine)

Monkey out of man

Let me pause and reflect for a moment to explain the great "Monkey Trial," that the news media helped to win, years ago. In my opinion the whole thing was presented and was won by **sensationalism among the news media, poor science,** a **jury of airheads** and a **dumb judge**.

The Scopes trial (1926) was held with William Jennings Bryan as the prosecutor who stood for the Christian faith, versus Clarence Darrow representing what might be called the first of the ACLU, what is in my opinion the **A**nti **C**hristian **L**egalistic **U**nion, defending an evolutionist teacher John Scopes.

The primary purpose of this trial was to put God out of schools, and to uphold the "solid" science of evolution: **Presented was the Nebraska man, and Cain's wife.** The Nebraska man who was put forth as evidence of evolution was nothing but a mannequin made from the mind of an ignoramus with nothing to go on but the molar of a pig. That is right brethren! The ***weak minds of the day*** all rallied around what was later found to be a pig's tooth, and made a man out of it, **which they said proved the prior existence and evolvement of mankind,** and some lame brained judge allowed it introduced as evidence. When DNA emerged, a lot of this tom foolery has been put in the garbage can. Today "I am told" that the Nebraska Man, if it even still exists, was retired to some store room on the University of Nebraska's campus.

There was, as pointed out earlier, one further introduction given to William Jennings Bryan, which he could not prosecute effectively: Where did Cain's wife come from since she is not covered is Scripture. We will examine that a little later when we cover the sin of Cain.

I want to make it known that there is an organization who defends those who the ACLU tries to sue. **The American Center for Law and Justice, ACLJ is an organization dedicated to the defense of constitutional liberties secured by law.** A visit to their web (**www.aclj.org**) might be of value later.

"You cannot put one little star in
  Motion;
You cannot shape one single forest
  Leaf,
Nor fling a mountain up, not sink an
  Ocean,
Presumptuous pigmy, large with
  Unbelief
You cannot bring one dawn of regal
  Splendor,
Nor bid the day to shadowy twilight
  Fall,
Nor send the pale moon forth with radiance
  Tender;
And dare you doubt the one who has
  Done it all?"
                    Sherman A. Nagel, Sr.

ESTIMATED TIME LINES

If science is honest there are several things which cannot be ignored.

The Azoic Era is said to be three billion years ago when rocks first formed. Are there any fossils found? No!

The Archeozoic Era was supposedly two billion years ago. A little evidence of water plant life found.

The Paleozoic Era was five hundred and fifty million years ago. **Now in the Cambrian period** which I am told was the first division of the Paleozoic Era, fossils are now found, and they are **suddenly highly developed animals and of the greatest profusion.** Know something else? A "Good Scientist" will aver that there is absolutely no evidence to support the wildest speculation that any

intermediate fossil animal has ever been found or ever existed. No matter what time line is discussed, when a genus appears anywhere on earth it is complete and fully organized. I will repeat that. **When a genus appears anywhere on earth it is complete, and fully organized.** I know that I have repeated that before; however, some evolutionists just do not seem able to accept that fact. Anyone that says different is to me, totally out of their educated mind. This lack of progression is <u>not my opinion</u> alone, but receives the acknowledgement of even the evolutionist **as a problem**. There is not one creditable scientist, who will even hesitate to acknowledge that there <u>has never been one shred of evidence to support one species "evolving" of itself or into another species.</u>

No one, including creation scientists, disputes or tries to show that so-called **"micro-evolution and** I have heard it called **"micro-morph"** (variation within a type of organism) and I have heard it called **"micro-mutation,"**(supposed to be caused by natural selection) **has ever occurred**. I want everyone to understand that all the "theories" in the world have only proven that **natural selection happens within a known and existing genius**, and it is certainly not responsible for even one genius let alone the large number of genius' on earth, but rather it is variations **found within a type;** That is to say within the canine family, the reptile family, the birds, the insects... etc. All touted "evidences" for evolution are of this category (like Darwin's finches, the "peppered moth", or bacteria that become resistant to antibiotics) have long been refuted. It is important to note that **"micro-evolution"** **is a misnomer, as it implies that "<u>a little</u>" evolution** is taking place; In actuality, **NO evolution is taking place,** as no increase in complexity (such as the development of a new organ) is being generated, but merely the emphasis of some already present traits over others. By traits I mean, color, size, dexterity, and adaptability as examples. I do not mean one genius to another.

Evolutionists acknowledge this is a "<u>research issue</u>". Even non-creation scientists (such as Denton and Behe) have written books giving the hard scientific facts that document why <u>evolution is impossible</u>.

Michael Behe is Associate Professor of Biological Sciences at **Lehigh University**. He received his training in biochemistry at the University of Pennsylvania (Ph.D., 1978). His research, investigating the structure of DNA, is currently supported by a grant from the **National Institutes of Health.** His new book, **Darwin's Black Box**:

The Layman

The Biochemical Challenge to Evolution, published by **The Free Press**, argues that discoveries at the molecular level have cast the neo-Darwinian picture of life into grave doubt.

Behe goes further, arguing *"that the structure of life at the molecular level is best explained by intelligent design."*

Michael Denton is a Senior Research Fellow in Human Molecular Genetics at the **University of Otago**, New Zealand. He received his scientific training at Kings College of the University of London (Ph.D., 1974). He is the author of **Evolution: A Theory in Crisis:** (Burnett Books, London, 1984). Surveying a wide range of evidence at both the molecular and organismal levels, Denton argued that *"**the chance and contingency outlook of Darwinism is profoundly mistaken.**"* (Emphasis is mine)

I respect these gentlemen. They may, or may not, believe in my God, and His creative work, but they are not swayed by theoretical nonsense, emanating from those who possess little empirical knowledge.

As I say. Good science is worthy of consideration. Today's unlearned are not worth the breath to dispute them. Even the "Great Evolutionist" Charles Darwin in **"The Origin of Species"** dated 1859, stated in Chapter 10 *"Geology assuredly does not reveal any such finely graded organic chain and is perhaps the most obvious and gravest objection which can be urged against **my theory**."* (Emphasis is mine)

I can at least respect Mr. Darwin for following good practice. He clearly states "My Theory", then sets out to disprove his assumptions and lays the framework for which it is to be proven, or disproved. It appears to me that it is today's introverted scientist and educators who want to make a name for themselves who make a monkey their father.

Well for a long time "Science" said that there had not been sufficient investigation to prove this right or wrong. Today there have been billions of species uncovered from every corner of our globe, and a "Good Scientist" will tell us that not one shred of supporting evidence have ever been found to warrant even fantasy of an evolutionary act. So today, knowing that the more evidence that accumulates, the more that evidence proves evolution wrong, what do these "die-hards" do?; They start amalgamating in the term "Natural Selection." It is so sad that they waste their genus on a pipe dream.

GOD STARTED WITH LITTLE THINGS

*"How complex are the tiniest living things? Even the simplest cells must possess a staggering amount of genetic information to function. For instance, the bacterium R. coli is <u>one of the tiniest</u> unicellular creatures in nature. Scientists calculate it has some 2,000 genes, each with around 1,000 enzymes (organic catalysts, chemicals that speed up other chemical reactions). An enzyme is made up of a billion nucleotides(*the central part of a living cell*), each of which amounts to a letter in the chemical alphabet, comparable to a byte in computer language. These enzymes instruct the organism how to function and reproduce.* **The DNA information in just this single tiny cell is "the approximate equivalent of 100 million pages of the Encyclopedia Britannica"** (John Whitcomb, **The Early Earth,** 1972, p. 79*).* (Emphasisis mine)

This could not be the earliest life as we know it. A virus is a parasite. It must have living organisms to exist. So what is next?

Allow me to relate what a past genus Robert W. Faid**, (**author of ***Scientific Approach to Christianity****, New Leaf Press),* taught me about the complexity of simple life.

The simplest form of life that Mr. Faid discussed is the Amoeba Protozoa. It is filled with a clear substance which I believe science calls protoplasm. Within this little critter there is, as Mr. Webster says, *"A complex, usually spherical, protoplasmic body within a living cell that contains the cell's hereditary material and controls metabolism, growth and reproduction."*

The Amoeba crawls around by a foot which it extends, seemingly, from any part of its body. When it detects food, it scoots to it and then allows the food to enter its membrane by a sort of osmosis. If the food is mobile, the Amoeba has another foot that it extends outward, surrounds the food and then consumes it.

An amoeba can breathe: It has no lungs, it has no gills but it utilizes the oxygen in its environment by osmosis.

The amoeba consists of protein molecules. **Funk and Wagnall's Encyclopedia** defines protein as *"Term applied to any of numerous, exceedingly comples, organic chemical compounds, characterized by the presence in the molecule of amino acids joined together by a peptide linkage. Proteins*

The Layman

always contain nitrogen, carbon, hydrogen, and oxygen; they usually contain sulfur; and they may contain other elements such as phosphorus, iron, or copper

No scientist on earth can explain what we learned in school. When the Amoeba reproduces, it divides itself in half, whereupon the two halves then grow and repeat the operation. We have all heard my little professor extorting the lightning bolt and the amino acid, well this little feller has proteins which in themselves contain peptide linkage.

Though programmed differently, the Deoxyribonucleic acid (DNA for us unlearned) in the Amoeba is just as complicated as it is in us, and all of the listed elements are absolutely essential for our little professors lightning bolt to create life. Not only do the elements have to be present, **they absolutely have to be in the exact combination, the exact proportion, and leave a DNA program for others to follow**. Are we getting a picture of the smoke screen evolutionist are throwing up?

MY PROJECT

With your permission, I am going to set up an analogy which I feel will satisfy, in part, this question of why God started with little things.

Let's start by pretending I am the richest man in the universe, and have dedicated One Hundred Billion Dollars to accomplish my project.

I have the largest research facility that the world has ever known. It is one mile on a side and one hundred stories tall with the last two stories containing penthouses furnished to the extreme.

Within the confines of my facility I have every known scientific device, chemical, mineral and substance known to mankind, which will be available in any quantity desired in order to complete my project.

I shall enlist every scientist on earth who holds a Master degree or higher. I shall explain that it makes no difference their discipline, only that they must prove a genus by modern standards.

No expense will be spared, all their expenses will be paid, and every desire, within bounds of reason will be met, should they decide to undertake my task.

Here is my Project:
I will give 100 billion dollars to the team who will create for me a colony of **Specters**, **Spirits**, or **Ghosts** which have the capability to

70

communicate with me, each other, and have free will to do what ever becomes necessary to sustain their existence; that is, they will, at first, be provided with what ever energy sustaining substance that they require, until they can learn or be taught to furnish the same for them selves.

The team must define what they consume, how they digest what they eat, how that intangible is transferred to and is a contributor to their existence, and finally the properties and chemistry of their waste.

The team must define how they see, feel, sense, think, and logically satisfy every day trials. They must have feelings of comfort, and or discomfort for which the team will insure they will be mentally and emotionally equipped to cope with either or both.

There will have to be certain laws which will govern these identities. The team will insure that some laws will be instinctively understood, while others will be social restrictive. It is anticipated that some of the colony will naturally follow these laws out of devotion to me and they shall be accordingly rewarded: however, there will be some of this creation who will disobey the laws and must be appropriately punished.

Response:

Out of, say, 100,000 geniuses, how many would accept my requirements; **would you, could I?**

We are flesh and blood animate beings. The only Spirit which anyone knows of is the identity of God, and no one has ever seen Him, so where does one begin to create something that has never been brought into existence.

Question:

1. When creating a Specter, how does animate make life from something, and have it remain nothing, yet obtain the awareness and exist as we do?

2. How does Spirit make something from nothing to remain something?

EXCELLENT REASONING

Are we beginning to see why God took His time in creating something totally alien to His Spiritual being? He must first define what life is, then how to feed it after He determines what it is going to be. There is and has always been a master plan and He is not in the dark as our geniuses were in.

There is one thing about my "Project" that is missing. As one of my requirements I defined certain criteria which the specters must adhere to.

There are several problems, which must be addressed:
1. How will I know their eating habits; what they like; don't like?
2. How do they see and what do they see?
3. How do they feel?
4. How do they sense and deal with things as situations?
5. How do they apply reasoning to what they are told?
6. How do they think, and what modifies that thought?
7. What makes them happy, or what makes them sad?
8. What makes them comfortable/ uncomfortable?
9. Why do some obey my laws?
10. Why do some disobey my laws, and is there a reason?
11. How would I reward those who do as I say?
12. How would I punish those who do not do as I say?
13. How do they respond to pain, do they feel pain?
14. Do they feel love?
15. Do they feel fear, and why?
16. Do they hate, and what causes that to exist?
17. Are they lonely, content, or always sad?

I have considered this, and the only solution that makes any sense, so I can truly know each one of these parameters, is to become one of them. So I now **"know,"** as an animate being **I must become inanimate: a Specter,** otherwise I really will **not know,** and can not assure them that I know, without **having been there, done that.**

My suggestion is that our Father worked out His DNA program one step at a time. He started small and ended up with what we today call the dinosaur and biped, (cave man?) along with the many varied forms of terrestrial and aquatic life we call pre-historic.

I know this analogy will at first bring the gray headed pastor slam out of his seat. I know it is a simple approach to a humanly insolvable problem; however, when that pastor gives me a DNA program for a Specter--- I think we can leave it there.

God is Spirit, we are flesh and blood, and there is absolutely no comparison between the two. There was a transition that had to be made by a genus that the universe itself will never duplicate, and He, our genus, did it as He chose: how He chose; when He chose; for each **perfect** step, and God became flesh. OH! How I delight in my God's wisdom.

No intelligence in the universe could possibly entertain, even if, but for a moment, the preposterous idea of evolution.

I can see how it might be possible
For a man to look down upon the earth
And be an atheist.
But, I cannot conceive how he can look up into the heavens
And say there is no God.

Abraham Lincoln

A THOUGHT

We know that God created bipeds, dinosaurs and a host of other creatures. We do not know how long ago each existed, and for that matter we know only a little of what we have been able to discover about them. What the whole population was and did is mostly a mystery. If, say, we find relics from the past, we are prone to try and tell what the whole earth was like at the time of its existence and if not careful, someone will evolve that primitive creature from there through the ages until they go from the mental capacity of a chimp to the genius of Albert Einstein, depending upon who is doing the analysis. With such samples, all we can say is that God made something that existed, and we think it was such and such an estimated time.

If science would ever take Scripture as their base line and proceed to show truth, we would know so much more of our past than we do now. There has been a dramatic change on our earth: that is most evident in all life forms whether they are animal, vegetable, or mineral; that is a fact which cannot be denied, and can only be explained by God's creative act.

If clergy would take the findings of good science as their base line, we would not loose out young people to the secular world. Take a look at the **Grand Canyon, Bryce Canyon, and the Painted Desert** for starters. There is layer after layer, after layer of **sediment** that has been deposited over hundreds of millions of years to form

73

these geological wonderers. **The flood would only cause one** that may or may not be composed of a mixture of soil, **not layer upon layer**.

It is evident that the Dinosaurs roamed the earth, the seas had life, and the earth had abundant vegetation. Primitive Homo erectus (If that is all that was here) coexisted with the dinosaurs.

One final thought before we continue. It is most evident that our Father had good reason to know that the "next" creative act would have to be different than the first. He and the Lord our Savior already knew what it was going to take to save our unwilling souls. It was evident the Lord was needed even before Gen 1. Why was it evident that the earth would need a Savior? Let us look at a passage we have quoted before: Revelation 12:7 *"And there was war in heaven: Michael and his angels fought against the dragon; and the **dragon fought and his angels**."* (Emphasis is mine) These are the angels who followed Lucifer in his fall. This is but another reason it is felt that the creation of Gen 1:1 was destroyed judgmentally.

The battle here in Revelation, I feel, is to gain control of the heavenly realm in order to destroy, again, the earth and all its inhabitants through God defying sin.

Our Father knew, and knows the battle that has existed from millenniums past, to time eternal. The Trinity was prepared for the period of grace, far before the Phase I, Phase II creation, or the restoration. That is why we read in; Romans 8:29 *"For whom he did foreknow, he also did predestinate to be conformed to the image of his Son, that he might be the firstborn among many brethren."* I recognize that this speaks specifically of the Apostles; however, the *"first born of many brethren,* speaks of us. (Emphasis is mine.)

Our Father is not without a plan. So who did He choose to usher in this Kingdom? **He chose the lowly foul mouth fishermen, a teenager, a thieving tax collector, a doubting Thomas and a murdering Roman.** These were chosen before the original creation and confirmed their need from that point on. He foreknew them from before the womb: He foreknew them before creation. My friend He knew us endless ages ago. Every soul that has ever been created is recorded in the "Book of Life." Please don't let any of our names be blotted out: Not after our loving Father has done all this to save our retched hides.

I tell of helping a family in Albany Georgia. There was no husband or father, and for the most part, was left alone. I would provide, as best I could, a humanly love to them. I and my parents financially helped when it was a necessity. All the while, I should have thought, "You may be wasting your time, money, and efforts on that family." Was I right? I suppose to some extent, **yes!**

The point I want to make is this. I suspected that all the effort that I made in the world was not going to change them: then why? Well, I don't know everything, but our Father does. I suppose, looking back on it all, I was hoping for a million to one chance of success.

Would I do it again? **Yes.**

One must see, our Loving God does not tell us to help those who will succeed: He tells us to help.

Our Heavenly Father knew from the first who of the angelic host, and every created soul were going to succeed or fail. If we can look at our children and in most cases, predict which one will most probably succeed, and which one will be a bum, why do we in our wildest moment limit our Precious LORD God?

Does the parent prevent the birth of their baby, knowing it has a birth defect? The parents, who tearfully sang Amazing Grace to their dying child, saw his defect years before his execution; yet they loved him to the end and to the grave.

Our LORD God, knowing your faults and mine, is giving both of us the very best chance to come to Him. He has put us in the exact country; in the best location; in the best city, or town; in the best home; to the best parents; in the exact year; in the exact month; in the exact week; in the exact day; in the exact minute; in the exact second, to give us absolutely no excuse to pull from His loving, caring arms. We need not kid ourselves here.

I related helping the one family, if they failed, they could not say I failed them. See the parallel? Our loving Father does even greater things for all of us every day. If we should fail, we will never be able to look at Him and say He didn't try. **No we can not do that**.

Most important! He is not wrong about us at the present moment. He gives each of us the absolute best environment to succeed. We do not, will not, ever have a valid reason for failure, and our success is only through **His** Tolerant Grace.

There is a question which must be asked of ourselves; the answer to which we sometimes fear to seek. It is a question which sometimes haunts us, and for me it will for the rest of my life. It is a question that if it is not address, will result in all efforts, no matter how pious, turning to rubbish.

What must **I** do to be saved? **No,** that is not the question? "Well I believe that Jesus was and is the Son of God, born of a virgin, lived a sinless life, died a substitutionary death on the cross, physically died, was physically buried, physically rose the third day, and was seen upward of five-hundred before ascending to right hand of the Father." **That is pretty good, but not good enough.**

Precious brethren, don't we think **Satan knows all that? Is that going to save him?** Satan knew who God and Christ were before the foundation of the world, he saw Christ's birth, life, death, and resurrection: He was there.

So what is the question?

"Do I believe, or <u>do I just believe</u> I believe, and <u>what have I done with it?</u>" Does one only accept the fact that there is Father, Son, Holy Ghost, and an angelic host? I accept the fact that there are planets. I do not know or believe there are planets in space because I have not <u>experienced</u> them for myself, only earth. I accept the fact that there is a moon; I have not walked on the moon as our astronauts have, and though they can now say <u>they</u> believe there is a moon because they have experienced it, I only accept the fact that there is something there. I accept the fact that there is a sun. I feel the heat and it supposedly consumes hydrogen, but if science changes and says that the sun burns methane, I don't care, because I know nothing but what I have been told of the sun, but I accept that something that everyone calls the sun is there.

One would say, "But I have evidence that there is a God;" that by itself still means little. **Food on a table will not save one with lock jaw.**

There is absolutely <u>no way</u> a follower of Christ can live in this world today and not be persecuted by someone or some organization: All the way from what in my opinion is the **Anti Christ Legalistic Union**, to the next door neighbor. When I graduated from high school, they called me preacher Mac. That is not to my glory, but to His and the parents who raised me. They also put a statement in the part of the year book where one makes predictions of ones future that hurts even today.

We are so bound to quote Scripture that fits our lives that we miss God's messages. How many times has someone quoted this Scripture? Eph 2:8 "*For **by grace are ye saved** through faith; and that not* *of yourselves: [it is] the gift of God:"* Eph 2:9 *"**Not of works**, lest any man should boast."*(Emphasis is mine)

I asked the question before, do I believe, or do I <u>just believe</u> I believe, and <u>what have I done with it</u>? How many pastors dare to teach the verse that follows **Eph** 2:9?

Eph 2:10 *"For we are his **workmanship**, created in Christ Jesus **unto good works**, which God hath before ordained **that we should walk in them"**.* Then we have:

Jas 2:18 *"Yea, a man may say, Thou hast faith, and I have works: <u>shew me thy faith **without thy works**</u>, and I will <u>shew thee my **faith by my works**</u>.*

Jas 2:19 *Thou believest that there is one God; thou doest well: <u>the devils also believe, and tremble</u>.*

Jas 2:20 *But wilt thou know, O vain man, **<u>that faith without works is dead</u>?***(Emphasis is mine)

This is Salvation's "litmus test;" If we have it, we can not hide it; if we do not have it, we can not fake it. Oh! Precious brethren, **we cannot be saved with a dead faith.** But Churches shy away from this teaching; know why? The people will leave and go to another church which places no demands upon them; the collection plate will suffer, and they will hire another entertaining pastor for their itching ears.

We can have all the head knowledge in the universe, but my precious friend, **if all we do is go to Church on Sunday**, and have never expended one effort towards His Kingdom, we need to re-read what has just been said.

One can sleep in a garage, but that does not make them an automobile. All my life I have heard preachers aver, "Be on fire for the Lord." Well being a match doesn't mean one has a fire. For a match to start a fire it must give itself, **totally, to the task**, and it will be changed forever.

If we are saved, it is not because of anything we have ever physically accomplished on this earth, and we have not earned that salvation through works, but my friend <u>if</u> we are saved, <u>we cannot keep from working no matter how we try.</u>

When Jerusalem was utterly destroyed, the Romans were so obsessed with the Christians, and knowing that the Mount of Olives was a symbol to them, the big honcho ordered every olive tree cut to the ground. What he did not know was that the olive tree springs from roots better than seed. The resulting saplings which sprang up profusely everywhere were given the name "**Netver**," much as some would call them "crab-grass." In Central Texas we would call them

The Layman

hackberry, or yucca shoots. Netver was the term given the Christians, because the more one tried to kill them off, the more they grew and spread all over the place. Think on that.

When I was in Israel, I walked around that Olive Garden. Those ugly old olive trees stood in the midst of Netver sprigs that were as thick as weeds in any field.

I know that I again broke continuity, but perhaps not at all. I must impress upon all that the existence of this universe was not an after thought of our God. It was and is a deliberate plan to gather around Him a group of souls that want nothing better to do than love and serve Him.

Will we be one of them?

Intoxicated with unbroken success,
We have become too self-sufficient
To feel the necessity of redeeming and preserving grace,
Too proud to pray to the God that made us.

Abraham Lincoln

PHASE II CREATION II: WORLD II

Hebrews 1:2 *"Has in these last days spoken unto us by his Son, whom he has appointed heir of all things,* **by whom also he made the worlds;"**

Now allow me to explain "Phase I, and Phase II Creations". The Scripture we just read tells us that there were two worlds; however, the original world was created by the Phase I Creation I: World I that we are not given its creative sequence. The six day "Phase II Creation II: World II" is what we are not addressing. Remember the earth was not destroyed, only made "Void and Without Form", and it is for that reason Scripture identifies the two events, now, as worlds.

I have explained that in my opinion there was a preexisting occupied world: the one before the six days of the Gen 1:2. I have not placed a time upon it, nor do I think anyone can. We can only imagine the eons which may have past, that is if we can yet use the term eon. Time is time, but before time, how long something was has no meaning. Time cannot be assessed by us when it did not exist; then, perhaps, time did exist in the world before, and paused during the "Void and Without Form."

Having covered the period of time before the "Void and Without Form", I will present, in summary the five separate creative events:

1. The first Phase I Creation I: World I, we have covered.
2. Then, next, there is Phase II Creation II: World II.
3. We will later cover the Restoration.
4. From there we will discuss the Renewal.
5. Finally we will develop the Reorganization, and one or two interludes.

The first, which was "**Creation I**", the events occurring before Gen 1:2, we have briefly discussed, now for Phase II Creation II." Let me show a chronology of the next events of the seven days. I repeatedly hear: "God has never needed more than seven thoughts, each a nanosecond long (Billionth of a second), or seven anything's no matter their duration, to create the original heaven and earth, or to complete the second." I insert that because it would be common acceptance by many to assume He just "Zapped" everything into existence here. That might well be the case if it were not for His self established natural laws, **which He has most always followed**.

The Phase II Creation was done in seven of His days, whatever that time period was. Observe : 2Pe 3:8 *"But, beloved, be not ignorant of this one thing, that one day is with the LORD as a thousand years, and a thousand years as one day."*(Emphasis is mine) What Scripture is telling us here is that God's time periods are not necessarily ours. He can do, and most probably has done in one day what would take all else one thousand years to do. By the same token, since He is eternal, a thousand years does not exist to Him. It must be inserted; He could, but if He did, He would then alter His natural, well working, laws He established in the first place. Why should He get in a hurry? Our Father set up His natural laws from the beginning, so why not let things "Perk" as they still do, and enjoy His creativeness? I appreciate that I keep repeating that, but it is most important and we must never lose sight of that.

I fully recognize the argument that supports this as a "solar day." There are those I highly respect for their knowledge of Scripture which are quite dogmatic on this; however, the sun was not created until the fourth creative day; it was not until then, days, that is to say, days we now recognize, **could ever have begun**. I do not think that each of the days mentioned hereafter in Gen 1:2 refers to a 24 hour day, rather to a creative phase. God does not put things in Scripture to flower it up, and when time is explained by Peter, I think it is telling all of us, God does not have yesterday, today, or tomorrows.

One must recognize other examples here: This will make the gray headed Baptist pastor jump clean out of his shoes. I used to make home made wine. It would take me months to get the wine to age after initial fermentation so it had the flavor I would accept. **Jesus turned water into wine instantly** and the governor of the wedding feast declared it as the **best "hooch"** he had ever drunk. **Jesus healed the sick cast out demons and raised the dead**. I know these are verifiable examples of our Lord modifying His natural laws, but one must remember, why? It was to introduce the Gospel.

Consider if He went into details and explained all that occurred during these initial phases, it would boggle the minds of every one in the world.

In Genesis we have the following sequence of events: God creates heaven and earth, (Gen 1:1); It becomes "Void and Without Form"; God operates in the first of three of His offices, (Gen 1:2);The presence of <u>His light,</u>(Gen 1:3); and <u>God invents time,</u>(Gen 1:5); <u>God creates the sky,</u> (Gen 1:6); God <u>separates the earth from the waters,</u>(Gen 1:9,10); and <u>makes it fruitful,</u> (Gen 1:11,12); God forms the <u>lights,</u> (Gen 1:14-19); <u>Animals</u> created, (Gen 1:20-25); God <u>makes Male and Female</u> "in our image," (Gen 1:26-28); <u>Food appointed,</u> (Gen 1:29, 30); the work of <u>creation ended and approved,</u> (Gen 1:31), and <u>God rests on seventh day. (Gen. 2:3.</u>

The world of Gen 1:1 and that which we are now seeing in Gen 1:2 are a sequence apart. The void world lay in disarray; how long; how many possible millenniums could have lapsed, we just do not know. When I say it lay in "Void and without form", I mean that it stayed as it was. No morph, evolution, or microbial evolution was, or ever has been here.

When God decided, enough is enough, the Spirit of God makes His presence known and is now upon the scene, and we are now addressing, what I call Phase II Creation II: World II and God uses one of the 10 "lets" **(X01)** *

*(I want to make a note of the "X's I am using. I am going to continue using them as benchmarks. I will discuss them more later, but we need to remember them and where they are.)

Let there be light.

Gen 1:3 ¶ *"And God said, <u>Let there be light</u> (X02): and there was light."*
Gen 1:4 *"And <u>God saw the light</u>, that it was good: and God divided the light from the darkness."*
Gen 1:5 *"And <u>God called the light</u> Day, and the darkness he called Night."*

Before we continue I want to clarify the "Lets" of the first chapter. Who or what is God addressing when He says, "Let?" Are we to assume **He is asking that it be allowed**? Of course not; **He is in unison with His Son**. I have never heard one pastor even stop and address that. It has seemed to me that Pastors present this, almost as if God is solo here.

When I was a lad, when my dad wanted the lawn mowed, all he would have had to say when he left for work was, "Let's get the lawn mowed today son." When mom wanted the garbage taken our, all she would have had to say was, "Son, let's take out the garbage before we go to school." If I needed to make my bed, all she would have had to said was, "Let's get our bed made son." Did my dad mow the lawn; did my mother take out the garbage or make my bed? Neither my mom nor my dad **commanded** me to do those things; it was my love and respect for them that I did them. Can we not but see that it was our Lord's love, faith, and respect for the Father that exists here?

Now why do I bring this up? Look at the following:

Psalms 148:5 *Let them praise the name of the LORD:* **for he commanded, and _they were created._**

Isaiah 42:5 *Thus saith God the LORD,* **he that created the heavens,** *and stretched them out; he that* **spread forth the earth** *and that which cometh out of it;* _he that giveth breath unto the people upon it,_ **and spirit to them that walk therein:**

Isaiah 45:12 **I have made the earth,** *and created _man_ upon it: I, even my hands, have _stretched out the heavens,_ and _all their host have I commanded._*

Ephesians 3:9 *And to make all men see what is the fellowship of the mystery, which from the beginning of the world hath been* **hid in God, who created all things _by Jesus Christ:_**

Colossians 1:16 *For by him _were_ **all** _things created,_ that are in _heaven,_ and that are in _earth,_ visible and invisible,* **whether they be thrones, or dominions, or principalities, or powers: all things were created by him, and for him:**

Revelation 4:11 *Thou art worthy, O Lord, to receive glory and honour and power:* **for thou hast created all things, and for thy pleasure they are and were created.**

Revelation 10:6 *"And sware by him that liveth for ever and ever,* **who created heaven, and the things that therein are, and the earth, and the things that therein are, and the sea, and the things which are therein,** *that there should be time no longer."* (Emphasis is mine) It is God who is the architect, and the LORD who is the builder.

I want to impress this upon the reader, because there are a couple of things later that are difficult to understand unless we realize the creative acts here. Then we will see the LORD God acting: LORD in saving mercy; God in definable laws, and judgment.

In Gen 1:1 it states ¶ *"In the beginning God created the heaven and the earth."* Now if God created the earth, then He was present. If He was present His "light" would be present; however, after the explanation that the earth became *"Void and Without Form"*, His presence was obviously removed, and we now see the spirit of God moving over the face of the waters and His presence returns with the command "Let there be light," and God uses the first of His 10 "lets"(X02) of creation. So! The first thing that God put here in this phase of restoration was HIS LIGHT. This light was <u>not the sun</u>. We will cover that later, and He said "light" and not "Lights." That light was <u>God's presence where ever He may be</u>, and that "wherever" is now that His Spirit is once again on His earth.

LIGHT

There is a difference in the terms used to describe light that might be of interest. Here, in these verses, it is **"Ore"** (Strong 216), Speaks of a light Giver, or <u>light itself</u>. When speaking of the sun, **"Maor"** (Strong 3974), is used, in that it is a light holder or a <u>luminous body</u>. A lamp would be "Maor." Again, the word **"Ore"** is used as the identity of light itself. This light, **"Ore,"** was the presence of God, **His Shechinah Glory.** Now one won't find the word Shechinah in the Bible, but it was a Chaldee word used by the Jews to designate the visible symbol of the presence of the invisible God. This light was the total light which flooded the earth during the first phase of its existence. 1Jo 1:5 *"This then is the message which we have heard of him, and declare unto you, that God is light, and in him is no darkness at all."*

God's Spirit, this light, is now returning after a span of time beyond our ability to know, returning to a **"tohu," "bohu" earth.** We have, as I understand it, different divisions of light. Allow me to give examples. The Bible makes a clear distinction between **the light and a light giver.** There are at least four divisions of light as we know them.

1. We have the light of God's presence wherever He is.

2. We have the emitted light of the stars, our sun being but one of them.

3. We have natural light existing by certain animals, as the fire-fly, glow-worm, and several sea creatures.

4. We have light emitted from manmade devices.

5. We have His enlightening presence that light which shines in **our hearts** to give us understanding.

I would give reference to, Ps 74:16 *"The day is thine, the night also is thine: thou hast prepared **the light and the sun.**"* (Emphasis is mine) Again we have the "And" word. It defines what we are talking about in that <u>they are two distinct identities.</u> "The day is thine, the night also is thine: thou hast prepared the light and (**then**) the sun." (Emphasis is mine)

If the new heaven and earth are full of the "Light Giver" then <u>the opposite</u> would be the case with Satan's realm.

The Layman

Re 16:10 *"And the fifth angel poured out his vial upon the seat of the Beast; and his kingdom was <u>full of darkness</u>; and they gnawed their tongues for pain,"* (Emphasis is mine)

There was a time when one strayed from God. It would take a book to explain why. I will only say this, they express that while they moved from the Father they had never known Spiritual darkness until they were within its confines, and it surrounded, and grasp their very soul. They sought help from every professional, without comfort. I will not take the space to give the details of it all; however one would ask, "Did they return?" Oh yes; however, I will tell everyone that will listen, that bright relationship that they once shared with the heavenly Father has never been quite the same. Some pious one will say that "He is faithful and just to forgive." That is true, and He will remove the sin as far as the east is from the west; however, sometimes we are never able to forgive ourselves.

Friend, with all that lies within my soul, I beg all to stay within His light.

Jesus relates in Scripture to <u>both light and darkness as coexisting</u> within the evil. Mt 6:23 *"But if thine eye be evil, thy whole body shall be full of darkness. If therefore the light that is in thee be darkness, how great is that darkness!"*

If there were divine judgments upon the first earth, and I believe that as a possibility, then God's light, His Spirit, departed. "Well." One would say. "You said that Satan could have done it" I said it could have been either one, but in either case, God had to allow it to happen, or to have done it; therefore, God must have left, because He is now coming back.

We should never loose our understanding of His will. I am repeating this because it so easy for us in a seeing, touching, hearing and smelling world to lose sight of our awesome God and His foreknowledge and eternal plan.

1. There is the direct will of God; His established universal laws governing both the cosmos and mankind.

2. There is the permissive will of God; those of storms, floods, earthquakes, thorns/thistles, disease and general mayhem brought as a result of sin. One could write volumes explaining each.

We have discussed that God knew the first world was not eternal. There was a morning star singing off key and there were some of the sons of God who lacked the shout of a champion. Satan was one of the brightest and with him one third of the inhabitants of God's realm would fall. It was Satan's prideful subsequent fall which ultimately caused chaos upon the first creation.

I cannot imagine what must have transpired during the time span of the first earth, to have caused such a violent ""Void and Without Form"." But I am thankful that our God's "light" is here now.

TIME

We now have the first mention of "TIME". Before we have a sequence of events, but now God has "**an evening then a morning of the first day.**"

Gen 1:5 "*And (*then*) God <u>called</u> the light Day, and (*then*) the darkness he called Night. And (*then*) the evening and (*then*) the morning were the first day.*" (I have inserted the term "then" to emphasize its value. <u>I will do this only once more</u> since I feel it may distract from the Word.)

I cannot elaborate any further than what was first said; **before God created it, time did not exist.** That is the reason that even though the Word tells us that Jesus Christ was the "beginning of the creation of God, without time He is eternal past, present, and eternal future; Therefore, He is and has always been eternal. God made time so we wouldn't go nuts. Try to imagine life without the base of time. I bet one could not stretch their mind to even fathom it.

I know this to be redundant, but it would serve us well to be cautious at this point. Let us not forget Peter's definition of a day for God. **When speaking here, of a "day," we should not pin this down to a twenty-four hour period of time**, rather it should be seen <u>as sequence of event.</u> It could be further elaborated on by the statement "He was quite a man <u>in his day</u>."

Someone asked Dr. J. V. McGee to explain, "Eternity vs. time." Dr. McGee said, "*Picture, if you will your life as being contained within a long, long box. One end is when you are born, and the opposite end is when you die.*" He paused a moment for mental pictures to develop, then continued; "*Now eternity is the same thing. It is the very same box, except it now has both ends knocked out.*"

Firmament in the midst of the waters

(X03) Gen 1:6: ¶ "*And God said, <u>Let there be</u> a firmament in the midst of the waters, and let it divide the waters from the waters.*"

The Layman

Gen 1:7 *"And God made the firmament, and divided the waters which [were] under the firmament from the waters which [were] above the firmament: and it was so."*(Emphasis is mine)

I know that water is composed of two parts Hydrogen, to one part Oxygen. I also know that separated in the exact proportions they are in, if mixed and ignited, they would burn intensely, but when combined, they put out fires.

I well remember my Physics teacher demonstrating this phenomenon. With electrolysis he separated water into Hydrogen and Oxygen. He then directed the two gasses through tubes that mixed the gasses. At the output, he lit a match and there was a small flame, and little drops of water would form within the flame and drop to the floor. But that does not make Oxygen.

Now if anyone wants to research "Photochemical dissociation breakup of water molecules by ultraviolet and Photosynthesis sunlight and organics" there are good papers to be had. I think there are those who would thoroughly understand these, if I could understand it sufficiently myself I would present it here; however, I do not understand it.

I read a lengthy article where science is quoted in saying that without the ultraviolet rays of the sun beaming down upon the earth that the oceans of water would separate and form the oxygen we breathe. This breakdown would also provide enrichment to the atmosphere with carbon dioxide which would in turn enhance enormous vegetation growth. I do not know the natural "perk" when it comes to our atmosphere, so I will only say that we have atmosphere and leave it there.

There is one thing in this sequence that should be noted, and I have termed it "Perk." Our Father knows how His laws function, that is the reason, when science says it took one hundred million years to originally build up earth's oxygen levels, I do not dispute them; however, I feel oxygen has still here from that of Gen 1:1.

Could God make oxygen? I would not even answer that. What I keep emphasizing; "Why Should He?" He set up His natural laws, and for the exception of where our sins have altered them, they are still working: why not just let it happen like He planned no matter how long it took? We want to speed things up, because we are under the influence of time; our Heavenly Father was not, and is not and will not be. Now after saying that, I feel the air was still here from Creation I.

LAND

God separates the land from the waters. God defines the dry land and seas**(X04)**. **Gen. 1:9** ¶ *"And God said, Let **the** waters under the heaven be gathered together unto **one** place, and let **the** dry land appear: and it was so."*(Emphasis is mine) Again it is the way things are said in the Bible which are of the most importance. God did not say let us make land, dry it out, and call it **dry land**. It is stated as if dry land was already there, preexistent; all that need be done is let it surface. I am not saying that God kept mud puddles off of it while it was beneath the sea. I am emphasizing the term "let **the** dry land appear."

One with my same heart has logically put for the axiom, "If I have a jar full of sand and add water, does the sand become wet? Or does the water simply cling to the dry sand? Valid point.

To appear, something must have been in existence prior to this point; otherwise it is manifested, created, or called into being. It must be noted that the same expression used to relate to "the dry land" is used to relate to "the waters;" that is "let **the** waters," "Let **the** dry land." **If these were not preexisting**, it would seem that water and land would have to be first in creative sequence, then He would start from there. **In other words**; **let there be** waters, and let the waters under heaven be gathered unto one place. **Let there be** Land, and let the dry land appear.

Please do not get bogged down here. The point I am making is that by using the expression, "Let **the** dry land appear" it is evident that "dry land" **pre-existed**, and surfaced from a **preexisting body** of water, which had to be there before the "Void and Without Form." Precious brethren, I know that He does not have to tell us every detail. This is but another thing in a chain of events that has no explanation if one denies the first world's existence, and I mention it for the reader's consideration.

Gen 1:10 *"And God called **the** dry land Earth; and the gathering together of **the** waters called he Seas:"* (Emphasis is mine)

I find no one disputing that order. It is not until later that modern man has his problems with a supreme order of events.

Was the dry land "Pangaea" as stated by some? We will discuss this later when we cover Noah, but note that God did not say let the dry land**s** appear. However, the term, dry land, could be global, not regional; I am not encouraging one to be dogmatic here.

The Layman

God does not explain how He did these things and to say exactly how would be beyond our grasp; However, I feel it would not violate anything to say that possibly the fountains of the deep were formed at this point. The fountains would absorb vast quantities of water which would in turn provide the natural means for the dry land to appear, and later these same fountains would be used to cover the earth anew at the flood, and then return once more to wherever He holds them. We are talking about vast quantities of water that boggle my mind. Mount Everest is 29,028 feet above sea level. The flood was 22.5 feet above that, all over the earth, or 22.5 feet above whatever the level of the highest mountain **was at that time**.

Then again, we do not know at that time, what elevated level the land was in relation to the sea. All I can say is that there is a bunch of water stored somewhere. The South Pole has vast quantities of ice stored. In places it is over a mile deep. Well suppose that the whole earth was covered at the same one mile depth; there would still have to be 23,770.5 more feet of water to come from somewhere **if** our mountains were as high as they are today: **I suspect they were not.**

This would seem out of place, and perhaps should be discussed when we cover the flood, but I have put it here, and we should remember it because I will not cover it in detail there. It is most important for us to understand what is left out, and this is one: what ever amount this vast quantity of water was, it is still here somewhere.

There is another discussion to be explored, and we will address that in more detail when we get to the subject of the flood. We then will discuss the "Catastrophic Platonic" theories that may tell us that this great depth may not have been necessary.

DID IT RAIN

While on the subject of water, I want to express something that I want everyone to understand, that I can no more prove what we are about to discuss, than a "turtle can fly."

The next subject we are going to address is God's bringing forth vegetation. We know that in the second chapter of Genesis it tells us that there was no rain. Allow me to say that between the beginning of Gen 1:1, the first Phase and the beginning of Gen 1:2, the second Phase, cover **hundreds-of-millions-of-years.** Remember the dinosaurs were here 215 million years before Gen 1:2.

88

The reason I feel that there was rain until Gen 2:4: is that vegetation, animals, male and female need water, and since nothing is said, I feel it is another between the lines item. Vegetation, man, or animals cannot live without soil, food, and water. There is also the need for erosion, and most probably 90% of that occurred during the first Phase and the second Phase. There is an often overlooked item here in Phase II, if the land was submerged under salt water, the, now, dry land would need fresh water: to leach out the salt; to allow plants to grow; to refill the fresh water aquifers, and the occupants of the second Creation would need it to drink.

When we get to Gen 2, it will tell us of rivers that flow as a result of a mist which rises from the earth. I do not dispute the fact that the LORD God could have dredged the river beds, but again, why? If it rained here in Gen 1:2, then there would be natural channels for rivers to flow in, even if they were in Gen 2 supplied by the dew then available. If it rained in Gen 1:2, this would fill aquifers which in turn would, later, be replenished by the dew of Gen 2.

Reason with me here:

When we think on all these things, we should seriously ask ourselves: Did God take His hands and crush rock to make soil? Did He scoop up ocean water, distill it, then pour it on earth to carve river beds, or did He dredge river beds with a stick? See how silly these suggestions sound when someone hints that this was miraculously done in 7/24 hour days? If this is a 24 hour day, then this is exactly the way God would have to do it. I pray none who read this would accept such an approach.

I can only subjectively ask why God should do this when He has already set in motion His natural laws during the original creation. Why wouldn't He just enjoy watching it all happen? He could enjoy the rivers, water falls, and watch the tiny little things exist, all the way to the dinosaurs.

Allow me to dumb it down so even I can understand it. Why do people build elaborate **"Rouge Goldberg" devices** that work for hours and do absolutely nothing? It is because these creations always bring delight to the builder. They and we and our God all love to watch the product of our hands. We are in His image; do we not think He enjoys watching what He has set in motion, work?

VEGETATION: Gen 1: 11—12 **(X05)**

During WWII, most families had what were called "Victory Gardens." During the spring, we would take seeds and plant them in tin cans, which we would place on every window sill we could find. It was always such a thrill to see the little shoots stick their heads just above the soil; almost like saying hello to us all. We would then plant the seedlings when the warm weather was near. Each day mother would take buckets of water to the garden and water the little fellows. First, there were strong stems, then blooms, then fruit. No one will ever forget the fresh taste of garden fruit and vegetables. We kids ate vegetables. Tomatoes made your mump glands smart; peas did not turn to mush when you bit into them, and green beans weren't little green tasteless rubber tubes.

Today, we go to the nursery and buy a full grown plant with tomatoes already set, but in our hearts there is never the joy of what we did with our own hands, and the taste is not equaled.

I see my Father patiently watching each layer of earth piled upon another, each plant spring into the fresh air, and remember what the first world was like in pristine beauty.

Gen. 1:11 *"And God said, Let the earth bring forth grass, the herb yielding seed, and the fruit tree yielding fruit after his kind, whose seed is in itself, upon the earth: and it was so.* Gen. 1:12 *And the earth brought forth grass, and herb yielding seed after his kind, and the tree yielding fruit, whose seed was in itself, after his kind: and **God saw that it was good.**"*(Emphasis is mine.)

I studied a work, which was most interesting. (**Rightly Dividing the Word,** by Clarence Larkin, 1920) *"The work of the "Third Day" was twofold, the emergence of the land from the sea, and the reappearance of vegetable life. Gen 1:9-13. This was not a new creation, but a RESURRECTION. The earth rises up from its "Watery Grave," and seeds, and the roots of plants and herbs and trees that were in the earth sprang into life as they do in the spring of the year after the winter is over. This reveals the fact that the Pre-Adamite Earth was clothed with verdure, and covered with plants and trees like those of the Present Earth."*

There being a Pre-Adamite world, there were seeds, even though the seeds lay dormant for no matter how long, given the opportunity to grow, they sprang forth. Hence, God said "Let" the earth bring forth, not an evolutionary act at all, but another of His natural laws.

There are others who support Mr. Larkin's discussion of the establishment of vegetation after the "Void and Without Form"; however, it was still at the command of God, (the architect) to the LORD God, (the builder), as one of the "Let's" in Genesis.

Many who read this are familiar with seeds. I do not attest to be an expert, but I will tell what little I do know. Each year, my fields are attacked by thistles or weeds. One year the thistles were of such profusion that one could not set two fingers on the ground without touching one of them. The next Year it was dove-weed with few thistles present, the next year it was sunflowers with no thistles and few dove weeds; this year it was broom weed and then cockleburs. I have lived here for 12 years and have never, before had one single cocklebur, in addition to that, I have not had one thistle again.

The cycle continues. The seeds lay in a dormant state until just the right, whatever, happens, and then they attack. I have been told that seed can remain in the ground for hundreds of years until the right timing occurs. If we take seeds from archeological digs, plant them, they will grow. I remember reading when archeologists first opened the tombs in Egypt, and found a variety of seeds. There was great jubilation when they planted some, and they grew. Ask any farmer, and he would have told them that.

I remember, years ago when it rained on one of our driest deserts. Looking at the puddles, people were amazed in that they saw little shrimp like creatures swimming near the edges. These little fellers had survived for years without water and 120/140 degree summers, and frigid winters, but when the right time came, they came to life, bred, laid eggs in the sand, and then died. We will never grasp all of our Fathers wonders.

The LORD God did not "re-plant" the earth after the flood waters abated: did He? When we get to Noah, I will mention this again, but I want to start everyone's mind to thinking here.

Pal-ecologists have long said that the fossilized vegetation is similar **but not all** of that seen in today's plant life. This is most evident when imprints are found within coal. That does not dissuade me in the least. What they are saying is those that they have found do not all agree with today's plant life, and a lot of preexisting plants, simply did not make it through.

Take a second and think of this: How long does it take an acorn to grow into a tree which will produce an acorn? God said "let"

91

The Layman

the earth bring forth, and we try and cram this all into a 24 hour period of time.

The SUN, MOON, and STARS: (X06)

God creates light (Maor), and stars.

Gen 1:14 ¶ *"And God said, <u>Let there be lights</u> in the firmament of the heaven to divide the day from the night; and let them be for signs, and for seasons, and for days, and years:"*
Gen 1:15 *"And <u>let them be for lights</u> in the firmament of the heaven to give light upon the earth: and it was so."*
Gen 1:16 *"And <u>God made two</u> great lights; the greater light to rule the day, and the lesser light to rule the night: he made the stars also."*
Gen 1:17 *"And <u>God **set** them</u> in the firmament of the heaven to give light upon the earth,"* (Remember "set" later when we discuss the sun, and the moon.)
Gen 1:18 *"<u>And to rule</u> over the day and over the night, and to divide the light from the darkness: and God saw that it was good."*
Gen 1:19 *"And the evening and the morning were the fourth day."* (Emphasis is mine)

The sun and the moon are now present. The sun is appointed to provide the earth with a 24 hour cycle. The moon is appointed to provide the earth with a 27.2 day cycle. However, **that does not put our Father within these time frames.**

This **light** (Maor) **is a creation** as well as time: Light is what is called a 'Photon' and travels lickedy-split (That's real fast). Now this is different from the light (Ore) of Gen 1:3 which was God's presence. This is the photon light (Maor) from the sun, stars and reflective light of the moon and planets.

THE SUN

The sun converts 600-million tons of hydrogen, into 596-million tons of helium every second. The resulting **four million ton** loss, because of this transformation, is **converted into energy every second.** Our sun would have long been reduced to a dwarf or gassy giant or completely extinguished by now if it had been here and lit 4.5 billion years. It is most difficult to know how to put a time upon fiery

92

orbs; however, when speaking of our sun, here are two theories for consideration:

First: THE SHRINKING SUN THEORY.

It is reported that a British team has been measuring the sun since the eighteen-hundreds and they say that the **sun is shrinking** by five feet a day. 4.5 billion years of shrinking at 5 ft. a day would have made the original sun 1.5 billion miles larger back then, which would have put the planet Jupiter somewhere deep within its surface. I do not see our solar system existing if this were the case; however, if this were a constant, it certainly proves the sun was not here 4.5 billion years ago.

Second: THE EXPANDING SUN THEORY.

I further read where other astronomers, as well as concurring scientist, say that with the weight of matter being consumed, 4 million tons lost every second, the mass of the sun is less and less which, due to the loss of mass, lends to less and less gravity and makes it expand, so they say the **sun is expanding**.

We now must consider that **we** have the 4 million tons consumed per second and if this were the case 4.5 billion years ago, because of the additional gravitational forces exerted by this enormous mass, we would have had a star that was several magnitudes hotter than what we see today. Excluding the additional heat for now, that doesn't bother me as much as to figure out the mass of the earth, the projected gravitational pull of such a star , and how fast our orbit would have to be, or how far out in space we would have to be in order to obtain equilibrium.

Let me give an example here. Remember the little toy paddle and connected rubber ball on the rubber band? We used to twirl that little ball around and around, faster and faster, and the little ball would go further and further away. What we were doing was obtaining equilibrium between the pull of the rubber band and the weight of the ball. Now picture this: substitute that rubber band for a strip of rubber cut from an inner tube. How fast would we have to twirl that around to get the ball to fly out at the same distance as before? With this increase of gravitational pull, we would be really flying, and this does not consider what we are going to do with the other eight (excuse me, now seven) planets while we settle down.

I personally follow the expanding sun theory in that less mass produces less gravity and therefore the sun, obviously, would expand with age; However, if that were so, 4.5 billion years of expanding, and with it only as big as it is today the original mass would be enormous.

I can well imagine that if we were in the same orbit 4.5 billion years ago, five trips around the sun could equal one of our present days, and with the gravitational pull exerted, I highly imagine the earth would be much as the moon in that we would face the sun with no daily rotation at all. Then, how about centrifugal force? We would have been like a lawn sprinkler in space at those speeds. I know that this does not make sense when we think of 4.5 billion years, and science knows it doesn't make sense, that is the reason I say that the sun may have been here, but **it was not "lit" 4.5 billion years ago**, and without it, only the Shechinah Glory of God could satisfy.

I want to add here, there is a study which suggests that before the moon came upon the scene, the earth did orbit the sun, I think it said, six times a day. I do not want to leave any hole unfilled.

Armed with the understanding of either the shrinking sun, or expanding sun theories, it really makes no difference in the end which one we choose to believe. I read an article that said scientists are unable to account for the sun's existence for more than a few thousand years anyway.

What is even more puzzling, I understand that some scientist cannot explain why the sun consumes hydrogen at all. I am told that it is a suspected, if not accepted fact, using our current technology that the sun is not large enough to possess sufficient gravitational forces to start or even sustain a nuclear fusion state. So then why does it: Known only to God.

Another word shift:

I would point out another word, "Asah." Genesis 1:16 "*And God made (Asah) two great lights; the greater light to rule the day, and the lesser light to rule the night: he made the stars also.*

This word (make--Asah) does not necessarily mean to "create," but as **Strong's** (6213) interpretation also says, "*To accomplish, advance, fashion, appoint, or bring forth.*" This could indicate that the sun may possibly have been somewhere, as well as the moon, since the word applies to both.

Gen 1:17 And God brought them forth or set them in the firmament of the heaven to give light upon the earth.

It appears by Scripture, that:

1. Wherever they were, or if already here, God either appointed them or fashioned them to the task.

2. God <u>set</u> them in place, He then lit the sun and let the (Maor) light reflect off from the moon.

Isn't He so wonderful!

THE MOON

There are six predominant scientific theories on the origin of our moon.

1. **The Fission Theory:** In 1878, George Howard Darwin, no, not the evolutionist, but his son, theorized that the earth at its beginning, spun so rapidly that the gravitational force of the sun, and the centrifugal force of the spinning earth, caused a mass of the earth to separate and form the moon; this was known as the "**Fission Theory**." This theory, believe it or not, lasted all the way into the twentieth century.

2. **The Snare Theory:** About 1909, an astronomer named Thomas Jefferson Jackson See, set forth the theory that while the earth was forming, a smaller planet was also forming close to our orbital path, and as the two neared each other the mutual gravitational attraction snared the moon into an earth orbit. It was commonly known as the "**Snare Theory**."

3. **The Co-accretion Theory:** Then appeared another astronomer called Edouard Roche who set forth the theory that the moon and the earth independently formed, yet coexisted at the same time. This was known as the "**Co-accretion Theory**."

4. **The Big Whack Theory:** As a result of collaboration of several astrologists, among who were W. K. Hartmann and D. R. Davis who studied the work of a Russian astrophysicist, by the name of V. S. Safronav there arose what was affectionately called "**The Big Whack Theory**."

5. **The Giant-Impact Hypothesis Theory:** Then after the Lunar Lander missions when they brought about a half of a ton of rocks back to earth the "Big Whack" was given a more dignified title of "**Giant-Impact-Hypothesis**."

This theorized that an object two or three times the size of the planet Mars struck the earth and not only fused with the earth, but also caused ejection of the earth's surface to form a debris cloud which was

95

termed a "Proto-Lunar Debris Cloud." This cloud was void of any iron
due to the earth's iron core fusing with the iron core of the object, and
the remaining cloud, which later formed the moon would be composed
of the earth's crust, and the outside of the colliding object.

There arose an argument about the collision of such an object
with the then developing earth that would not account for the present
tilt of the earth in relation to the axis of its orbit about the sun. Also an
object that size, hitting the earth would cause the earth to spin much
faster than it does today. This rapid rotation of the earth would not
prevent life, as known in this period, to have existed once the
atmosphere and climate once settled.

6. Well there was one who questioned, just one impact,
Astrophysics' Robin M Canup. Her calculations showed a flaw in the
original thinking of the Giant Impact. She addressed the problem of an
object large enough to form the moon, striking the earth would in fact
make it spin much faster than it presently does. She introduced the
"Big Whack II." She said that for the earth to have its present angular
tilt of 23.5% off the orbital path around the sun it must have, later,
been struck by another object which slowed the earth's rotation to
approximately what it is today.

One thing which she did not explain, and if so, I did not
discover the answer, just what was the second impact's composition
and what happened to the ejected debris from this impact.

I am not going to cover the different **"Capture theories"** since
they vary in complexity with the author of each. It may be summarized
by saying each; essentially say the same thing; the moon formed
elsewhere and the gravitational pull of the earth "captured" it.

The term used in Genesis does not necessarily indicate that
God created the moon at that specific time, but assigned it the task at
that time. Both the sun and the moon could well have been present
and fully functional until God decided to appoint them their rolls in
creation; **the earth had to orbit something**.

We sometimes fall prey to picturing God sitting down at His
work bench and randomly forming the cosmos, one bit at a time; now
I do not believe that. Do we stop and realize He made a star called
"KY Cygni." KY Cygni has a diameter of 1.3 billion miles. According
to the new study it is determined to be about 1500 times larger than the
Sun. Its size is so large that it would completely engulf the orbit of
Jupiter if it were located in our Sun's position. Considering that, now
picture our Father at the other end of the creative work bench,

designing a tiny "Quirk" that is so small that it can penetrate our atmosphere, go through the center of out earth, and exit the atmosphere on the other side, having touched nothing.

That would bring to the forefront of our thinking, what then is a Quirk made of? It is easy to say our planets are made of such and such material, but let us look at the opposite end of creation. It is easy to say a Quirk is just a charged particle, OK! What then is that particle made of, or what is holding the charge, or what is a "charge"?

There is no end to our universe in the infinite to the infinitesimal. No matter how far out into space one would go, there is something on the other side. No matter how small one could search there is something it is made of, of something, of something.

When we try to impress others with our lack of understanding, it becomes meaningless. We cannot, we have not, and we will not figure out God's natural laws. It is fun trying, and there are many who enjoy untangling what isn't tangled in the first place, and I admire them. I only wish they could see that all this wonder could not have happen by its lonesome, and just quit trying to fight the obvious.

Let's look at the moon as science sees it today. If we were to take the billions, even millions of years that modern man says we were on the earth and apply it to the moon, the moon would be in deep trouble. Now it is a fact that the tidal movement of the earth, gravity, and the relation of the moon to the earth have an effect upon each other. The moon's orbit is changing, and its rotation has long stopped to equal its orbit around the earth, so only one side is seen from our surface. I have been informed that the moon is moving away from the earth at a rate of 1.5″ a year: **today**. The rate at which the Moon is moving away from the Earth (due to tidal friction, and the mutual gravitational fields, slowing its orbit around the earth) places a limit on the age of the Moon, within present knowledge, of **no more than 20-30,000 years.** This time period is to be remembered when we discuss the Neanderthal man later.

THE STARS

Let's look at the stars. I do not really think that the stars were made at this time, rather at an earlier time. Let me caveat that statement by saying I really do not have proof either way; however, if the universe is supposedly 12/15 billion years old, the stars must have been here at that time. Scripture only tells us: Genesis 1:16 *"And God made two great lights; the greater light to rule the day, and the lesser light to rule the night: **he made the stars also**."* That simple statement tells us He is not going to get any deeper in explanation.

LIFE ON OTHER PLANETS

Joh 14:2 *"In my Father's house are many mansions: if it were not so, I would have told you. I go to prepare a place for you. Joh 14:3 And if I go and prepare a place for you, I will come again, and receive you unto myself; that where I am, there ye may be also."*

For those of us who believe the Bible, there is no argument that there are other "abiding places" in God's universe. We do not know, because we are not told, if they are presently inhabited or not. Mankind, and I embarrassingly must add my name here, says "our universe." My friend, it is God's universe because, except for the myriads of litter we are depositing about our little planet, we have not, as yet, ruined the universe.

There are many things we will never know about the heavens until we are in them. I laugh at man when he wants to "discover" **if there is life in the universe other than us**. I heard an old preacher respond when asked about flying saucers; if he believed there was life beyond our planet. He quoted John 14:2 and said "I would love to think that there are millions of worlds out there, and that we are the only one who have sinned against our God."

I would not take the fore front and try to imagine when God started this entire universe. It is for Him to know and for me to find out when I get the chance to ask Him. Even then He may choose not to answer. How could God explain timeless events to one who is bound to time tables? Perhaps when I become eternal, He can explain things eternal. I love Him, and that is enough.

Someday man will detect something which he thinks is evolutionary life on one of the planets. My little professor will "toot" that "we are not alone, we knew this all along and **that proves evolution is everywhere:** What are you creationists going to say now?" My brother in Christ, modern man will never believe that he is not the smartest thing in the universe. Man will find primitive life on Mars; know why? It is not that Mars is closest to the earth in environmental possibilities, it is because, science knows, that spores in our atmosphere have been picked up since day one, by solar winds and are scattered throughout the solar system. They will scratch the dust of Mars and someday find an area where a greater population of these spores has landed. Boy what a donkey-pony show they will put on then. They could find the same thing, and in much greater quantities on the moon, but that would be too obvious wouldn't it? I mean, that would tip their hand and ruin there show. Remember the probe to Mars where some of the scientific community, was quoted as saying that they had indeed found life? Then Good Science proved that it was due to instrumentation, and contamination which caused the result.

One would aver, "I know that there are most probably millions if not trillions of spores that are being picked up by solar winds, but what are the odds that they would find their way to Mars?" Well I do not have a clue as to the odds, but speaking of odds, how about the miraculous rock from mars finding its way to earth? Not only do they know it came from Mars, since they have so many rocks to compare it too, but they also say they know how it got here. They say it was because of a glancing blow of a comet or meteor smashed into the planet and catapulted it to earth where it was, perchance, discovered. They even know <u>when</u> this happened. They can't date a live mollusk, or seal accurately, but they sure must be good at dating falling rocks. It won't be long until someone will aver that they have even found the crater on Mars from which it came.

They date this rock by sedimentary layers of ice where the thing was found. Of course they don't know how fast it was traveling, how hot it was when it hit, therefore, how deep it settled; perhaps, it ricochet off of two walruses a wooly mammoth and a polar bear before settling down. Who is to say that this "rock" did not come from somewhere else in the universe just because it had similarities to mars?

One little rock hidden under tons of ice and they can't find a four hundred, fifty foot wooden ship under ice on a known mountain. Isn't that amazing? I bet if we sit one of those fellers down, he will tell us whether it was a Yankee rock, or a Rebel rock. If someone doesn't think Satan is working in the minds of some men today, they are very naive indeed. It will benefit us all to remember, Pr 15:2 *"The tongue of the wise useth knowledge aright: but the mouth of fools poureth out foolishness."* They could be honest and say that "It **seems** to be like samples we took from mars." Who can prove them wrong?

Please do not lose sight of one fact; Jesus has already told us there were many abiding places in the universe. **He did not say** that

The Layman

there was nothing on them, in fact, by saying they were mansions, or abiding places, He left the door wide open to the possibility. If science could show there was life anywhere else, that **does not** take away from my faith in Scripture, on the contrary, because **Scripture does not say we are alone.**

I love this quaint saying of a dying man, who exclaimed:

"I have no fear of going home; I have sent all before me;
God's finger in on the latch of my door, and I am ready for him to enter.

"But" said one, "Are you not afraid lest you should miss your Inheritance?"
"Nay," said he, "nay; there is one crown in heaven which the angel Gabriel could not wear, it will fit no head but mine.
There is one throne in heaven which Paul the apostle could not fill; it is made for me, and I shall have it."

Dr. Scofield

GOD CREATES LIFE

THE RAT

Now this will tie into our discussion quite nicely. Poor scientist in their "wisdom" has now put forth the hypothesis that all, now living things, evolved from a little rat: can you imagine that?

Hadrocodium (having the definition of full head), which is more than I can say for the somewhat lacking intellectual that dreamed up this primordial fairy tale. This little rat was so small that its estimated weight would have been less than a thumb tack. Since it is the first little critter that "evolution science" can find, which they say was here 65-million years ago when at the Yucatan Peninsula, an asteroid struck and all life on earth was destroyed: All but the little rat of course. Scientist says it lived "deep" within the earth and survived the asteroid strike.

They then jump on the evolutionary train and says that we all come from him. See? We were always taught our ancestor was a monkey, now we know our grand-daddy was a rat; however, there is no DNA to prove that. Oh bummer, we have to go back to God again.

Why do they do this? Well to admit total extinction, they would have to admit that there is a Living and True God. The amazing thing is that they can show absolutely no evolutionary evidence which would show where everything originated, yet they will keep up the dialogue.

It is a fact of human behavior, if a lie is repeated often enough to the same people, they will accept it as fact; however, scientists are going to have and show me how the little feller morphed into an elephant, rhino, tiger, kitty cat, puppy dog, then you and I; and they can not. The sad part is they know they can not. DNA disputes them at every turn.

There are approximately 500 species of rats in the world today, and if someone came up with a magic bullet that would kill off 90% of them, they would reestablish the predator, prey ratio within one year. One pair of rats can procreate 350,000,000 offspring in three years.

Know something else? **They are still rats** and haven't evolved into anything else for the six to ten thousand years we have observed them.

FISH AND FOWL: Gen1:20 (X07)

Gen 1:20 ¶ *"And God said, Let **the waters** bring forth abundantly the moving creature that hath life, and fowl that may fly above the earth in the open firmament of heaven.* Gen 1:21 *And God created great whales, and every living creature that moveth, which the waters brought forth abundantly, after their kind, and every winged fowl after his kind: 22 And God blessed them, saying, Be fruitful, and multiply, **and fill the waters** in the seas, and let fowl multiply in the earth.* (Emphasis is mine)

He says "multiply, and fill the waters in the seas, and let fowl multiply in the earth." He does not say "Replenish." The reason is that these are for the most part new creatures, with possibly a few aquatics which may well have survived the "Void and Without Form" period. Recent finds have indicated this as a possibility; **however, most all of the creatures we see today, are all new.**

At this point we don't have, as yet, anything on land except, possibly the birds. Remember those "uneducated" men of old which said 1Co 15:39 *"All flesh is not the same flesh: but there is one kind of flesh of men, another flesh of beasts, another of fishes, and another of birds."* (Emphasis is mine) Isn't it amazing? They didn't have DNA investigative equipment, they didn't have autopsy evidence, and they didn't have electron microscopes. Wonder who told them all this? We know who it was, the revelation from our LORD God.

I cannot stress the importance of everything in order, and in balanced harmony. Man could not dream this sequence, and this is the only supported order of life that could have existed on the planet.

ANIMALS CREATED: (X08).

Genesis 1:24, 25 **God creates animals on the earth. (XO8)** Gen 1:24 ¶*"And God said, Let the **earth** bring forth the living creature **after his kind**, cattle, and creeping thing, and beast of the earth **after his kind**: and it was so.* Gen 1:25 ***And God made** the beast of the earth **after his kind**, and cattle **after their kind**, and every thing that creepeth upon the earth **after his kind**:"*(Emphasis is mine)

No one will ever convince me or or anyone else, that these animals were of the Tyrannosaurus Rex variety. I think they were sheep, goats, horses, cattle, and the like. They were all graminivorous, including the Lions, Bears, and Tigers. We do not know if these creatures were all new creatures or if some were probably being made after known species which God had made at Gen 1:1. I don't know, and only tantalize thoughts along these lines. I think there may be arguments for both, but may I remind all that when fossils are found, few are of the "restored" creatures, some exceptions being, the cat, rat, dog and a few other present day ones and such as the aquatics.

We must take note that He said **"the"** living creature, **"the"** beast of the earth. We do not hear Him say **a** living creature, **a** living beast of the earth. Is this reason enough to speculate that some were a known creature from another time? The way it is presented, follows the same pattern, but again, if they are known species He did not make all of the ones that He made from the past.

There are many animals on earth today which appears to have duplicates in the distant past: The cat, dog, oxen, rat, reptilians, primates, and then the fish that either survived the void, or were brought forth again.

I want the reader to make a note here that animals are created at this sequence, and will be out of sequence later in Genesis 2 with Adam in the Garden. (It is important to remember the sequence in relation to man's creation. **The animals were first in order here**, and then the next verses tell us about man. I put a mark there, **(X08)**, so the difference may be seen later.)

Back on page 62, I wanted to remember the discussion of the animal population after the meteor impact, when science did not understand why animals did not over populate the land. We have just discussed the Phase II Creation of fish, birds, and animals by one of the "Lets" of creation. What I am reminding the reader is that science is **still holding to evolutionary** ideas when they discussed those smaller animal's inability to produce great numbers. If science would read Scripture they would know that God, here, created the same and different creatures during the Restoration. When we understand that fact, then what science has found agrees with Scripture; however, evolutionists are as hard headed as some of us are.

MALE AND FEMALE CREATED

Gen 1:26 ¶ *"And God said,* **Let us make man** *in our image, after our likeness: and* **let them have dominion** *over the fish of the sea, and over the fowl of the air, and over the cattle, and over all the earth, and over every creeping thing that creepeth upon the earth.*
Gen 1:27 *So God created man in his own image, in the image of God created he him;* *male and female created he them."*(Emphasis is mine)

Let us: (X000) One should note that it is no longer the single "Let", but it is now "let us." This is the first introduction of the whole Trinity. Note it is not let you and I create; it is not you create, it is "let us." Man is and has always been a marvelous creation of the Trinity. I have made a break here, and used three "0's" for the Trinity. X000 represents the trinity, and X0001 is for male and female's creation. I hope this is not too confusing. A Quick look at Figure 1, on page 150 will help keep it straight.

Make: (X0001) If we will look at this word in Strong's Exhaustive Concordance, (6213) we will find that the closest meaning here would be to *"bring forth."* This is interesting, and of importance when we get to the second chapter of Genesis. Here, God **brought forth man:** how? Therein lays the mystery: either by thought; personal activity, or command.

Man: This is an act of the Trinity(X000), but still one of the "Lets" of creation, even though it seems to be the apex of this creative venture.

GOD DEFINES THE ROLE OF MALE AND FEMALE

Now that, **Male** and **female** are created **(X0001)**, in the image of God**(X09),** I want to call attention to a couple of points here.

1. Gen 1:28 *"And God* **blessed** **them,** *(X010) and God* **said unto** **them** *(X011), Be fruitful, and multiply, and* **replenish** *the earth* **(X012),** *and* **subdue(X013)** * *it, and have dominion over the fish of the sea, and over the fowl of the air, and over every living thing that moveth upon the earth."*(Emphasis is mine)

(I know this is a lot to remember with all the X's, but perhaps one should "dog-ear" the pages so they can flip back and forth. It really is important that we compare the relationship between here with male and female, Adam and Woman, and later, Noah.)

2. God created male and female, Not Adam then Woman. I also want to remember the sequence, **plants, animal, male and female, blessed them, said unto them, subdue the earth,** and the part about **replenish.**

I will repeat verses 26 thru 28 and highlight what we need to concentrate on for our later Scripture comparisons.

Verse 1:26 ¶ *And God said,* **Let us** *make man in our image, after our likeness: and let them* **have dominion** *over the fish of the sea, and over the fowl of the air, and over the cattle, and over all the earth, and over every creeping thing that creepeth upon the earth."*

Verse 27 "So God created man in his own image, in the image of God created he him; **male and female** *created he them."*

Verse 28 "And *God* **blessed them,** *and God* <u>said</u> *unto* **<u>them</u>**, *Be fruitful, and multiply, and* **<u>replenish</u> the earth**, *and* <u>subdue it</u>: *and* <u>have dominion</u> *over the fish of the sea, and over the fowl of the air, and over every living thing that moveth upon the earth."*(Emphasis is mine)

<u>Male and Female</u>, are in Gen 1:26 to subdue it and by subduing it they will **have domination** of the earth. Later in Gen 2:19-23 we find that <u>Adam</u> is to **rule** as his lot, and later yet, in Gen 9:2 with <u>Noah</u> we will see that "Into your hand are they **delivered.**"

These are deliberate differences, or one would have to assume that God was confused when He had it all recorded: may He forgive me for even using such a statement; precious, **we know better.** They are different offices, ordained by the Father, to different individuals, and one must assume, different dispensations.

Another interesting thing to note is the fact that there is no set hierarchy between male and female here, they seem to be completely on the same level of leadership.

We should note yet another subtle difference here. Referring back to when God says He created man in His image. Please note it isn't necessarily, in this case, what God says as what He does not say that is of importance. "**Let us make man.**" Notice He did not say let us make **a creature** and call it a man, and make them in our image. He did not say let us make "**a**" man, and make him (or in this case, them) in our image. "Let us make man," <u>as if man was a known identity</u>, and I think man was just that. Remember; "<u>let **the** waters</u>" and "<u>let **the** dry land</u>."? From the other side of "Void and Without Form", I am convinced God foreknew man (even if he was Homo erectus), waters and dry land.

There is another thing about this "let" which was discussed before; "Let **us make**." God is speaking in the office of the Trinity, and He did not use the "let the--bring forth," but He now says "let us **make**." Man was made; he was created.

Remember the "Logo?" Well here is another one. "Gen 1:27 *And God created man **in his own image, in the image of God created he him**;*"(Emphasis is mine)

God was making man in His image, but whether man, (if in fact he did exist on the first world), was in God's image before the void, we have no way of knowing. Christ is the corner stone, God is the structure and He is telling us that mankind is, and possibly was a part of something very special. God started a beginning with an ending; Jesus started an ending with a beginning.

I briefly covered this when discussing the earth of Gen 1:1. There are **supposedly** man's footprints in the river bed of the Paluxy River near Glen Rose, Texas. One can find pictures of them on the web. We will discuss "Catastrophic Plate Tectonics" later. I will say this now. If there were Homo sapiens on earth before Gen 1:2, I feel we will never prove that because all evidence of such would be beneath the earth mantle during what we will cover later; subduction.

I bring this up because of Isaiah speaking of Lucifer "which didst weaken the nations!" It is most difficult for me to determine where prophesy divides; **now; later, or before**. Without venturing into the misty isles of the lost continent of Atlantis, may I only say, this is a question which may never have an answer for us: I have thought of it often.

Looking at what science presents of the world before the "Void and Without Form", it is indisputable that after extinctions, the earth was re-populated by creatures that were **more**, and **more complex**. One has only to consider creation from algae to the Homo erectus to see what I am saying. **That would be weak evidence** to indicate that there was a creature science calls "cave man." If there were, and taking Isaiah's discourse with Lucifer, when speaking of "didst weaken the nations," I am at a total loss to present anything about that. I submit it only as a LAYMAN who can later say, "My studies have indicated that all along." **Take it in that light**. It is my S.W.A.G.

REPLENISH

Here in Gen 1, God is talking to them both, and then **blesses them**. Gen 1:28 *"And God blessed **them**, and God <u>said unto **them**</u>, Be fruitful, and multiply, and <u>**replenish**</u> the earth..."* (Emphasis is mine)

The other striking thing is the phrase He uses **"replenish"** the earth. I want to quote another passage then comment. Gen 9:1 *"And God blessed Noah and his sons, and said unto them, Be fruitful, and multiply, and **REPLENISH** the earth."*(Emphasis is mine) Both verses, separated by more than two thousand years, and the identical thing is said, "Replenish the earth." **This is <u>not</u> the case when we get to Adam.**

Scofield says of the word Replenish, *"To replenish the earth with a new order--man;"*

Easton will not touch the word; neither will Unger. I wonder why?

Strong's Exhaustive Concordance has many interpretations for the word, but the only ones which come close in this case would be, *"presume, replenish, satisfy, and take a handful."* I don't know why Strong used replenish to explain, replenish, but he did.

Webster's dictionary has *"To fill, or make complete **again**."*(Emphasis is mine)

We find in the book of Isaiah the word used closest to Webster's. *Isa 23:2 "Be still, ye inhabitants of the isle; thou whom the merchants of Zidon, that pass over the sea, have replenished."*

We discussed this at the first of the book. How many commentaries have we studied in order to get a clarification about a hard subject such as this, only to find each author skips the very void we wish to fill? Here also is the case. For my part, I pray that this will fill such a void and that I will be forgiven for those voids which I have left. I am also guilty of such. I get so excited over showing something that I also fail to see the in-betweens. Forgive me if I have done so.

To replenish something, one must first have the thing, and then it can be replenished because it has been depleted. Is this what our God is saying? **If male and female are to replenish the earth, then they are to populate it with what was here before them.** The earth was destroyed and I want to fill it up again. I want you to **replenish** it. **I do not know** if there was Homo erectus (bipedals) on earth, or Homo sapiens (humans). This is something which will have to be answered at a later time, possibly never.

The Layman

I think on these lines, because God said the very same thing to Noah and we know there were people on earth before the flood; Therefore, Noah was told to **fill it up again**, that is, <u>I destroyed the earth's inhabitants with the flood, now, I want you to fill it up again.</u> The word "Replenish" is only used two times in Scripture; Gen 1:28, Gen 9:1. The term "Replenished is used five times, and has the same meaning.

I call attention to the command of God to the fish and fowl Gen 1:22 *"And <u>God blessed them,</u> saying, Be fruitful, and multiply, and **fill** the waters in the seas, and let fowl multiply in the earth."*(Emphasis is mine) God blessed them and they were to fill the seas, and fowl to do the same on the earth. He does **not** tell them to replenish because there may well have been some of those who survived the earth's destruction, along with others that He put here anew.

But I must hasten to take notice He says the similar things to animals. Gen 1:25 *"And God made the beast of the earth after his kind, and cattle after their kind, and every thing that creepeth upon the earth after his kind: and God saw that it was good."* Different terms are used here for a reason. These are some of the same and arguably different animals: The elephant verses the mammoth; the tiger verses the saber tooth tiger etc. This is the reason they were to fill and not replenish. If they were to replenish, then we would have the same animals living today which made fossils yesterday. I trust I have not confused the reader here.

The Father closes the book on evolutionist here. We either believe the Bible, or evolution, not both. By God saying *"After his kind,"* there has never been, nor will there ever be, an evolutionary act.

I know there should be a more in-depth discussion here, but I don't think myself qualified. What I am saying is that I can fill your glass with tea. I can replenish the tea in your glass. If I put milk in your tea glass I have not "replenished" your tea. So if you want milk, you will have to say "will you fill my glass with milk," that way I then am not replenishing your tea, but now filling your glass with milk.

If someone were to ask a bartender to "Hit me again," he would ask, "What are you drinking?" I figured most of the tea-toddlers out there would understand that example.

Replenish, is Replenish; Fill is Fill. Remember this when we get to Adam and Eve where it is **not said,** then to Noah where it **is said,** because Adam has a soul.

There are so many hints to this separation of the creative acts that I don't think it can be ignored. Am I right in my assumption? I am convinced I am or I wouldn't be writing this, but I have been wrong many times in my life and caution the reader to seek the Holy Ghost for the final answer. One thing for sure; salvation does not depend upon it either way and that is the paramount objective of Biblical studies.

FOOD APPOINTED

Male and female

Now here, again, is yet another significant difference that I want us to remember as well: We called it pencil mark**(X014)**. Gen 1:29 ¶ *"And God said, Behold, I have given you* **every** herb *bearing seed, which is* upon the face of **all** the earth, *and* **every** tree, *in the which is the fruit of a tree yielding seed;* to you it shall be for meat. *"*(Emphasis is mine)

I want us to remember that God gave **them every herb, and every tree."** What tree did He withhold from **them**? I don't know, but I didn't read of one here in my translation.

For animals: Gen 1:30 *"And to* **every beast** *of the earth, and to every fowl of the air, and to every thing that creepeth upon the earth, wherein there is life,* **I have given every green herb for meat: and it was so.** *"*(Emphasis is mine)

Another key point

1. This is not said again about the **animals**; **not in the Garden**, and **not after the flood.**

2. Here in Gen 1 God gives "**male and female**" all the trees.

3. In Gen 2 God commands the **Adam not to eat** of the "tree of the knowledge of good and evil."

4. To Noah it is given; **Genesis 9:3** *"Every moving thing that liveth shall be meat for you; even as* **the green herb have I given you all things.** *"*(Emphasis is mine.)

Precious brethren, there are definable differences:

1. In Gen 1, God **told both the male and female this**. If He had just told man, He would have said "and God told man."

2. In Gen 2, God tells only Adam.

I am convinced that Scripture is saying **what** happened, and **when** it happened, and **to whom**. I know there are going to be skeptics who will jump up and say that the lion was a meat eater and his system would not tolerate vegetation. Lions were never graminivorous.

Dr. Ironside was giving a sermon and read the scripture, Isa 11:7 *"And the cow and the bear shall feed; their young ones shall lie down together: and the lion shall eat straw like the ox."* After the sermon this well dressed man approached the podium and with a loud clearing of his throat in order to gain the maximum of attention, said;

"Dr. Ironside! I have to tell you that I am Dr. "So and So" in the discipline of Zoology. I am here to tell you that a lion can not, could never, and will never be able to eat straw as an ox." Dr. Ironside looked at the gentleman and said, "Sir! I will make a wager."

"What is your wager, sir?" He replied.

"Well" Dr. Ironside's continued, "**You make** a lion, bring him to me, and I give you my fervent word that I shall then make **your** lion eat straw like the ox"

With that the man, recognizing his error smiled and turned away. We all must never forget that it is the architect who designs the building for His purpose; it is the builder who follows the plans, and it is only when the tenants change and use it differently, that makes the building unsuited for occupancy.

I need to start developing a thought here. There was a humanoid on earth, the Neanderthal, approximately 30,000 years ago, **after the "Void and Without Form"**. We will discuss more of the Neanderthal later; however, I feel the male and female are what science has called the Neanderthal. For now, just holds that thought and we will, later, explain this in more detail.

BEHOLD IT IS VERY GOOD

The next thing we have is "Gen 1:31 ¶"And *God saw every thing that he had made, and, behold, it was very good"*. (Emphasis is mine) And the evening and the morning were the sixth day. I highlight the "very good" because I want to stress the point that a Tyrannosaurus who supposedly killed for food could not be called "Very Good." I am not sure that old Rex isn't given a bad name. I really think he was a two short arm, and two long legged buzzards. I think he was a scavenger and didn't kill for food at all, but then I haven't any proof to tell that, but using others privileges, if **I can't be proven wrong, I am right**.

AUTHORITY

Before I go any further, I want to make clear, if one has not ascertained it already, is that I believe the **King James** Translation of Scripture as the only Authorized Version. I say that for several reasons which I will not elaborate here; however one will notice the oft occurring "¶" symbol that is present with quoted Scripture. I have one King James Version which does not contain all of them. I do have my study reference which does, as well as my KJV 2000, my Bishop Bible, and the KJV1611. **Without these marks, one is helpless to ascertain the time and thought differences between verses.**

I know there are many who disagree and to them I say that is their opinion, and they are their own guide, I am not one to say I am right and they are not. I do not agree with them in the least, but then I am not their final judge; am I? If anyone has such a translation and they read it with joy in their heart, I say to them **Amen-Amen-Amen.**

It was A. W. Pink's in his works on **Genesis**, who said that one **should note every comma, every change of tense, every time the Scripture gives a number, and every time Scripture notes a name, place or thing, it has meaning.** I thoroughly believe that, and for me the other translations have removed many of these stepping stones in an **honest** attempt to "clarify" the meanings, and simplify the language.

I call attention to that because of what I am about to point out, but first we must understand one thing more. The Scriptures are divided into Chapters, and verses, which have little to do with the original separation of such. In fact only the book divisions were first known. It is my understanding that Robert Stevens was riding back to Paris, got bored and divided the Scriptures much as we see today, so he could find things easier. **I do not know** whether that incident is true or not; however, lets examine a possible coincidental example as follows:

> What is the **shortest chapter** in the Bible? (Answer - Psalms 117)
>
> What is the **longest chapter** in the Bible? (Answer - Psalms 119)
>
> Which **chapter is in the center** of the Bible? (Answer - Psalms 118)
>
> Fact: There are 594 chapters before Psalms 118
>
> Fact: There are 594 chapters after Psalms 118

Add these numbers up and we get 1188 what is the **center <u>verse</u>** in the Bible? (Answer - Psalms 118:8)
How many chapters in the Bible? (Please don't say 1188, someone forgot to count Psalms 118)
594+594+ (Psalms 188) = 1189 chapters

Is the division of the scriptures for a divine purpose, or is it coincidence? I don't know, but the above illustration is given **only** to make everyone keenly aware that it is God who is the final authority, not us. He could have guided that gentleman's work as well.

When we read Scripture it is important that we note the little "¶" that occurs every now and again. That is the beginning of another **thought**, a division **of facts**, another **time**, and many times a break to reemphasize something further. I say this because the first chapter of Genesis should really end at chapter 2:3. Then we will see the little "¶" which is the start of the second thought with Gen 2:4. In Gen 1, there are 10 little "¶" up to this point, each with another time, thought, and presented will of God. These "¶" marks were not inserted by the translators, but were in the original text.

If we stop and consider that with each **"¶" there could have been a lapse of time that we have completely failed to consider.** From the very onset we do not know how long God's Spirit moved upon the earth. We do not know how long it was before His light shown, nor do we know how long His light was present before the next sequence of dividing the firmaments.

Go through each of these events of chapter 1, and ask, do I really think this was in a blink of an eye. He says that it was the duration of a "day." Can we say that this is a 24-hour day or perhaps it could well be as, Acts 17:31 *"Because he hath appointed **a day**, in the which he will judge the world in righteousness by that man whom he hath ordained; whereof he hath given assurance unto all men, in that he hath raised him from the dead."*(Emphasis is mine). **Day here is a period of time for the promise to be fulfilled.** In this passage I understand that this is much the same as "He was a winner in his day."

Do I attest that this is objective? No! It is totally subjective and I would have the reader only to consider it. I know I am redundant at times, well quite a few times I suppose, but I would not lead anyone astray for fame or fortune. We are all in this world to support each other, not bury one another; however, I for one, <u>will never be convinced that what we have been addressing is a twenty-four-hour day.</u>

GOD RESTED: X015)

Here is the part that I said some had never thought about. <u>Have we ever asked ourselves how long He rested?</u> Gen 2:3 *"And God blessed the seventh day, and sanctified it: because that in it he had <u>rested</u> from all his work which God created and made."*(Emphasis is mine)

Now may I ask, what time frame is there between the seventh day, and when God wasn't resting? I do not think the term "Rested" meant that God was worn out, tired, or even winded. I think it simply means He stopped what He had been doing at that phase.

One would wonder why? Well He has already set in motion salvation through grace, even though we learn of that later, it has none the less, been accomplished. I feel He is **still resting**, and **invites us** to join Him in that rest. Consider this:

Heb 4:3 *"For we which have believed do enter into rest, as he said, As I have sworn in my wrath, if they shall enter into my rest: although the works were finished from the foundation of the world."*

Heb 4:9 *"There remaineth therefore a rest to the people of God."*

Heb 4:10 *"For he that is entered into his rest, he also hath ceased from his own works, as God [did] from his."*

Considering Gen 2:3, <u>I am amazed at what the Bible says, by not saying it.</u> So many of us miss many jewels when we don't ask ourselves **what wasn't said**. Notice that there is "And the evening and the morning were the first day"; "second day"; "third day"; "fourth day"; "fifth day"; and the "sixth day." Now look at the following. Gen 2:2 *"And on the seventh day God ended his work which he had made; and he rested on the seventh day from all his work which he had made. Gen 2:3 "And God blessed the seventh day, and sanctified it: because that in it he had rested from all his work which God created and made."*

Did everyone notice, **it does not say** anything about the "evening," **nor anything about** the "morning." It is incomplete as it stands when we look at the careful arrangement of the preceeding verses. It is much the same as when the LORD says in Revelation "Re 1:11 Saying, *"I am Alpha and **Omega**, the first and the last:.."* The **Alpha** is spelled out, but **the letter** for **Omega** is used. Why? Well He is the beginning, and the present, but He has not completed the part covered in Re 10:6 which says *"And sware by him that liveth for ever and ever, who created heaven, and the things that therein are, and the earth, and the things that therein are, and the sea, and the things which are therein, **that there should be time no longer."**(Emphasis in both verses are mine)

I think, as in Revelation, God leaves out the time period here on the seventh day for a purpose, and says nothing of evening and morning, because He is still in that "Rest." He did not finish it because it was and is stll going on. Will we enter into His rest? I am trying, I pray all who read this are also.

We don't know what this original time frame was, and my Father doesn't tell us. It is within my mind that He just let things perk, and enjoyed the fruit of His labor.

WHO WAS THIS MALE AND FEMALE

Were they the Neanderthal man? Before we define this being, I have emphasized this, and will again and again, this creature, whatever anyone wishes to call him, <u>existed</u> on this earth, and doing so **was created by my Father** for His supreme purpose. I am told that every time we take a breath, we breathe in a molecule of nitrogen, and that, tiniest of molecules has at one time or the other, been inhaled by every air breathing creature that is or has ever been on this earth. I say this again, it is so complicatedly simple, simply complicated; I love it.

When I say Neanderthal man, I am **not** saying that this creature is in fact, **by name**, the identity which we seek when referring to male and female of Gen 1; however, **I do say** that this creature's existence simply **falls within a historical sequence, which is consistent with the thrust of this work.** However, if I were not convinced that these first humanoids were the male and female that God created, there would be a hole in this work that could not be plugged. Let me explain a little of this humanoid, and allow me to, later, put this in perspective with the first of Genesis

NEANDERTHAL

The extraction of mitochondrial DNA (MtDNA) from a Neanderthal fossil has caused considerable discussion recently. Neanderthal was a group of hominids very close to human beings, and in fact, is **often considered to be human beings**. The DNA results tend to suggest that Neanderthals were intermediate to humans.

Some data that seems to support this theory is given in an article in **Science vol. 277 July 11, 1997**, pp. 176-178. *"The method used to extract the DNA was the polymerize chain reaction, which on old and damaged DNA is highly error prone. The DNA was in fragments about 100 base pairs long, which had to be pieced together into a region 379 base pairs long. This process of piecing together took three months of work. Among the fragments found were some that looked like modern human DNA, but these were considered to be contamination. This process was done twice, and the same sequence was obtained both times. The resulting sequence was compared with 986 distinct sequences from living humans. The sequence differed from these in an average of 25.6 positions. Living humans differ in this region in an average of 8 positions, <u>but the maximum difference is 24 positions</u>.* **But the pattern of mutations in the Neanderthal sequence was different than in modern humans."** (Emphasis is mine)

Could this have been the 500,000/600,000 years that evolution science says that there were those resembling man upon the earth? I <u>do not</u> think so. I rather think the time frame would more approach 30,000 years for the "Neanderthal" man.

If the species was limited in size, <u>genetic science</u> says 30,000/10,000 BC would come close to his existence. Perhaps the Neanderthal man did start that far back, and faded out shortly after Adam came upon the scene. He might have faded before the LORD God formed Adam, but **I have a reason not to think so.** I have another reason to feel that the "Neanderthal" man was here when Adam and Eve were here, and I will cover that later.

If someone wanted to do research on this genus, they would agree that more and more findings suggest that the Neanderthal man lasted until around 10,000 years B.C.

I want to slow down here and ponder something. <u>Why did our leading scientist stop with saying that they may have lasted as long as 10,000 years ago</u>? I know that some of their data indicated a little different story, but if science were truthful, they would admit that the **Neanderthal existed much longer**; however, that would then bring them in <u>direct conflict with what the Bible says as the beginning of man:</u> this is defensive in that **scientists feel** if they can hold a separation between the two disciplines, even though they do not know where they came from, they can live in their own little world, and **theologians** can live comfortably in theirs with no barrier to cross. In other words, they can say **theologians are all wet**, and theologians can say **scientists are all wet**. I guess that means we are the only ones that

The Layman

know the real truth, so we can now say **they are both all wet**. Now that should put us right in the middle of the discussion.

What is MtDNA/DNA/RNA

Let's examine why there is no evidence that modern (Adam) and Neanderthals are related. Mitochondria DNA **(MtDNA)**, is not transmitted through nuclear DNA (nDNA), and in most multicultural organisms, virtually all mitochondria are inherited from the mother's ovum and is passed on to the **daughter.** Sperm cells, except through the Y gene do not contribute any X gene mitochondria. It is more common that the female MtDNA is used to track ancestral linage. The DNA that the male carries in the X gene, inherited from his mother, contributes to genetic traits, that is to say with the Y gene, sex and physical features.

DNA (Deoxyribonucleic acid) is a double stranded helix which is contained in each of the estimated 10-trillion cells of the body, and is packaged within the chromosomes, and carries approximately 4-billion code of genetic information. This is mixed with the female's DNA and as stated, contributes to physical features

RNA (Ribonucleic acid) is a single stranded molecule with less nucleotide, and is important in the process of translating genetic information from DNA and the protein synthesis complexes known as ribosome's, and acts as an essential carrier molecule for amino acids to be used in protein synthesis.

There is a very interesting discipline called Morphology. Morphology, as I understand it is the process in which DNA is passed on to each generation and with each passing, the DNA contains accumulating defects. This defect will carry on and on, accumulating from one generation to the next, until the species reaches **equilibrium** at which time it can no longer have offspring, and then cease to exist.

This Morphology slams the door on evolutionists: here is why; for any species to have existed in the first place, the creature must contain a **perfect DNA** strand. From there, by the very nature of morphosis, which by its own definition causes each successive generation of DNA strands to accumulate errors, or in short, DNA never goes from "corruption to perfection as evolutionist would have us believe, on the contrary DNA does exactly the opposite, it goes from **perfection, to corruption**. This is a proven, scientific fact. So

116

how can evolutionists justify their theories without denying the very science, which they have said proved it??

Dr. Lubenow, a creationist, and author of "**Bones of Contention**," makes the following observation. *"Neanderthals get more severe in their archaic morphology as they approach the end of the Neanderthal sequence,* **the opposite of evolutionary expectations**, *this would seem to indicate that the Neanderthals were degenerating and not evolving to become more fit.* (Emphasis is mine)

Based upon these findings of Dr. Lubenow, and his research, Dr. Mark Stoneking, **associate professor of anthropology at Penn State**, had this to say, *"These results indicate that Neanderthals did not contribute mitochondrial DNA to modern humans, Neanderthals* **are not our ancestors.** *The findings will cause reconsideration of the current consensus that Neanderthals became extinct only 30,000 years ago and co- existed for some time with modern humans in Europe. The new research indicated that Neanderthals and modern humans diverged genetically 500,000 to 600,000 years ago. While the two species may have lived at the same time,* **Neanderthals did not contribute genetic material to modern humans."** (Emphasis is mine)

There are genetic studies which have been evaluated that dispute this early date of modern man and the Neanderthal man's coexistence. These dates **do not agree with the 500,000 to 600,000** year theory. If they would take the DNA and backtrack using it, they would find that **modern man** could not have existed on earth more than 10,000 years ago. This has evolutionist screaming "FOUL, FOUL." This means that **every time line outside of scripture that has been established for mankind is false**.

We have discussed both sides of the argument concerning the dates of the Neanderthal's existence. Both of these studies agree on the demise of DNA over time, but one is using a larger populist, than the other, in determining the dates of existence.

Realistic population growth formula, accounting for wars, etc., give the result that only **several thousand years** as needed to produce the current world population (not millions of years). It is my somewhat limited understanding of DNA, that if a population is very small, then the species will not survive as long as if the population is vast. Perhaps this "Neanderthal" man never reached great numbers and was therefore due for extinction more rapidly than imagined. I hold to the 30,000 to 10,000 years BC for his total existence with him becoming extinct sometime around the time of the flood. But how do we have a time line for Adam of six to ten thousand years then? I will try and show this when we get to Gen 2: when we discuss what I feel is another dispensation.

I started this discussion much earlier about the Neanderthal man. I said at that time that I do not try and designate this created being as anything but having appeared at the time sequence that fit's a part of Genesis. Please do not lose interest and prejudge this now. Let me develop my thoughts along these lines, and then everyone form their own opinion.

For all the "genius" of modern science, the Neanderthal man just seems to have appeared, and then disappeared with no trail either way. The biped is not genetically linked to Neanderthal, and Neanderthal is not linked to modern man: Adam.

This man was called Neanderthal because it was the Neanderthal valley in which the first remains were discovered. Far earlier and more reaching information has been uncovered in many parts of the world which makes the first area of discovery pale in importance in our study of this being. There are works that aver his first name given as, "Neanderthal", and was later changed to Neandertal. Why the name got changed from Neanderthal to Neandertal, I do not know: I use Neanderthal.

Now having said that; there are yet other reasons I believe that which is **called** the Neanderthal man closely fits the Male and Female spoken of in Gen 1:27.

It has been verified that the Neanderthal man had;

1. A primitive **family life**.
2. Evidence shows that he was a **communal being**.
3. Evidence shows "**he buried his dead**".
4. **He cared for the sick** and handicapped of his association.
5. The **female was of a large pelvic** region which indicates, to me at least, that child birth was not to be "*in sorrow thou shalt bring forth children*," as placed upon Eve.

There is no such evidence to support any of these findings for the biped sequence, with the possible exception being the size of the female pelvic region.

The Neanderthal man **suddenly appeared, fully developed,** and had intelligence which exceeded the gradual learning curve in which science says as the normal educational range expected. Later it was discovered that this "subspecies" wasn't as dumb as some would like him to be. We still have much to learn from his existence, but overwhelming evidence proves he was a being who was as entirely different from the biped, as Adam was from him. This change <u>did not</u> come on gradually. Can we not see that there are sudden, drastic changes in our previous world which evolution makes itself an echo of ignorance each time it attempts to justify?

On one hand we have in the biped of Gen 1:1, what for all practical purposes, and supported with what has thus far been found, is a ignorant being who hunts, gathers, and seems to even rob for his survival. There is no evidence to support anything short of a somewhat organized hunting pack when communal behavior is addressed. There is in fact evidence which shows that the only time male and female came together, was for procreation.

The "Void and Without Form" happens and the biped is no longer; however, there is another who is coming upon the scene, and we now have the one science called, "Neanderthal man." There is no evolutionary process, when discovered the Neanderthal man is **complete**, and **fully developed,** and I believe this is the Male and Female of Gen 1:27.

I do not want one to view this group of individuals as being ready for modern living. For all practical purposes, they may have been two notches above a head of lettuce. There is, however, evidence that they were quick learners, made tools, and in comparison only to the biped, could be seen as a parallel to modern man.

As puzzling as it may seem, the Neanderthal man was not depleted from earth by a comet, an Ice Age, or climatic changes; he just disappeared. It is the conclusion of some, and I include myself into that group, to a point, that he lost his identity by inner marrying with the Cro-Magnon man, or the flood got him. I am of the opinion that the procreation of the Neanderthal with the Cro-Magnon partially was to blame, however, there is another reason, and that is, there was **war** between the two that could ultimately have caused this extinction.

I think the Neanderthal fits the sequential time frame of the male and female who were created in Gen 1:27; however, wait until we have time to explore more Scripture. Then it is the readers absolute right as a Christian to disregard everything in this writing. I will still love them as brethren.

There is abundant evidence to show that the Neanderthal was mostly a gatherer. By that I mean he was not a hunter. Would that not fit in with what God said would be his food? I know that there is

The Layman

scattered evidence of carnivores in the population, but how can one tag the whole Boy Scout organization for what one troop does?

CREATION RECORD:

Before I begin to explain my difficulties with the creation record **which I have been taught,** I want to make one thing perfectly clear. God did not make me a Prophet, I am not an Apostle, and I do not hold myself in any special esteem. I have had no vision while sitting on a lotus blossom, I have not been smacked in the head with a rock and started prophesying, I have not been told a special addition to the Scriptures which the LORD must have left out and now reveals to start another sect, and I have not seen aberrations of a virgin who has had seven children, appearing to disclose another dot, or tittle. I am just a LAYMAN, one who tries in my sinful way to love and follow the LORD God in His strength. **I fully realize that I emphasize this over and over again.** I must be redundant to insure for myself that no one thinks more highly of me than I am worthy. **We each believe what the Holy Ghost reveals to us** and nothing else.

It is impossible for me as a human being to tell at once whether an event is from God or Satan. God is pure light; there is within Him no darkness. Satan is pure darkness; within Him is no light. I do not go around "tooting" that I know His action or lack of it when I undertake a project. When we try and convince someone that our work is something approved by the LORD, and we cannot tell perfect Spiritual light from absolute demonic darkness, we need to be very cautious with our accolades. It is for that reason that I caveat this work.

I know there are some who will jump up and swear that they are in personal contact with the LORD and know immediately what is and what is not of the LORD. I must caution everyone on such a statement. I knew a fine Christian woman who when asked about temptations of Satan made the statement, "He won't mess with me." When asked why, she answered "Because he knows who's the better man." I lived to see that wonderful saintly person tormented for most of the rest of her life, and finally burned to death in her sleep.

I was looking at motor homes one day and as I and the owner of the lot, which sat in a large field next to his farm, was discussing one such item, when a car pulled up, and four or five people exited. "We have been sent by the Lord to buy a van for our church" This person exclaimed.

120

The owner asked to be excused and he would get another salesman to assist them. Before he got three steps from where he was standing, this same person said. "The Lord has lain it upon my heart that this is the van we need," Pointing to one on the lot.

Another salesman then appeared, and the owner requested that he tend to the party. Before they disappeared into the office, the same person turned and shouted, "Is that house over there for sale?" pointing to the owner's house, just west of the field.

"Everything is for sale if the price is right" He responded. "May I look at the house?" they queried

With that he phoned his wife and explained the situation, then addressed the person, "My wife will be glad to show you the house, Go on over."

Walking toward the house the person once again exclaimed, "The Lord has laid it upon my heart to buy that house."

The owner looked at me, smiled and said, "I hope the Lord has laid within their pocketbook, the money I am going to ask for it."

I tell this true story to impress upon all; I believe what I am presenting here in this work, with all my heart. Others do not have too. I lay claim only one thing. **God does not damn a turtle because it cannot fly, but I wouldn't want to be an eagle that didn't try**. I feel as a turtle with this presentation.

The person in the story I presented was, as far as I am concerned, "Off their rocker." No one has a direct, "open line" to our Father or our Lord. If He openly told you something, He would have to talk to all of us. It is so sad that people use His name in vain in that way.

I have spent years researching the contents of this work. Others who compose books seem to have not problem grinding them out in speeds which seem like days. I trust the reader will understand my reluctance to hurry, because what is presented here is beyond anything which I have ever read, or I have been taught.

I want to bring something to everyone's attention here. **It is my belief** the Neanderthal **were God created beings**. Their MtDNA would not match that of Adam (modern man), but that did not make them Homo erectus; **they were still Homo sapiens**. They were a different race, but Homo sapiens, and if, Male and Female, in His Own image.

Whatever existed on this earth over the millions of years was created by my God: for His purpose, and at His directions.

121

The Layman

I will explain why the genetic code was so very close to modern man, yet different, when we get to the Cro-Magnon man later, but now we have yet another dispensation: the Restoration.

The difference between the Anti-Christ and Christ
Is that one gives you a number
And the other gives you a name.
When Jesus comes, will your name be called?
Or will your number be up?

Adrian Rogers

THE RESTORATION

Gen 2:4 *"**These are the generations of the heavens and of the earth** when they were created, in the day that the <u>LORD God</u> made the earth and the heavens,"* (Emphasis is mine).

Allow me to pause here and point out that this is the first introduction of our Lord God, by name, in Scripture. I have read the many wonderful explanations of each word here, and I really think they are absolutely correct; however, when I see God in Scripture, I see judgment and law; when I see Lord I see mercy, when I see LORD God I see our Father in judgment and law, viewing us through our Lord in mercy. I don't want my Father to look at me any other way.

Now back to the sequence:

Remember when we discussed the "Let" of creation in Gen 1? If we can not understood that God along with the LORD God was working there, it would sound like this chapter had been put in Scripture to explain some thing which is out of sequences with the first chapter: that we all know is not so. Here the office of the LORD God is setting the stage of another creative event. **In the first chapter, it was God the architect and the LORD God, the builder. Here it is the LORD God, the builder, with God the architect.** I think of this part of Scripture much the same as one watching a play. The curtain closes on scene one, and opens on the next scene: though different rolls are played out, the characters are the same, and are vital to the play itself.

The Lord God is here, summarizing in capsule **all the creative events to this point**. It is not in error when He says that He did the creative events up to this point, and we pointed that out when discussing Gen 1.

It would serve us well to remember the summation the LORD God is giving us here, because when we discuss Gen 5 later, we will be introduced to yet another and **final summation <u>of all three stages</u> of their wonderful acts.**

Having readdressed this summation, we will continue. These are the generations (**plural**) of the heavens (**plural**) and the earth (**singular**) when they (**collectively**) were created, in the day (**period of**

123

event) that the <u>LORD God</u> (**office change from Gen 1**) made the earth (**singular**) and the heavens (**plural**)

To complete this thought as written we would have, these are the generations of the heavens, and these are the generations of the earth. I must add here that if we were to substitute the word "then, "we would have, these are the generations (plural) of the **heavens** (plural) **then** these are the generations of the **earth** (singular). (I know that I said I would do this once more, and this is it.) The term "generations" applies to both heavens and the earth.

ORIGINAL HEAVEN

In Gen 1 we are only told that this was a creative act in the beginning with no creative explanation and no time put upon it. Here in Gen 2 we will discuss the three heavens, in addition to these, there are two abodes which are never fully explained.

We will start our explanation with Mr.Scofield, who says that <u>heaven **one**</u> is our cloudy heaven, <u>heaven **two**</u> is the starry heaven, and <u>heaven **three**</u> is God's abode. I have reversed Scofield's order in the following, **and included possibly two other realms, which are not as we normally consider heavens,** and perhaps we should address them as abodes.

First: There is the third heaven, the realm of "***our Father which art in heaven.***" This was the original and well must be the realm of the entire heavenly host, and is related to as, singularly, heaven. This is where, as Enoch calls them, "The Watchers" are. This is the Godly government if I may say so. What all happens there is quite mute and should be. We are given only a small glimpse in Job 2:1 "*Again there was a day when the **<u>sons of God</u>** <u>came to present themselves before the LORD</u>, and <u>Satan came also</u> among them to present himself before the LORD.*"(Emphasis is mine)

It is of this heavenly realm to which Paul relates of his vision, 2Co 12:2 "*I knew a man in Christ above fourteen years ago, (whether in the body, I cannot tell; or whether out of the body, I cannot tell: God knoweth;) such an one caught up to **the third heaven.***" (Emphasis is mine)

Second: There is heaven two, the starry heaven which we see only a small fraction of every starry night. It is therein which our LORD has given insight as having many mansions *(Or as some explain, "Abiding Places)* of the Father. Joh 14:2 "***In my Father's house are many mansions***: *if it were not so, I would have told you. I go to prepare a place*

124

for you. And if I go and prepare a place for you, I will come again, and receive you unto myself; that where I am, there ye may be also."(Emphasis is mine) It is this time, distance, continuum which drowns man in broad speculation.

Third: There is the cloudy heaven, **the expanse(X03) of our earth (sky).** This is the one where clouds of unimaginable shapes and awesome power of wind, storm, and pleasantness abides. It is the least, but most important to us on earth. One has said to describe the vastness of our sky; they should take a globe from the class room and spray it with a protective layer of paint. The vastness of our sky would be less in relation to the earth than the layer of spray paint they have on the classroom globe.

There are two other realms: I do not classify them as heavens, but they are abodes that I feel we should mention at this time.

Fourth: There is a realm which is really never fully explained and it is where the fallen angels are, who fell with Satan. They are called "Evil Angels", a "Lying Spirit", Legion, and are seen throughout the Scriptures as opposing the world and its governments. This is the realm which Satan commands and we are warned in 1Pe 5:8 "*Be sober, be vigilant; because your adversary the devil, as a roaring lion, walketh about, seeking whom he may devour.*" There are other spirits that are mentioned in,

Mt 8:29 "*And, behold, they cried out, saying, What have we to do with thee, Jesus, thou Son of God? art thou come hither <u>to torment us before the time?</u>*"
This is Satan's realm. He is called "Prince of the devils in Mt 9:34, 12:24. Satan is called **"Prince of this world** in Joh 12:31, 14:30 and 16:11.

Fifth: When the sons of God were involved in an adulterous union with the daughters of man, there was a realm discussed where they were reserved in chains until judgment. 2Pe 2:4 "*For if God spared not the angels that sinned, but cast them down to hell, and <u>delivered them into chains of darkness, to be reserved unto judgment;</u>*"

Generations:

Let's look at the plural of generation. "The generations of the heavens:" These are the generations (**plural**) of the heavens (**plural**). If in Scripture we only have the term, "generation" then there would be no need for this work. I emphasize this because the term "heavens" alone without the plural generations, would only mean the sky and the abode of our LORD God as having only one generation. With the usage of "generations," it is evident that we are addressing far more. I stress again, the term generations; That is to say, from the birth of one, **to the birth of the other:** the first ones to the birth of the reordered ones.

If there was a perfect heaven at one time, and that heaven became divided because of Lucifer's pride, to keep one from reflecting upon the other, there would of necessity be two generations. We know all things were at one time perfect in heaven, and it could be well said that the same was true upon earth, perhaps before the introduction of the first man.

How do we know things were perfect? Look at the book of, Job 38:6 *"Whereupon are the foundations thereof fastened? Or who laid the corner stone thereof;* Job 38:7 *"**When the morning stars sang together, and all the sons of God shouted for joy?**"* (Emphasis is mine) There was then *"the morning stars"* singing, as we discussed earlier, but there is no singing, or shouts of joy from the "sons of God" in heaven at the time in which we are now looking.

I see another squirrel that needs shooting here. There are songs in our books at Church that need be removed. "**Hark the Herald Angels Sing**" is at the top. In the account of the earthly birth or our LORD, it is Lu 2:13 *"And suddenly there was with the angel a multitude of the heavenly host praising God, and **saying**,"* (Emphasis is mine) but we must romanticize Scripture so it is "sweet." Another on my list would be **"This is my father's world."** I did not capitalize father because it has to speak of the wrong father, and not my Father. The LORD God gave the earth to our grandparents. Our grandparents gave it to Satan through their sin. My friend, it has been said and I concur, if this is my Fathers' world, He just isn't doing a very good job of it. **The LORD God lives in the heart of the believer, not in a sinful world**. We need not kid ourselves about that. We need not blame our Father for what the seed of sin has raised. At Christmas we sing "**Joy to the World."** This song speaks of Christ's **return** in Revelation, not as his incarnation in Bethlehem. We do so much without thinking.

RESTORED HEAVEN

There now is a different heaven: Restored to a different order, if you please. In the first is when the Stars of God sang, one of them was no more sincere than Judas was at the Last Supper, and no more serious, I must sadly add, than a lot of folk are each Sunday. God chained some of the angels up before the flood, and others He allowed to remain within limited bounds, free.

This is a new order for Heaven. Where there was once singing, and shouts of joy, I suspect that now there is solemn dedication to fulfill the unfolding will of the LORD God.

I can't say much more of this division and the generations of heaven. We just aren't given that insight. I think we are given sufficient information to make certain subjective findings:

First: We do know it was pure at one time because God does not make sin. We know it fell, in part, because of Lucifer and the fallen ones. We know it will be pure again.

Second: The realm where the fallen angels were chained may or may not have existed. It may have been an abode which was made to accommodate them in there fallen state. I personally think it was there and was brought up to habitation when God put them in there.

We must never forget that God is never taken by surprise: He already knew there would be cracks in the character of His angelic staff. He knew that Adam would fail; He already foreknew his disciples, Eph 1:4 *"According as he hath chosen us in him before the foundation of the world, that we should be holy and without blame before him in love."*;(Emphasis is mine) My precious brethren, He foreknew each of us from ages past. He knew that some of the angelic host would fail and would have to be kept until the Gospel was finished on this earth. Lastly, my friend, He knew, knows, that some of us would fail, but praise His Holy name; He still gave us the best chance not to.

Fourth: There is the starry heaven which we view each night. I have no Scriptural evidence to say whether the foundations of the universe were removed when the rebellion occurred. **Scripture does not seem to indicate the universe was a part of that event**; I personally do not think it was; however, I know that it will be in the end, since Scripture tells us in Rev 6:13 **"And the stars of heaven fell unto the earth, even as a fig tree casteth her untimely figs, when she is shaken of a mighty wind."**

Fifth: There is the "Sky" which sustains us. I think generations also apply to this. There is a complete difference in the heavens because in Gen 1 it is evident to me that God reorders the air itself: Gen 1:6 *"And God said, Let there be a firmament in the midst of the waters, and let it divide the waters from the waters."* Gen 1:7 *"And God made the firmament, and divided the waters which were under the firmament from the waters which were above the firmament: and it was so."* Gen 1:8 *"And God called the firmament*

127

The Layman

Heaven." If life were to exist before the restoration, I have stated elsewhere, I think it rained. It is clear in the reordered work of our LORD God that we now address, there is no rain.

THE GENERATIONS OF THE WORLD

I know this is a repeat of this Scripture, but I think it important to emphasize, "Generations." **Heb 1:2** Has in these last days spoken unto us by his Son, whom he has appointed heir of all things, by whom also he made the worlds: **Earth is planet; World, is the inhabitants.**

I see this as meaning from:
1. The birth of the first earth, in Phase I Creation I: World I, which is the original creation of Gen1:1,
2. to the earth in Phase II Creation II: World II. This is given to us in Gen1:2-Gen 2:3,
3. And, finally, where we are about to discuss, the "Restoration" of world II.

An Unknown Interval
I feel there was a "Gap" in time between male/female and Adam. That span of time could have been of any length; I personally think it was about 30,000 years, and this has been verified by DNA evaluation. The Homo sapien that science calls the Neanderthal, suddenly appeared about that time. Then, for no apparent reason, though some have elaborated that the Cro-Magnon man killed them off, and he disappears, or almost disappears from the scene.
I say almost because I am not sure all the Neanderthals were killed by the Cro-Magnon man. We must remember that when the Neanderthal came on the scene, we were at the tail end of the Pleistocene ice age.

It is as if the Phase II Creation took place and then there is an unknown period of time, and the world goes on as planned. How long this period was, we really do not know. We do not know how long each of the six creative days were, but I suspect that for whatever length those days were, that the seventh is not of the same length, or as I have suggested, each represents a sequence and the 7th is still running.

Recap.
It is well that we take of inventory of what we do not know, so we can try and find out. what I feel we are lacking in:

1. We do not know how long God took to complete the original creation of the **earth**, (world I).

2. We do not know what steps He took in that creation.

3. We do not know what creatures, other than the skeletal remains we have found, existed at that time.

4. We do not know how long the first earth existed before everything became, or was caused to become "Void and Without Form."

5. We do not know how long the earth lay in a "Void and Without Form" state.

6. We do not know the length of each creative day of Phase II Creation II event.

7. When speaking of God resting we should stick with what is given in Heb 4:3 *"For we which have believed do enter into rest, as he said, As I have sworn in my wrath, if they shall enter into my rest: although the works were finished from the foundation of the world."* (Emphasis is mine)

8. We do not know how long 'male and female' lived before Adam.

THE TERM IN THE DAY

Gen 2:4-6. 4. *"These are the generations of the heavens and of the earth when they were created, **in the day** that the LORD God made the earth and the heavens."*(Emphasis is mine) I have again redundantly, highlighted the term "day" to show this is a summary of the creative events: the term "day" includes a vast period of time and many creative events.

Now with the start of Gen 2:4 we will introduce the work of the LORD God with the Father, where we have an entirely different sequence of creation, and it is evident that there is a dramatic change here.

OFFICES OF GOD

In Gen 1, we saw God bringing the world out of judgment. Now in Gen 2 we see the office of the LORD God, restoring the world to a different order; an entirely different scene.

Albert Barnes has this to say about the title change. *"The document upon which we are now entering extends from **Ge 2:4** to Gen. 4. In the*

The Layman

second and third chapters the author uses the combination יהוה םיהלא *yehovah 'elohym* **"the Lord God,"** to designate the Supreme Being; *in the fourth* he drops םיהלא *'elohym* **"God,"** and employs יהוה *yehovah* **"the Lord,"** alone. *So far, then, as the divine appellation is concerned, the fourth chapter is as clearly separable from the second and third as the first document (1ˢᵗ* Chapter*) is from the present (2*ⁿᵈ* Chapter*). If diversity of the divine name were a proof of diversity of authorship, we should here have two documents due to different authors, each of them different also from the author of the first document (1ˢᵗ* Chapter*).* **The second and third chapters, though agreeing in the designation of God, are clearly distinguishable in style.***"* (Parenthesis and bold type are my insertions for clarity)

He is explaining that:

1. The first chapter and the second chapter are vastly different in that the office has changed.

2. He, further, states that the second and the third differ from each other also,

3. Lastly he states that the fourth differs from the rest.

It must be read, and re-read in order to understand his explanation and to get the full meaning. He wrote in proper, educated English, and the reader is burdened, by now, to my usage. I present this; redundant as it is, to show the reader what I am presenting is not as a lone wolf in a snow storm. These chapters are arranged in the most perfect order, and must be considered unbiased by the reader.

THE OFFICE OF "THE LORD GOD"

In Scripture we have the office of GOD, God, LORD God, Lord God, LORD, Word of God, Lord, Christ, Jesus Christ, Messiah, Father, and Jesus; plus the many attributes describing each.

The office of the LORD God (Jehovah Elohim) is now preparing to usher in another creative sequence which is quite different from the first. We now are viewing the LORD God "formed", "caused", and "made" everything that is to be in this new phase, which is the hands on, forming of man and personal preparing of vegetation, animal and woman.

Scofield's notes, on the usage of LORD.

"(1) The primary meaning of the name LORD (Jehovah) is the "self-existent One." Literally (as in Ex 3:14), "He that is who He is, therefore the eternal I AM:" But Havah, from which Jehovah, or Yahwe, is formed, signifies

also "to become," that is, to become known, thus pointing to a continuous and increasing self-revelation. Combining these meanings of Havah, we arrive at the meaning of the name **Jehovah. He is "the self- existent One who reveals Himself."** *The name is, in itself, an advance upon the name "God" (El, Elah, Elohim), which suggests certain attributes of Deity, as strength, etc., rather than His essential being.*

(2) It is significant that the first appearance of the name Jehovah in Scripture follows the creation of man. **It was God (Elohim) who said, "Let us make man in our image"** *(Gen 1:26);* **but** *when man, as in the* **second chapter** *of Genesis, is to fill the scene and become dominant over creation, it is* **the LORD God (Jehovah Elohim)** *who acts.* **This clearly indicates** *a special relation of Deity, in His Jehovah character, to man, and all Scripture emphasizes this."*

(3) **Jehovah** *is distinctly* **the redemption name of Deity**. *When sin entered and redemption became necessary, it was Jehovah Elohim who sought the sinning ones Gen 3:9-13 and clothed them with "coats of skins" Gen 3:21 a beautiful type of righteousness provided by the LORD God through sacrifice Ro 3:21-22. The first distinct revelation of Himself by His name Jehovah was in connection with the redemption of the covenant people out of Egypt Ex 3:13-17."* (Bold type and underlines are my insertions)

Even Dr. Scofield takes note that there is a distinct difference between male and female of chapter 1, and the man of chapter 2, by saying it was God (Elohim) who made man (male and female). Then Dr. Scofield continues, to show the distinctive separation when stating that it was the LORD God (Jehovah Elohim) who acts in forming Adam.

We now are introduced to an entirely different sequence of creative events of the LORD God. Repeating Gen 2:4 *"These are the generations of the heavens and of the earth when they were* **created**, *in the day that the LORD God* **made** *the earth and the heavens,"* (Emphasis is mine)

I want to be cautious here; He is bringing us up to where His creation is at this point: it is a summary of **all creation up to here**; if you please.

In the first of the verse we have the following order; the heavens; then the earth, and then the term **created.**

In the second part of the verse we have the term **made**, then the earth, and then the term heavens.

131

The Layman

These are the generations:

Here we are addressing more than one generation, and if Gen 1:1 to Gen 2:3 is one of those generations, then in Gen 2:4 to Gen 2:22, would bring light upon the second generation.

Follow the sequence here:

A. In Gen 1:1 we are introduced to God, "in the beginning," creation, of Phase I, world I.

B. In Gen 1:2 to Gen 2:3 we are introduced to God in recreation phase II world II, coming from judgment, and the creation of our heaven.

C. In Gen 2:4 to Gen 2:22 we are introduced to the LORD God in the restoration of the second world where the earth and the heaven are not recreated, since they are already here, but **made**: to a different order.

If I am correct in my assumption the LORD God has purposely **used the term made** rather than created because He is reflecting upon **a total dispensation**; that is "In the day." They really reflect upon a span in time, and to use both terms, "created" and "restored" in the same statement would open doors He chose not to make so plain, and uses the term made. This event of Gen 2:4 includes the six day "lets" of Gen 1:2 through Gen 2:3.

If there was rain in Gen 1:1 to Gen 2:3, then **the heaven** would have to be <u>changed</u> in Gen 2 by the LORD God, because it should now, not rain, but produce only a mist from the earth, so the heavens were in Gen 2, not created because they were already here, but made to a different order.

The reversal of the order is keeping with what happened in this new generation. Careful consideration should be given to the use of the term "<u>made</u>." Not to be confused with the first chapter, where with the creative "Lets" we have plants, animals, male and female. Here in Gen 2:4 we will see the creative events are "made", and the sequence is; Adam, plants, animals, then Woman.

I can only cautiously offer this explanation on such a profound Scripture. When He uses both the terms "<u>created</u>" and "<u>made</u>" almost in the same breath, it is monumental.

Let's look at the Scripture again and how this unfolds. Gen 2:4 *"These are the generations of the (1)heavens and of the (2)earth when they were*

132

created,(God with the LORD God) *in the day that the LORD God* (with God) ***made*** *the (2)earth and the (1)heavens,"* Gen 2:5 *"And every plant of the field before it was in the earth, and every herb of the field before it grew: for the LORD God had not caused it to rain upon the earth, and there was not a man to till the ground."*(Emphasis is mine)

IN THE DAY

1 In the day that the LORD God <u>made</u> the earth and the heavens.

2. Every plant...every herb of the field <u>before they were in the earth...before they grew</u>. The Geneva footnotes have this to say here, *"many prefer to render the original, "And no plant of the field was yet in the earth, and no herb of the field yet grew,"*. Now remember in Gen 1: God said "let the earth bring forth" as if the seeds were already present.

This verse of Gen 2:4 does not incorporate Gen 1: 11. We are now discussing the explanation of **new plants** for the Garden. One could assume that there was little growing in Eden at that time and for good cause: Why? Because this dispensation coincides with the end of the last recorded ice age which began years earlier. It is for that reason I feel the LORD God is preparing another group of plants. We are not trying to say that **all** plants died off, but that the LORD God is preparing different plants. One would be the tree of life which wasn't in the first chapter, then the other would be the tree of the knowledge of good and evil which was not in the first chapter either. If all the plants were different, or not, is only speculation, but then why would Scripture call it out if it were the same? Why not say that He took choice trees, grass, and herbs from the earth and caused them to grow here?

Not a Man to Till the Ground

Now I have you." One would say. "You have said that there were male and female on earth before Adam, and now it says "Not a man to till the ground." Well I have said that, but let us look at that in more detail before we get a mind set.

1. Here is a possibility, giving the thought that Scripture is **not** telling us there was no life. The part of Scripture we are looking at is the statement, "<u>man to till the ground:</u>" This has a broader meaning. The first, "male, female" were not farmers, and were considered <u>gatherers</u>. If this is the meaning, and I am sure it is they would not be considered as being those who would be "tilling the ground." Remember **God gave them all to eat**, Genesis 1:29 *"And God said, Behold, I have given you **every herb** bearing seed, which is upon the face of all the earth, and **every tree**, in the which is the fruit of a tree yielding seed; **to you it shall be for meat**."*(Emphasis is mine) If they are given everything that is growing, why grow anything? We must also remember that God did not tell them to till or tend anything.

2. Adam is formed, and then the garden is planted. At this point in Gen 2:5, there is no man here.

3. Gen 2 we have another event, we will be introduced to Adam and he is to till, or dress the garden. This garden will be planted in a land called Eden: Using that logic, we are safe in making the statement that before Adam, there was no man to **till** the ground.

With every "theory" there is subjective analysis until it is revealed by the Holy Ghost, and becomes truth. I stand upon the premise within my presentation of these phases of creation; however, **it would be unfair to fail and point out its holes.** That is the reason I have made a point, of the verse; "man to till the ground." Perhaps there are those who can provide further insight here, and if so, it is my prayer that they should pass it on. Perhaps it is the hole in the dyke which destroys the entire dam. The reader will have to judge for themselves. I would reemphasize that there is a difference between a gatherer and a farmer. A farmer <u>tills</u> the soil, plants the crop, weeds the field, and hires <u>gatherers</u> to reap the crop.

When I was young, the guys would go to what we used to call "The Wrecking Yard," and start picking up pieces of what would later be put together and it would become a car, well that is what we called them anyway. Some cars were made with parts, motors, and drive trains from every manufacturer, with this part bolted to here and another bolted to there, and when the bolt holes didn't match, you drilled new ones. You didn't have one of those fancy electric hand drills. Our drills were hand driven and looked like a converted egg beater. I remember a car my friend made. It had a city park bench for a front seat, no doors, sides or top. It did have a "bug screen" which we learned later was called a wind shield. You didn't have safety inspection stickers then, and you didn't have to have insurance. You could get a license plate for anything you had guts enough to drive. Do you know we loved those old rattle traps more than any new shiny car we purchased later in life?

I remember one such car a friend and I had. We cannot get together even today after 50 years, and not start laughing over that "beast." The driver side window fell out in Atlanta Georgia, and would have clipped the feet of a nimble footed cop had he not learned to jump so well. The battery shorted against the horn in Greenville South Carolina at one-thirty in the morning. And the emergency brake, which was not located within the back brake as today's are, but were wrapped around the drive-shaft: Ours never worked, well not until it finally burnt all the oil out of it, then decided to grab hold. This sent us into a spin, which nearly caused us to hit a frantic truck driver. One said it looked like a lone Indian circling a wagon.

Know why we loved those old death traps? Why? Because we put our creative hands on each part and formed that old wreck. My LORD God wanted a personal touch when He made us, He really did, and he loves us even if we are old wrecks too.

God is not some cosmic kill-joy
Every time He says, "Thou shalt not"
He's simply saying, "don't hurt yourself.
And every time He says, "Thou shalt,"
He's saying, "Help yourself to happiness."

Adrian Rogers

THE LORD GOD FORMS MAN

In the first chapter we had the "**Let**" acts of spoken creation, in Gen 2:4, we now see the LORD God **"Forming," "Planting"** and **"Made Restorations"**. Back in Genesis 1 we are told that God said "Let us make man." Now in Gen 2:4 we have the LORD God "forming" man. Strong's definition (73) here says that this word means to *"squeeze into shape," "to mold."* My friend there is a vast difference in speaking something into existence, than to squeeze it, or mold it. It is important to see the differences between these two chapters.

The LORD God now takes a personal approach to what is happening. There are no "lets" here. The LORD God formed, made, and planted. Oh! That I could dive ever deeper into His treasure chest here, but alas, I can only scratch the surface.

Adam

Gen 2:7 *"And the **LORD God formed man** of the dust of the ground, and breathed into his nostrils the breath of life; and man became a **living soul.**"* (Emphasis is mine) Not in His image as Gen 1, but here it is said He breathed into his nostrils and man, (not male and female), became a living soul. This is the first mention of man's soul in Scripture.

Gen 2:8 *"And the LORD God **planted a garden eastward** in Eden; and **there he put the man** whom he had formed."* (Emphasis is mine) Have we already asked ourselves a question? The LORD God forms Adam, **then** the LORD God plants a garden **with seed**, and **then** the LORD God puts the man in the garden to dress it. In Gen 2:8 is a summary statement that will be amplified in Gen 2:15 later.

1. What time elapsed after the LORD God formed Adam did He wait to start the garden?

2. Where was Adam all this time? It is explained the LORD God planted the Garden Eastward. Adam must, therefore, have been westward, but how far west, we do not know. (Remember this later when we discuss the term "father and mother.")

136

3. How long did it take for the seeds to grow into fruit bearing trees? Have we ever known of someone who planted an acorn, apple, peach or a pecan tree; how many years did it take before they bore fruit? I sure do not know; however, I am smart enough to know that it did not happen overnight. Could He have done it and violate existing natural laws established? Why should an eternal LORD God do that? He is later going to put an eternal Adam in there. What's everyone's hurry? Consider #4 below.

4. What total time frame are we talking about, between the LORD God forming Adam, to the point that Adam is to dress and keep the garden? I mean he has to have something to dress. Now please, don't try and take the "God can do more in a nano-second than we can do in a lifetime. Then if that were true, we must ask ourselves, why did the LORD God **plant seed in the first place?** I take pure delight on watching a tender little plant send its exploring sprout through the surface, and say "hello" to the universe. The Godhead has a set of rules that need not be broken. What would be the hurry? I think our Lord just delighted in watching it all grow, and, **to let Adam do a little ("Walk-About") exploring of earth.**

Later there would be a couple, in the garden He has planted, who would be His earthly descendants, and in the New Testament, He comes back to finish the job of sowing a very different kind of seed, and to harvest a very different crop, precious brethren: You and Me, and it takes a lifetime for us to mature as well.

Let's look at His work:

Gen 2:9 *"And out of the ground **made** the LORD God **to grow** every tree(X0014) that is pleasant to the sight, and good for food; the **tree of life** also in the midst of the garden, and the **tree of the knowledge of good and evil**."* (Emphasis is mine.)

In the chapter we are now addressing **we have man**, then we **have vegetation**, then we **have trees for food**, and **we don't have any animals**. Has the reader noticed, **There is no female as of yet?** Is everyone still with me?

There is a difference here so obvious that a blind man could see it with a walking stick. Is that difference just an amplification of what has been said previously? I do not think so, and will never be convinced that this dispensation is the same as Gen 1: it is for that reason this work is presented.

137

The Layman

There must be harmony between these two dispensations, and there is <u>none</u> **unless** they are understood as <u>two separate events</u>, occurring years, perhaps centuries apart. For me to believe otherwise would cast doubt on its authenticity. We will show the differences in a comparative chart a little later.

THE LAND OF EDEN

We must take note that the "garden" <u>was not a land</u>. The "garden" was a part of a land called Eden. I cringe every time I work a crossword puzzle and it gives the question, "A perfect place," and they want the answer to be "Eden." If it were a perfect place, why would the LORD God have to renovate it?

Gen 2:8 *"And the LORD God planted a garden eastward in* <u>Eden</u>; *and there he put the man whom he had formed."* Eastward from where: I think it was eastward from where we have been up to now. Where was that? There is a saying in Texas, "I ain't gonna run my hauss in that race." But there is again another "buzz" which our minds skip over because it does not understand what is being said. When we read about the garden, we narrow our attention to a lush garden, pristine in beauty that somehow covers the whole earth and we don't want anything to disrupt that thought; however, that is just what the LORD God is going to do by even telling us there are many other lands wherein water is delivered.

RIVERS WITHOUT RAIN

When I was a lad and lived in Georgia, I used to go to a place in Albany where there was this river that just boiled out of this deep black hole in the ground. We would dive into the currents and try to see how deep we could go, which wasn't really very far. It would feel like you were going ever deeper, but if you were standing up on the diving platform and were watching someone trying to do the same, you would laugh to see that person only a couple of feet beneath the surface just battling the current for all they were worth, only to pop to the surface the moment they ceased their efforts.

I said that because we know rainfall on the East coast finds its way into the aquifers and cause this phenomenon.

How does one have rivers without rain? This is why in an earlier discussion that I felt that it rained in Gen 1: To cut channels, and provide necessary erosion for the water to follow.

Water

I like to chase squirrels once in a while. We now have an additional characteristic of earth which is given here, and almost as if it is out of place. In the first chapter of Genesis, it never mentions how the earth is watered; now it becomes an important point. There must have been water for all the erosion to take place, and to mention it, would demand an explanation as to why it was stopped here.

Our Father and the Lord knew man would fail, and He was going to later give Noah a "Rainbow Covenant. Now if one has rain, and the sun shining, they are going to have a rainbow. So the heaven here in the 2nd chapter is made different, so the sun will not directly shine on the earth. It is the opinion of most, that there was a continual overcast over the earth at this Phase.

Well we are now going to show another difference between Gen. 1, and Gen. 2. And that is the discussion of the topography with rivers.

Gen 2:6 *"But there went up a mist from the earth, and watered the whole face of the ground."*

Rain does not fall, but a mist rises from the earth and a great amount of it because we then read, Gen 2:10 *"And a river went out of Eden to water the garden; and from thence it was parted, and became into four heads. Gen 2:11 The name of the first is Pison: that is it which compasseth the whole land of Havilah, where there is gold;* Gen 2:12 *And the gold of that land is good: there is bdellium and the onyx stone.* Gen 2:13 *And the name of the second river is Gihon: the same is it that compasseth the whole land of Ethiopia.* Gen 2:14 *And the name of the third river is Hiddekel: that is it which goeth toward the East of Assyria. And the fourth river is Euphrates."*

In Gen 2, notice that the river did not originate within the Garden, but <u>came out of Eden</u>, and having passed through the Garden it then branched off into four heads. This fog had to be far beyond what we see in early morning when, what we call fog, forms and drips off of everything; however, this quantity of water had to come from within the earth if there was no rain. That is the only way I know, to have rivers without it raining. For that river to flow of sufficient quantity to divide into four heads and water named lands leads me to believe this way.

The Layman

How closely do we read Scripture? Wonder why it never says which direction, or where it goes when speaking of the river Euphrates. I do not know either, but I assure everyone that there is a divine reason for that omission.

I remember as a Boy Scout when we went camping alongside a swamp in Florida. One morning everything in the camp was soaked. Our covers, our clothes, the very ground was wet, and the trees dripped all over us. Well, that fog didn't make a river, but it was surely wet.

If I am to believe that Gen. 2 is a recapitulation of Gen 1, then I could not have the same faith. It would be the same as the LORD God saying, "Well what I meant to say was."

Would I think of writing this and not take the time to do several drafts? (Some might at this point think I should have made a few more.) I cannot imagine my Father not knowing how to write what must be a first grade reader to Him, without editing it in the very first two chapters. I mean we are talking about the very first part of Scripture here. How can we imagine this all doesn't fall into a perfect pattern? If our LORD God cannot get the first part right, how are we to trust the rest? **He got it right my brethren, He really did.**

I know what we are addressing in this work, is not soul saving, or damning. Scripture is all we have and need today to bolster our faith. We **must believe it all or none at all.** No, my friend; I do not limit my Father. Sure, I find holes which I cannot plug, but I know there is a plug somewhere; I know there **is**, and with each hole, the plug comes from the Holy Ghost. Now let's look at:

NAMING OF THE LANDS

I want to make note of the lands which are related to here. They could have been named from the beginning, and only given here by the "then" name, or that may have been names given at Moses' time. I know that there are other names given by historians to each of these lands. I do not find significance in them, but if they are given in Scripture, there most certainly is a meaning I am missing. We must, however, always remember one most important truth, **one cannot have a kingdom without a king, and a king is not a king unless he rules a kingdom.** If there is a land, there is a border to that land. A border separates one or more lands from each other. <u>If there are no people on earth at this time, how can there be different lands?</u> Why

140

have the lands called out if they did not exist at that time and were only called into existence later? It stands to reason **if there were not lands at that time, then why didn't the LORD God just say "rivers flowed through the garden, then divided into four parts to water the earth"**? He said that they watered NAMED LANDS.

We do not know if the LORD is using the names Havilah, Ethiopia, and the land of Assyria which were predominantly used at Moses' time, or not. We do recognize the rivers, "Euphrates" and "Hiddekel" (later renamed Tigres), the others I don't. I think the important point here, that we must not let fall from our minds is that there were "lands" of different designation at this time, whether the names are the same or not, they were **still named lands**, and there is yet another land we will see later.

Now for the river, I do not know if the LORD God caused the river to start flowing when He planted the garden, or if He planted the garden around an existing river. I just wonder what the originating point looked like, and where it was. Wonder if it was one like the one in Albany?

MAN IS TO TEND THE GARDEN

Gen 2:15 *"And the LORD God took the man, and put him into the Garden of Eden to **dress it** and **to keep it**."* (Emphasis is mine)

Adam was to farm, and/or till the ground, or maybe just prunes the trees, there is no real definition given.

Have we ever asked ourselves what is missing here? How was Adam going to tend the garden? What tools did he have? The reader will never read Scripture the same again, I promise them. We must always remember that the Lord never assigns a task beyond our capabilities to carry it out. I do not know what Adam had, but he had something that would do the job.

I think Adam when he was on his "walk about" observed the male and female, and there learned about certain tools. I will have to leave it there because that is another S.W.A.G. on my part.

Man is given food to eat:

Gen 2:16 *"And the LORD God **commanded the man**, saying, Of every tree of the garden thou mayest freely eat:"* (Emphasis is mine)

Food withheld:

Gen 2:17 *"But of the tree of the knowledge of good and evil, thou shalt*

141

not eat of it : for in the day that thou eatest thereof thou shalt surely die." Here the LORD God talks to "Adam" and not as before in Gen 1,when "God talks to both the <u>male</u> **and** <u>female</u>."

How many times have we heard this tree called "The Tree of Knowledge," and the rest is left out? It has nothing to do with knowledge as we use the term today; it is what that knowledge is <u>about</u> that got us in trouble.

Now compare this with Gen 1:29 as God is addressing male and female; *"And God said, Behold, I have given you <u>every herb</u> bearing seed, which is upon the face of **all the earth**, and **every tree**, in the which is the fruit of a tree yielding seed; to you it shall be for meat."* (Emphasis is mine)

There is a difference between these two chapters: Notice that for **Adam**, while he was still <u>without</u> a "helpmeet" God <u>withholds</u> *"**the tree of the knowledge of good and evil**."* It doesn't even mention the tree in Gen 1:29, because it was obviously not there. The LORD God made the seed and planted it in the Garden of Eden. We must see the deliberate differences between these two events.

Sadly, Adam and later Woman also had the tree of life that they could also have taken, but the LORD God knew what would happen.

How many parents have ever told one of their children not to do something, and they knew before they told them not to do it, they were going to have to punish them for doing that very thing? OH! The love that He has is beyond our wildest imaginations. It is seldom recognized that today we have opportunity for such a tree of life?

Re 22:14 *Blessed are they that do his commandments, that they may have right to <u>the tree of life</u>, and may enter in through the gates into the city.* But alas, some chose otherwise.

In Gen 1, God makes man a <u>gatherer</u>, and in Gen 2 the LORD God makes Adam a <u>tenant farmer</u> or an orchard grower from the beginning.

The first <u>male and female</u> are given **all to eat**, and were not hunters, nor farmers, but gatherers. <u>Adam</u> is also a gatherer, and in addition the LORD God has him to dress and to keep the newly created garden. It is obvious that these are not the same events, and not the same people, if it were, why wouldn't it mention the garden in the first chapter? There is no mention of where the "male and female" are ever going to live; friend, my God is more organized than that.

I cannot be convinced that when the LORD God gets to the second chapter, He is saying, "Well now let me explain what I meant to say in the first chapter." If we do not see the differences here, then we must face another wall, and that wall would be that He got it mixed up and is now trying to get it straight. I choose my explanation rather than think the LORD God is unorganized: **and we shall not do that.**

DIFFERENCES OF GEN 1, and GEN 2

In Gen 1 we have:
1. **Vegetation;**
2. Then **Animals**
3. Then God <u>makes</u> male and female;
4. Then blesses <u>them;</u>
5. Then **tells them** to **replenish** the earth;
6. Then Gives them **everything to eat.**

Here in Gen 2 we have:
1. The LORD God <u>forms Adam</u>;
2. Then **Planting of the Garden** in Eden;
3. Then when the plants are fruitful, He puts **Adam** in the Garden to dress it;
4. Then Command of what <u>he</u> **can eat;**
5. Then tells him **what he <u>cannot</u> eat;**
6. Then **Animals are formed** out of the ground, which Adam will later name, then finally,
7. The LORD God clones **Woman.**

We note that:
In Gen 1, God is talking to <u>both</u> **male and female.**
In Gen 2, it is the LORD God who is **talking only to Adam.**
In Gen 1, God **blesses male and female.**

In Gen 2, it is never mentioned that the LORD God blesses Adam at all and it is not until we read in Gen 5:2 *"Male and female created he them; **and blessed them**, and called **their name Adam**, in the day when they were created.*
"

Why is it omitted until then? Because chapter 5 is again a summation of the total creative events from Gen 1:2 all the way **up to Gen 5:2**, and "Adam" is used there in the **generic sense** there to mean all mankind.

Here is another wall we have to deal with concerning the inerrancy of Scripture when studying the first two chapters. There are irreconcilable differences that can only be explained when one recognizes that they are two very separate events. If one refuses to recognize this, then they must accept:

      1. Moses did not accurately record the events as he was enlightened.

      2. The original translators went on coffee break between the two chapters and forgot where they were.

      3. There are some who would have to say, "We just do not understand want we have read."

Well **I do** understand, and feel the **reader does also.**

ADAM'S RULE

Next, we have "Gen 2:18 *"And the LORD God said, It is not good that the man should be alone; **I will make** him an **help meet for him**."* (Emphasis is mine) Looking in the margin of my reference/concordance, this word may also mean **"as before him,"** or "I will make him an helpmeet as man had before him"? I think that is exactly what is being said.

Gen 2:19 *"And out of the ground the LORD God **formed every beast** of the field, and **every fowl** of the air; and brought them unto Adam to see what **he would call them**: and whatsoever Adam called every living creature, that was the name thereof.*

Gen 2:20 *And **Adam gave names** to all cattle, and to the fowl of the air, and to every beast of the field; but for Adam there was not found an help meet for him."*

See how personal the LORD God has become here? He has put His personal seal of approval upon all things. **The LORD God "formed."** There are no "lets" here.

There is another difference here that we should take note of, in Gen 2:19 He is quoted as saying **"formed** every beast of the field **and every foul of the air.** In Gen 1 we are told Genesis 1:20 *"And God said, **Let the waters bring forth** abundantly the moving creature that hath life, **and fowl** that may fly above the earth in the open firmament of heaven."* (Emphasis is mine.

The first ruler:

Time is a very important point when we discuss Scripture. I have said elsewhere, that Adam was ageless when created. He was, I suppose, an adult, but he did not age since he was eternal, until his fall. How long did he tend the garden before he got lonely? How many days, moons, or years (if we can even apply that term yet) passed before he was to be joined by the creatures of the world? How long did the LORD God wait before He started forming the animals: I wonder if He brought cubs or bears, calves or cows, colts or horses? Did He bring all of the animals all at once or did He form them, and then bring them to Adam? In either case, Adam has a task in front of him.

Genesis 2:19 *"And out of the ground the LORD God formed every beast of the field, and every fowl of the air; and brought them unto Adam to see what he would call them: and whatsoever Adam called every living creature, that was the name thereof."*

Adam will name the animals, and we somehow seem to persist in our thinking that he is doing this before lunch. I don't see it that way at all. I see him studying each creature and naming them according to the character which the LORD God instilled within them. I don't see Adam as an air head at all, in fact as Luke calls him "The son of God." I rather see him as quite a bit more intelligent than I, and if it won't make someone mad, smarter than a lot of people I have met.

Now when I say that Adam was more intelligent, I do not say he was more educated. One must be exposed to many facets of life before even a genius can be called educated.

Today there are an estimated 5,416 mammal species on earth, and 9,800 for birds. That figure **does not include** the **vast numbers** that have gone extinct over the many years, and this present estimated number, I am sure is a conservative figure; however, using that as a starting point, if the LORD God formed one animal a day, and Adam similarly named them at that same rate**, it would take over forty years**, and two a day **would still take over twenty**. When we try and put time to something, that someone else has done, we sometimes lose perspective.

I heard about one preacher who said "The LORD God brought an animal to Adam to see what he would name him. Adam studied the animal for several days and when asked what he would call him, Adam said, 'Well he is as big as an elephant, smells like an elephant, and eats like an elephant, what do you think? Should we go with elephant?'"

I think it is a funny story and gets laughs, but Adam has an almost insurmountable job. We must remember that we are not in a hurry here: time as of yet has not started for Adam.

I appreciate the fact that I keep bringing this to the reader's attention, but **it is pivotal**. In Gen 1, our Father uses the *"Lets"* to

145

create. Here in Gen 2, our LORD God forms and the Scripture reads, *"Out of the ground the LORD God formed every beast..."* It is not one of the creative "Lets" of the first chapter. There is a difference, or the same language would be used. The LORD God personally "forms" these animals. I emphasize that He formed "**each**" animal, whereas in Gen 1 it seems to indicate that our God has the LORD God to form them all using the "Lets" with one directive command. How long it took for **either** creative event to be complete, **we do not know** because it is not told us. One should remember we are still within the garden, in eternity here in Gen 2.

I did not mention this when discussing the male and female at the sixth day of creation of Gen 1: however, I do not think they were as Adam; eternal, **but aged.**

I apologize for using days, months and years to describe the naming sequence. I just do not know of another way to explain this sequence, and the time it took.

Now we are going to discuss the ruler. Remember we discussed, "One cannot have a kingdom without a ruler, and they cannot have a ruler without a kingdom." Well we are going to have a ruler. (Ok! I know I changed the term from king to ruler. I do not think of Adam as a king, that's all.)

We now have a ruler who has come upon the scene, and **that ruler is Adam**. The first group, "male, female" were **given** the earth to **subdue and thereby have dominion,** but not the rule of it. **Adam is to rule** over the earth and everything in it. This will upset a whole lot of politically correct "Persons", but **Adam will rule earth, animal, and Woman.**

Let's look at Naming

When a king possessed a land or took a city throughout the Bible, **he would rename** the city and/or the land, which gave him the right to rule it. When a king took captives into his kingdom, **he renamed the captives,** and when we get to Heaven **we will be given a new name**; why? To rename a city made not only the city and the land, but also the inhabitants yours. When you renamed a captive that captive was yours to keep, kill, mistreat, honor, or dishonor. He was literally yours to do with as you chose. That is the reason we have so much trouble identifying places today; they have been renamed several times before. Many records etched into stone have literally been chiseled off to remove authority of the past and allow the new king, his authority.

If I were to relate the following: "Now among these were of the children of Judah, ------, Hananiah, Mishael, and Azariah: Unto whom the prince of the eunuchs gave names: for he gave unto ----- the name of Belteshazzar; and to Hananiah, of --------; and to Mishael, of ------; and to Azariah, of --------." Everyone would recognize the four names if I gave them. I am trying to impress upon everyons mind that this was the practice from time past.

Filling in the blanks for the above passage we have, Daniel 1:6 *"Now among these were of the children of Judah, Daniel, Hananiah, Mishael, and Azariah:* Daniel 1:7 *Unto whom the prince of the eunuchs gave names: for he gave unto Daniel the name of Belteshazzar; and to Hananiah, of Shadrach; and to Mishael, of Meshach; and to Azariah, of Abednego."*

The conquering king did this, and these fellows were his to do with as he chose: One later to the lions, three to a fiery furnace.
Here are more direct examples of naming:
2Sa 12:27 *"And Joab sent messengers to David, and said, I have fought against Rabbah, and have taken the city of waters.*
2Sa 12:28 *Now therefore gather the rest of the people together, and encamp against the city, and take it:* **lest I take the city, and it be called after my name.**
2Sa 12:29 *And David gathered all the people together, and went to Rabbah, and fought against it, and took it.*
2Sa 12:30 *And he took their king's crown from off his head, the weight whereof [was] a talent of gold with the precious stones: and it was [set] on David's head. And he brought forth the spoil of the city in great abundance.*
2Sa 12:31 *And he brought forth the people that [were] therein, and put [them] under saws, and* under harrows *of iron, and* under axes *of iron, and made them* pass through the brickkiln*: and thus did he unto all the cities of the children of Ammon. So David and all the people returned unto Jerusalem"* (Emphasis is mine)
Here is something in the believer's future: Re 2:17 *"He that hath an ear, let him hear what the Spirit saith unto the churches; To him that overcometh will I give to eat of the hidden manna, and will give him a white stone,* **and in the stone a new name written,** *which no man knoweth saving he that receiveth it."*
Re 3:12 *"Him that overcometh will I make a pillar in the temple of my God, and he shall go no more out: and I will write upon him* **the name of my God,** *and*

The Layman

the **name of the city of my God**, *[which is] new Jerusalem, which cometh down out of heaven from my God: and [I will write upon him]* **my new name.**" Re 22:4 "*And they shall see his face; and* **his name** *[shall be] in their foreheads.*"(Emphasis is mine)

I wonder what my Lord's new name will be; I know I will love it. He will give us new names and therefore have rule over us for eternity. **He will do unto us as He pleases for eternity.** We will be called by our new names; we will have the name of our God and the city of our God written on our foreheads. I don't know about anyone else, but I will be glad to know what my real name is; won't we all? I know when I read that "white stone," I will exclaim, "I knew my name was all wrong: This is who I really am."

The LORD God is giving the rule of earth and all that's in it to Adam, and Adam is **naming everything** so he can rule it and do with it as he pleases. Unfortunately, Adam will give it over to Satan later, but there again is another story.

THE LORD GOD FORMS WOMAN

Next we have Gen 2:21 "*And the LORD God caused a deep sleep to fall upon Adam, and he slept: and he took one of his ribs, and closed up the flesh instead thereof;*" (I know this breaks the continuity of thought, but I get a kick out of Scripture. It says that the LORD God caused a deep sleep to fall upon Adam, then it adds "**and he slept.**" What choice did he have? Do we catch these things when we study? There is a prophetic reason this is repeated, I just wish I knew what it and many others like it really mean.)

There is another similar expression: Isa 37:36 "*Then the angel of the LORD went forth, and smote in the camp of the Assyrians a hundred and fourscore and five thousand: and when they arose early in the morning, behold, they [were] all dead corpses.*"

Did we catch it? Now has anyone ever seen a live corpse? I know I read Scripture a little different.

Gen 2:22 "*And the rib, which the LORD God had taken from man,* **made he a Woman, and brought her unto the man.**"(Emphasis is mine) Please note that the LORD God brought her unto the man (Adam). Now precious, I do not put her in the same category with the animals, and in no way place her in any level of worth, but only to point out that **she was "brought unto the man"** by the LORD God: Why? This was an order of leadership, and Adam **was to name her** as

148

well, and Adam **called her Woman.** Also note that it is not recorded that the LORD God <u>talks to them</u> both as He did male and female of Gen 1.

Remember the words of Jesus: Mt 12:25 *"And Jesus knew their thoughts, and said unto them, Every kingdom divided against itself is brought to desolation; and every city or house divided against itself shall not stand:"* That goes for heaven, earth and the home.

I know this to be redundant, but there is nothing mentioned about procreation. One final comparison before we get any further, and that is to make a point that there is no mention of the LORD God **"resting."**

The following table (Figure 1.) will make a quick reference of the differences between the two chapters. I trust that it will clear up a host of difficulties which I am sure some have experienced following each of the "X's" within the text.

Gen 1:2/Gen 2:3	Gen 2:4/Gen 2:26
X0 Office of God	Office of the LORD GOD
X01 Let's of Creation	
X02 Let there be Light	Light already here
X03 The expanse of the air	The air is already here
X04 Let the dry land appear	The land is already here
X05 Let the earth bring forth vegetation	The LORD God prepares the seed before planting P133
X06 The Sun, Moon are assigned their roles	The Sun and Moon are already here
X07 The Fish and Fowl are created by the "Let's"	No animals yet
X08 The animals are created	No animals yet
X000 Office of the Trinity	No mention of the Trinity
X001 Male and Female are created by the "Let's"	The LORD God FORMS Adam from the dust of the earth P136
X09 Created in His image	Adam is made a living soul P136
X010 God blesses them	No female as yet
X012 God tells them to Replenish the earth.	The LORD God plants the Garden P136
X013 God tells them to subdue the earth and thereby have dominion	Rivers and land explained P138
X014 God gives them, and the animals all to eat	The LORD God puts Adam in the Garden P141
X015 God Rested	Commissions Adam to keep and dress the garden P141
	With holds the Tree of the Knowledge of Good and Evil P141
	The LORD God forms the animals P144
	Adam names the animals and becomes the ruler P144
	Female is cloned P148
	Adam names her woman P149

FIGURE 1

FATHER AND MOTHER

I know most of us have read this passage over and over and the problem with that is we "Buzz" over the passage. Here is another point which I think is completely overlooked. Gen 2:24 *"Therefore shall a man leave his **father and his mother**, and shall cleave unto his wife: and they shall be one flesh."*(Emphasis is mine)

We must ask ourselves, **if** Adam was the "FIRST" person on earth, how does he know about a father and mother? Remember that I asked everyone earlier to remember that?

Notice each of the following passages has a lapse of "time"
Gen 2:7 *"And the LORD God formed man of the dust of the ground, and breathed into his nostrils the breath of life; and man became a living soul."*
(This line represents the lapse of TIME)......................)
THEN:
Gen 2:8 *"¶ And the LORD God planted a garden eastward in Eden..."*
(This line represents the lapse of TIME)......................)
THEN:
.....and there he put the man whom he had formed."
(This line represents the lapse of TIME......................)
THEN:
Gen 2:19 *"And out of the ground the LORD God formed every beast of the field, and every fowl of the air; and brought [them] unto Adam to see what he would call them: and whatsoever Adam called every living creature, that [was] the name thereof."*
(This line represents the lapse of TIME.......................)
THEN:
Gen 2:22 *"¶And the rib, which the LORD God had taken from man, made he a woman, and brought her unto the man."*

It should be noticed that there was one of those "¶" at Gen 2:4: Gen 2:8; Gen 2:16; and Gen 2:18 and Gen 2:22. These paragraph divisions tell us that each is chapters in themselves and even though they are in sequence, they are separated by an unspecified length of time.

The LORD God formed Adam, "**then**" He planted a garden in Eden, "**then**" there He put man whom he had formed, "**then**" He forms the animals and brings them to Adam, "**then**" Adam names the animals, "**then**" He clones woman and brings her to Adam and he names her. How many years have passed between verses 2:7 and 2:22 no one knows.

151

Since the LORD God planted the seeds for the garden, it must have taken a while, (though to say so would place time on the event), for the trees to grow and produce fruit. Meanwhile where was Adam?

I have often asked myself, how many growth rings the trees had; only zero, in the thoughts of some.

I think that Adam knew of the other race of Gen 1:26, 27. I think that is where he knew about "Father and Mother." I mean; if I were saying the same as verse Gen 2:24, wouldn't I say, "Therefore will my son leave me and my wife and shall cleave to his wife?" This is the first time Adam **has supposedly** ever **laid eyes on Woman**, and he already has the whole thing down pat? <u>He doesn't even know he is necked, but he knows of father, mother, and wife.</u> I am convinced that Adam witnessed the life of the Neanderthals, where he learned these things, otherwise, how would he even know about a son?.

Then some would say, "Well Adam had great knowledge and wisdom, he probably was prophesying here." Well I will have to agree that he could have been using a Divine given knowledge, but if this were so, it is the only evidence, short of him renaming woman to Eve, ever recorded that we could attest to him.

We must stop romanticizing Scripture. I honestly think that some people vision Adam leaving a little whitely painted home with a flower filled, manicured lawn, to tending the garden on a John Deere® tractor and driving a Rolls Royce® auto to work. I am sure that he was a very fast learner and advanced rapidly, but he started from ground zero with only the clothes, the LORD God later gave him, on his back.

Adam knew more of the outside world than is being told to us. After all, the Scriptures are for our edification toward salvation, not a total science and history lesson. **Adam had to be somewhere** while the LORD God prepared and planted the garden. **Adam had to have something to eat, and he had to exist somewhere besides a newly planted Garden.** Scripture says that **after** the garden was planted, and that the LORD God was pleased with it, He then picked up Adam, from wherever he was at the time, and put him in the garden to keep and dress it.

ADAM NAMED HER WOMAN

Gen 2:23 *"And Adam said, This is now bone of my bones, and flesh of my flesh: **she shall be called Woman**, because she was taken out of Man."* (Emphasis is mine)

There is a wonderful slap at evolutionists here. Remember when we were in school and studied about "Chromosomes?" Well let me refresh our memory here, because I had forgotten. Humans have 23 pairs of chromosomes, with a diploid number of 46. Twenty-two of these pairs are called autosomes; these chromosomes serve the same functions in both male and females. The remaining pairs of human chromosomes are called the sex chromosomes, because they play a dominant role in determining the sex of the individual. Females have two copies of the female-determining, or X chromosome, while males have one male-determining, or Y chromosome, and one female-determining X chromosome.

What I want to emphasize is that **both** males and females inherit **one sex chromosome <u>from the mother</u>**, and it is **always an X chromosome.** Then from the father one sex chromosome, which is an X that he inherited from his mother. in the case of a little girl offspring and a Y that he inherited from his father, in the case of a little boy offspring.

Why is that important? Well evolutionist will leave this study alone, because there is no way that evolution could have worked all that out, let alone the MtDNA, DNA/RNA codes. Now if mankind were to first come from a common genius, there would never have been a male, because there would have been only the X chromosome, it is the male which determines the sex of the child, and the woman who holds the genetic recorded secrets. If evolution were to produce a single organism, then all offspring would be produced by "Parthenogenesis ;"(*Partheno* = *virgin*+ *Genesis)* this would be single sex birth.

Biologists have made a fundamental discovery as to why the "Y" chromosome, a genetic package inherited by the male alone, does not suffer "evolutionary" decay.

Before DNA decoding, we were not aware that the "Y" chromosome has been shedding genes at a furious rate over time, and is presently at a fraction of the size of the "X" chromosome carried by the Female. Remember it is the male who determines the sex of the child.

The decay of the "Y" stems, it seems is caused by its inability to unite with anything from the "X" of the woman. This would have the advantage of each member of the pair of chromosomes swapping DNA with its partner.

This swapping procedure, is what is known as recombination, and takes place between the inherited chromosomes from the mother's and the father's side, and is the first step in producing a fertilized egg. This enables bad genes, the ones damaged, to be replaced by its good counterpart.

God has prevented the "Y" chromosome from recombining with the "X" chromosome of the woman, except at the very tips. If it were otherwise, the "Y" chromosome would combine with the "X" chromosome and there would be only females on earth.

The amazing thing is, this lack of combining, has rendered the greatest proportion of the "Y" genes useless. At one time the "Y" and the "X" chromosomes were equal in the 22 base pairs, and each carried somewhere around 1000 genes. It is estimated that, presently, the "Y" carries around a hundred.

There is still another wonder of God, built within us. This lack of combining with the "X" is really no lack at all. The "Y" just recombines with itself. If a gene is defective, when the "Y" recombines it simply copies the good genes and discards the defective one. This process has been attributed to the survival of the male thus far.

There is another recent find that has puzzled science for some time, and that, of course, it "junk DNA." This is a vast stretch of genetic material, and was once just termed Junk. It now is becoming evident that it is not junk at all, but contains essential instructions for the growth and survival of people and a whole lot of other things as well. It seems to hold the key to our very immune system, and the inheritance of certain diseases as stroke, heart disease, and many other calamities. This material, though not as yet understood, seems to possess the instructions which tell the body how to use its genes, when to turn them on, and when to turn them off.

Eric Lander, director of genome research at the **Whitehead Institute for Biomedical Research** in Cambridge, Mass, when addressing this issue, is quoted as saying, *"My goodness, there's a lot more that matters in the human genome than we had realized. I feel we're dramatically closer now to knowing what all the players are."*

If one wants to pursue this subject and look at the failure of the theory of evolution, it might pay those interested to read, **A Theory in Crisis,** by molecular biologist Dr. Michael Denton, M.D. Perhaps an equal offering would be **Defeating Darwinism,** by Phillip Johnson.

Isn't God great? He is so smart!

Why did Adam name her? From the beginning she was **his to rule**. I wish I could carry that thought further, but that would take another thirty pages. I will say that **I do** not interpret this to mean that Adam was to "**Lord**" over her here. There must always be one leader, and everyone else has a pecking order. **Both king and queen comprised the royal household.** The king may have been an idiot, or a genius, but the queen knew, and kept her place in the pecking order. Now girls, do not get disturbed here.

A husband is instructed, according to Eph 5:25 *"Husbands, love your wives, even as Christ also loved the church, and **gave himself for it;**"*(Emphasis is mine) I have never met a godly woman who didn't sometimes dream of a man who would do just that very thing for her if necessary. This is the dream of young girls, that a boy would step forward and smack a forward jerk, and thereby saving her from her dragon. I delighted in listening to my precious daughters as they would describe a boy and why they liked him. As Dr. James Dobson has said about boys and girls, *"We are just wired different."*

Sadly, however, in this politically correct world we forget, Eph 5:22 *"Wives, submit yourselves unto your <u>own</u> husbands, **as unto the Lord**."* This is mostly misunderstood; our Lord does not <u>make</u> us submit, we do so because we love him enough to do so.

It is well to point out that if a husband or wife cannot follow what Scripture instructs, then it must be said, **they should have stayed single**. It might be well to declare to all, it is not easy to be a "Man of God" nor is it easy to be a "Godly Woman," but hand in hand, we will make it.

THE FIRST LIE

What was the first lie? I bet some will say, "it was when the serpent who was under the control of Satan said "Ye shall not surely die:" But that is not the first lie that was uttered. Know what it was? I know what it was, but do not know who first said it; I do know who it was recorded against. Woman said the words which were recorded. When Woman was telling the serpent that they could not eat of the tree of the knowledge of good and evil, she said Gen 3:3 *"But of the fruit of the tree which is in the midst of the garden, God hath said, Ye shall not eat of it, **neither shall ye touch it**, lest ye die."*(Emphasis is mine) Whoa! I don't find in my Bible where the LORD God said Adam couldn't touch it, play ball with it, or just watch it grow. He said not to eat of it.

How long, how many years Adam and Woman existed before this event, we just do not know. Remember, we discussed this before; they did not age because they were eternal. I know the Scriptures give an age for Adam at the birth of Seth, but it also eliminates his age at the birth of Cain and Abel. Adam and Eve could have lived a thousand years before they fell. Time in this part of Scripture is elusive at best.

There are four possibilities for this lie. Maybe more but I am writing this and I only know of four.

One: Adam and Woman already began the battle of the sexes, if you please. There could have been a rift between them over the restrictions of the tree from the very first. I suspect that woman's gaze fell upon that tree and the fruit, more and more often. It would stand to reason that Adam, to emphasize the danger of it all, may have added to what he told Woman about the tree, "And you can't even **touch it** unless you die."

We know, what information the woman knew of the tree, came from Adam, because the LORD God did not tell that restriction to Woman, only to Adam. **Woman had not been cloned at that point**.

Two: This will make some of the girls happy, but they know it is true. My wife would take something which I had done, normally something I goofed up, and **she wasn't in want of subject matter in my case;** anyway, she would so exaggerate it, to the point that it became a full blown catastrophe. Well maybe it was, but again it is my story, and explanation.

Three: There is a rule in marriage, **you do not** tell your mate **not to do a thing**, nor do you tell them **to do something**. Direct orders work in the military, but not in the home. I can imagine that Woman did not take the command from Adam lightly, and proceeded to usurp the authority shown by him.

Four: Woman could have added the "not touch" limitation when talking to the serpent, to show him that the only reason she had not recognized the value of the fruit was certainly not that she hadn't already known about it, but that the limitations were so unnecessarily severe that she had just not bothered. It is wonderful when we admit to our God that none of us are perfect, and of all souls, **I** freely do admit that.

One final comment that need be said: The LORD God is never recorded as having spoken to woman except in questioning her as to her guilt. The command, forbidding the consumption of the tree of the knowledge of good and evil was given to Adam, who passed it along to woman. **The point I am making** here, based upon Adam's given authority of rule, when he told woman the law that the LORD God gave him, it carried the same weight as if the LORD God personally gave it to woman.

What was that tree: All my life I have heard that Adam and Eve ate the forbidden "**apple.**" We have always heard that a man has an "Adam's Apple." They are going to have to convince me that an apple was what was growing on that tree. I think I know what that tree was, and I do not think it was an apple tree. Do we remember what Adam and Woman did right after they had disobeyed the LORD God? Let me refresh our memory.

Now the weight of disobedience is about to unfold.

Genesis 3:6 "*And when the woman* **saw** *that the tree* **was good for food**, *and that it* **was pleasant to the eyes**, *and a tree* **to be desired to make one wise**, *she took of the fruit thereof, and did eat, and gave also unto her husband with her; and he did eat.*

Ge 3:7 "*And the eyes of them both were opened, and they knew that they [were] naked; and they sewed* **fig** *leaves together, and made themselves aprons.*"

There is another, almost hidden support to my theory. In the New Testament, what was the **only thing our Lord cursed** while He was on earth?

Mt 21:19 "*And when he saw* **a fig tree** *in the way, he came to it, and found nothing thereon, but leaves only, and said unto it, Let no fruit grow on thee henceforward for ever. And presently the fig tree withered away.*"(Emphasis is mine)

I think that tree which was in the garden was a fig tree. It wasn't poison fruit that caused our parents to die; it was disobedience that caused the sin. I could support that through many thoughts, but I won't. Think on it, and study what emphasis is given to the fig tree and what it meant to the Hebrews in Scripture, and parallel that with our Lords visit to an unfruitful nation, and I think it will become clearer.

Can we feel the heart of our Lord here? Don't we realize that when he saw that tree mentioned in Mt 21, His mind spanned back in time to recall its significance? There is yet another memory to hurt Him; we will cover it in a moment.

Genesis 3:11-13 "*And he said, Who told thee that thou wast naked? Hast thou eaten of the tree, whereof I commanded thee that thou shouldest not eat? And the man said, The woman whom thou gavest to be with me, she gave me of the tree, and*

157

I did eat. And the LORD God said unto the woman, What is this that thou hast done? And the woman said, The serpent beguiled me, and I did eat.

There is a story giving the account of Adam and Woman facing the LORD God in the garden.

Well one day the LORD God was walking through the garden and could not see his two cherished people. "Adam, where are you?" He called.

"I am here under this tree. I heard you coming and I was ashamed because I am necked." Adam replied. And with that both he and his woman came crawling out from under the boroughs of the tree.

"Who told you that you were necked? Have you eaten of the tree which I told you not to do?" the LORD God asked.

"Well yes." Adam replied. "It was that Woman that you gave to me. She did give it to me, and I did eat."

Turning to Woman the LORD God asked, "What is this that thou hast done?"

Woman quickly responded, "Well it was that serpent over there. He beguiled me, and I did eat."

The LORD God turned to the serpent, and the serpent just didn't have a leg to stand on.

There is something else that most will miss in the story of the fall. It is a beautiful story, and one in which I feel the New Testament has reason to call Adam "the **first** man **Adam.**" 1Co 15:45 "*And so it is written, The **first** man **Adam** was made a living soul; the **last Adam** [was made] a quickening spirit.*"(Emphasis is mine)

"Well" One would say, "What is the parallel?"

Well, Adam was never tempted by Satan to disobey the LORD God by taking the fruit. Look at:

1Ti 2:13, "*For Adam was first formed, then Eve.*"

1Ti 2:14, "*And Adam **was not deceived**, but the woman being deceived was in the transgression.* (Emphasis is mine)

Adam was not fooled by the serpent. **Adam loved that little girl**, yes he did. If woman was going to die, so too would he, by giving his life for, or with her. Adam was a good man, he was in type a foreshadowing of our LORD, who Himself was not tempted, but willingly laid down **His** life for someone, and that someone was **you and me**.

I think in my heart that Adam suffered greatly at that moment. On one hand he had a personal relationship with the LORD God, and on the other hand, he had a human love for his little wife.

Genesis 3:14-15 *"And the LORD God said unto the serpent, Because thou hast done this, thou art cursed above all cattle, and above every beast of the field; upon thy belly shalt thou go, and dust shalt thou eat all the days of thy life: And I will put enmity between thee and the woman, and between thy seed and her seed; it shall bruise thy head, and thou shalt bruise his heel."*

WOMAN'S FOUR CRUSES

Eve suffers **four curses:** Gen 3:16 *"Unto the Woman he said, I will greatly multiply **(1)thy sorrow** and **(2)thy conception**; in sorrow thou shalt bring forth children; and **(3) thy desire** shall be to thy husband, and **(4)he shall rule over thee."**(Emphasis is mine)

We don't read Scripture as we should: let me explain. Genesis tells us where we have been, and it tells us where we are going. If we do not see **our** faults as a parallel relationship to the characters presented in this, the first book of the Bible, we should reevaluate our lives. **In Genesis we are told** of the first; lie, rebellion against God, murder, adultery, bigamy, disobedience to parents, lust, idolatry, sodomy, incest, and idol worship to name but a few. But we still do not learn.

1. *"In **sorrow"** thou shalt bring forth children;"* I am not going to get into the birth canal of woman and animals except to say that the Neanderthal had large pelvic regions and seemingly did not have pain in delivery where as, women from Eve on, does. I remember one lady telling me that throughout the hours of delivery, all she could think of was "Jim did this to me." Well, Jim must have been forgiven because they had other children later. When Carol Burnett was once asked what it was like to have a baby, she replied, "I think the best explanation I can give, is, it is like taking your bottom lip, and pulling it up over your head."

2. **"Thy conception:"** It is very rare for a lady to have a child without her entire body, at one time or the other, rebel against her. She suffers morning sickness, swollen ankles, and then there is the burden of carrying several pounds, up front, which constantly tries to tumble her forward. I left out the cramps, the cravings, the mood swings and the "I'll get you for this."

159

3. **"Thy desire"** shall be to thy husband… I will briefly touch on this, since it is a part of the failure of mankind; however, there is no way I can adequately address this statement here.

First of all I want to make it clear that it is one of **the most misunderstood statements in the book of Genesis.**

The desire that is addressed here is what made woman ultimately sin in the first place, and this desire was imposed as one of Eve's punishments. **It is not**, as supposed by some, that she will have a romantic attraction to her husband.

The desire which the LORD God is addressing is **very, very, similar, in every aspect** to the desire that Lucifer had, and still has toward, God. **It is the desire to be equal with if not above her husband.** When that is understood, we can see that woman's punishment is harsher than that given to Adam. For either the Lord God imposed this desire upon woman, or the Lord God was leaving it where it had already manifested itself, where it will continue to the end, and **she is, therefore, on her own, to be in obedience to the LORD God, and willingly to be obedient *to her own husband.***

Now girls, I am not in any way putting anyone down. What the Lord has done He has done and we both know it was for good reason. Today Satan is using this desire to the fullest. If one doubts this, look in the advertisements in magazines, news papers…etc. The first half is devoted to products used by the girls. Today's ads for new cars are addressed to the girls. Promo's on the televisions depict the girls in total control, and in some cases has the husband staying home while she enters a new car and drives to her company.

Today's "woman" has given up the feminine qualities that so long existed. She no longer wears an attractive dress, she now wears slacks, and in many cases she wears a three-piece-suit. The day of adorning hair has all but disappeared, and the crew cut is in fashion, low quarter shoes replace feminine wear. The tie replaces the flower on many, as if she is ashamed of the fact that she is female.

I was in an office one day and a woman came by and asked how I was; I replied "I am fine lady, and how are you?" I sat there for five minutes of instruction on how to address her, and "Lady" was not one of the methods. I was unceremoniously told I should address all females in the work place as Mssssss, or however one pronounces it.

I listened and simply told her that she should not address me in the future, and I would then not have to sit through all the reasons she did not like to be a lady. I've had that happen to me twice?

4. "And he shall rule over thee."

It is not the husband's responsibility to dominate his wife; it is **her responsibility** to the following:

Eph 5:24 *"Therefore as the church is subject unto Christ, so [let] the wives [be] to their own husbands in **every thing**."*(Emphasis is mine)

It is not Christ's responsibility to **make** us to be in subjection to Him, it is our responsibility in obeying Him, because **we love Him**, and keep His commandments, thereby resulting in our willing subjection and thereby **welcome His rule over us.** We know this was an issue between Adam and Woman because to the added statement, "neither shall ye touch it." There was a conflict from the very beginning, and it will continue until our Lord returns.

There is one thing our Lord saw we men needed, and that was the loving hands of a Godly woman. I do not want anyone to dare think I am brow-beating women; one has to feel my heart when I make the following statement.

"There is no greater blessing, given by God unto man, short of salvation, than that which is given, in a Godly Woman." The home, the family, and each member individually will feel that blessing; the nation as well, are all blessed. It is not easy to bear Woman's curse, and I am not trying to belittle it, **not one bit**. Quite honestly, I would not want to do it myself. I really don't know if I could either, but I would not be as foolish as some modern ministers who say that times and customs have changed and "modern woman is no longer suppose to." He needs a song book thrown at him.

One was quoted, so rightly, saying "As go the mothers, so goes the nation:" **How true**. Sadly, look at some "mothers" today; praise God not all, but many who put kids in the "lowest bidder's" care, and fulfill their earthly careers, while their offspring then learn the ways of a stranger. I know there are some precious ones who have no choice, **God love you**. As a man I have no concept of the burden you bear. I do know this, our Father knows, and if asked He will help, He really will.

Some time ago, I heard an inane person who was attempting to "woo" the working woman's vote, say, "It takes a village to raise a child." Anyone with the slightest bit of intelligence would know better than that; it is the world's influence on the children that is destroying their character now. We all know that all it takes is one Godly woman, and she can raise a village of kids. The problem today is that our children are shuttled between the lowest bidding day care centers, and have little or no stability while their parents are "keeping up with the Jones's.

What mothers are forgetting is the fact that a girl's body, between 9 and 14 is so messed up that she can fall in love with floor tile. Unsupervised for the 3 to 4 hours until you get home is an invitation for disaster, even for the best of young adults. They watch movies that were forbidden when I grew up, which contain every situation they are dreaming about. When she gets pregnant, disown her, she has brought disgrace on you and your husband: Amen?

Before I get back to the subject I want to tell everyone something they really do not know. I am serious about this. If Adam was made, and then Eve from Adam, know what that makes both man and woman when they are by themselves??? It makes each a "Half Wit." Know what they become when they are joined in matrimony? A "Knit Wit."

ADAM'S FIVE CURSES

Now Adam's turn. Gen 3:17 *"And unto Adam he said, Because thou hast **hearkened unto the voice of thy wife**, and hast eaten of the tree, of which I commanded thee, saying, Thou shalt not eat of it: **cursed is the ground** for thy sake; in **sorrow shalt thou eat of it** all the days of thy life;* Gen 3:18 ***Thorns also and thistles** shall it bring forth to thee; and thou shalt eat the herb of the field;* Gen 3:19 ***In the sweat of thy face** shalt thou eat bread, till thou return unto the ground; for out of it wast thou taken: for dust thou art, and **unto dust shalt thou return**."* (Emphasis is mine)

Cursed is the ground for thy sake.
1. *In sorrow shalt thou eat of it.*
2. *Thorns also thistles shall it bring forth.*
3. *In the sweat of thy face shalt thou eat bread.*
4. *Unto dust shalt thou return.*

If anything on this earth proves Scripture it is *"Thorns also thistles shall it bring forth to thee."* I can spray all the "Round-up®," "2-4-D®," or "Weed-Be-Gone®" in the world on my field, and thorns and thistles will return. A drought will kill crops in the field, and grasshoppers will consume them, but when one looks out upon the green that remains, they will not find your planted crop, but they will find "thorns and thistles" that even grasshoppers will not eat. A weed will grow out of concrete. Has one ever seen an abandoned airport? The runway will be completely destroyed by invading weeds growing in the expansion joints.

I have seen a thistle growing during a drought; beside a three foot deep hole I dug to replace a fence post. The ground was so dry even at that depth that I had to pour water into it so the posthole digger could hold dirt long enough to get it to the surface.

I have always said, "There are two things which to me, prove our Scripture correct; one is the Jew's survival with the world trying to eliminate him at every turn, the other is thorns and thistles which neither will ever be eradicated."

When I was in Israel, I told this to an Israeli, and he laughingly agreed. "We are like Netver." Then he took my hand, looked me in the eye and said "God bless America for your support." I told him, "NO! God bless Israel: If it were not for our support of Israel, we might well have lost our blessing."

There is another curse placed upon man that has no need of the LORD spelling out: I have felt it, as I believe most others have. There is a loneliness which resides deep within which one cannot quite put a finger upon.

Let me ask: When the last present is opened at Christmas, don't we feel that something we had secretly hoped for, was not there? Don't we feel that somewhere there was that intangible, which we, ourselves, cannot quite lay a finger on, but if we had it, all would be so very much different?

When Adam sinned, and the LORD God pronounced sentence upon him, Adam stepped from the eternal presence of our LORD God, into an alien world governed by time. There was a separation, which every Christian feels: almost a vacuum that can never be filled until we are back in His presence once more. That is what drives us to ever new expectation. We work for retirement, and when we retire, it is not what we expected at all, there is something still missing. That is what is missing at Christmas, or our birthday. That is what is missing when we finally get that one thing we have dreamed of, then, there is just that unexplained something that is still missing that we can not quite put the fingers of our hearts on, because that cherished wish, though finally realized, still lacks that intangible; the lost-personal-presence-of-our-LORD GOD.

It is the separation that happened when the LORD God pronounced the curse upon Adam. Adam was, and we as well, are now on our own, but not forever. **We will never have what we are seeking, until what we are seeking calls us home**.

The **last curse** we all know too well. We will all return **to the dust** from which we are made, unless the Lord raptures us before: I so long to see that moment. I will shout a shout that can be heard from here into eternity. Remember; turn to dust, for later.

ADAM RENAMES WOMAN: TO EVE

Remember that I said "Woman" was Adam's to rule? Well that was true when Adam named her, but Adam named everything, then Adam lost his earthly **rule** when he gave it to Satan because of his rebellion against the LORD God, but **not** his position within the family.

O, don't miss this; The LORD God gave **his first** pronouncement, back in Gen 3:15, that there would be a Savior coming into the world, by saying "**Her seed**."? It was after that when Adam "**Renamed**" Woman, and called her Eve which means "**Living**." Gen 3:20 *"And Adam **called his wife's name Eve; because she was the mother of all living.**"* (Emphasis is mine)

Man has the seed. How can woman have seed? Read the New Testament and it all comes together. The virgin birth of our Lord has, and will remain a stumbling stone for so many. Our Father knew the end before the beginning. This was after the fall, and after the LORD God progressed through the punishment of their sins

THE SECOND SACRIFICE

Gen 3:21 *"Unto Adam also and to his wife did the LORD God make coats of skins, and clothed them."* "Well I got you now" One would say, "When the LORD God sacrificed the animal(s), to make coats of skin that was the first sacrifice, not the second."

There was another sacrifice and it was 4.5 billion, possibly 12.5 billion years before this one: It was the **first** sacrifice. That is the reason I called this one the second. Look with me at Re 13:8 *"And all that dwell upon the earth shall worship him, whose names are not written in the*

book of life of the **Lamb slain from the foundation of the world."**
(Emphasis is mine) Christ was that first sacrifice, and this one of Gen
3:21 is the second. You then say, "But Christ wasn't put on the cross
until years later." Dr. McGee said, in his explanation about Abraham's
resolve to follow God's command in sacrificing Isaac, "*That lad was
sacrificed in Abraham's mind before they left home that morning for the mountain.*"
For, millions of years, our God looked at His son, our Savior, and
every time He did, He got prouder of what He saw, and in His mind,
He was sacrificed already. I made the statement about the heart of our
Lord, a while back when we discussed the fig tree. Join with me, but
for a moment and see just how perfectly salvation was planned.

When the LORD God sacrificed that animal in the garden,
which I know in my heart was a ram, He also looked forward to when
He would offer himself a sacrifice for the very ones He was now
attending. When He was on the cross, He reflected back to this very
moment, and this was a primary cause for the statement He made on
the cross.

**With a slight smirk on his swollen lips as he looked
through blackened eyes straight into the eyes of Satan and said
"It is finished."**

We must see the final stamp of approval of the Godhead. The
plan of salvation was finished, and for Satan it was his foreshadowed
doom and he was also finished. I can only imagine the total consuming
panic that Satan felt at that moment.

Satan now sees that his efforts to destroy, not as before the
world, but to destroy man who God loves so much, has utterly failed.
The damming part that pierced his black heart is the fact that he is now
allowed, by the Holy Spirit, to see the meaning of **Matthew 13:35**
"*That it might be fulfilled which was spoken by the prophet, saying, I will open my
mouth in parables;* **I will utter things which have been kept secret
from the foundation of the world.**" (Emphasis is mine)

Had he not caused our parents to sin in the Garden, he would
have succeeded: **one cannot save the saved.** The final thrust of the
sword of truth is now revealed. Had he not stirred up the hatred for
our Lord; had the crucifixion not occurred, the plan of salvation from
the foundation of the world, would not have been.

His every plan of jealous hatred had ended in his own disaster.
It is for that reason the Apostle Peter warned, 1 Peter 5:8 *Be sober, be
vigilant; because your adversary the devil, as a* **roaring lion,** *walketh about,
seeking whom he may devour:* (Emphasis is mine) I am of the

understanding that a lion is not stupid enough to roar until he feels the prey is helpless as he lunges for what he thinks is the kill

My precious brethren, our LORD God **started an ending right there in the Garden of Eden, with a beginning right here on the cross.**

What a privilege it is to be a part of this wonderful plan. A plan that was set in stone, eons before even the universe itself was brought forth.

I am of the opinion that the LORD God had Adam and Eve watch as He performed this sacrifice; not to punish them, but to let them see what death really was. What a stark awakening that must have been for them to watch life slip away, and death to become a reality, and knowing that they had caused it.

I know much of what they may have experienced, when in combat, I looked, for the first time, into the dying eyes of mankind. I will carry those images to my grave. That similar vision was carried by our grandparents to their grave as well: I know it was. And every day they wore those skins they were reminded of the fact, they had caused that suffering, death, and if I may say, the second sacrifice of the innocent for their guilt.

Now allow me to tweak everyone's minds. Adam and Woman did not age until they disobeyed the LORD God's command not to eat the forbidden fruit. Now! They eat the fruit, and their punishment is pronounced. They, now, **Adam and Eve**, are forced out of the Garden.

The point I have been making about not being told everything because it would bring up more questions, will now become more evident. Suppose Scripture now says that "Adam was fifteen months old when he knew his wife Eve and she conceived and bore Cain and Able, when **Adam was two years old: Well think on that**. I am not trying to be cute here; study why our Father has left so much out. If that were not enough, **think on this**: Adam was formed first, then Eve; however, **Eve was older than Adam** when Cain and Able were born.

In Gen 4:3, 4 we are not given the explanation of when, and how Cain and Able were given the method of, and the reoccurrence of the offering, and though we may speculate, we do not know what the offering was really for since the laws had not yet been given. It should be noteworthy that this rite was <u>not called a sacrifice, but an offering.</u> We may also note that it appears the proper way was given to them, because we note that Able' offering parallels, in part, those of the priests later, and almost out of defiance, Cain defiles the offering.

Concerning the offering:

For me to leave this part out would not be right, but to try and speculate when, what, and how it all came together, would be impossible for me, because I do not have proper knowledge here. It is most interesting to note that, in this case, God must have given them the rite. Now remember it is God who gives the laws, and perhaps that is one reason it is not fully disclosed here, since we are addressing the office of the LORD God. The rest is a mystery that we just do not know; however, it is this offering, which caused, but perhaps it was not the total reason for the following to transpire.

THE FIRST RECORDED MURDER

Gen 4:8 "*And Cain talked with Abel his brother: and it came to pass, when they were in the field, that Cain rose up against Abel his brother, and* **slew him**.*"* (Emphasis is mine) This is the first recorded murder and human death in Scripture. I have often wondered if Cain felt what is now sadistically called "closure" as he looked at his dead brother. I have never been able to hate a dead enemy soldier. He was someone's grandfather, father, brother, or friend: Someone somewhere suffered loss.

THE THIRD LIE

Gen 4:9 "*And the LORD said unto Cain, Where is Abel thy brother? And he said,* **I know not***: Am I my brother's keeper?*"(Emphasis is mine) First lie "not even touch it," second lie "thou shall not surely die," third lie "I know not."

THE FOURTH PUNISHMENT

Gen 4:11 "*And now art thou cursed from the earth, which hath opened her mouth to receive thy brother's blood from thy hand?*"
Gen 4:12 "*When thou* **tillest** *the ground,* **it shall not** *henceforth yield unto thee her strength;* **a fugitive and a vagabond** *shalt thou be in the earth.*"(Emphasis is mine)

167

The Layman

Able was a rancher, while Cain was a farmer. The very crops that Cain held dear, would now turn on him, and be one of the causes of his constant suffering.

THE FIRST CRY FOR MERCY

Ge 4:13 *"And Cain said unto the LORD, My punishment is greater than I can bear."* **The sad thing, if all noticed, is that the Office has changed to the saving name of LORD here**; what would have happened if Cain had asked Him for forgiveness. Have we ever thought; what if Adam and Woman had prostrated themselves before the LORD God and had asked for forgiveness?

My friend, have you asked the LORD for His forgiving mercy? Belief in itself, will save no one. Satan believes more than we ever will. Works will not save you, but faith without works won't save you either. "Faith, without works is **dead**." One is the test and the other is the proof: The litmus test of salvation. One cannot work for salvation, but if one has salvation they cannot stop working because of it. Let me put it this way: **If you got the mumps, you got the bumps.**

SECOND MARRIAGE

Gen 4:16 "And Cain went out from the presence of the LORD, and dwelt **in the land of Nod, on the East of Eden.**" 4:17 *And Cain knew his wife; and she conceived, and bare Enoch: and he builded a city, and called the name of the city, after the name of his son, Enoch."* (Emphasis is mine)

Has everyone noticed that everything is going east all the time? The LORD God placed the Cherubim's and the flaming sword at the East of Eden as well. I find it informative that we are not told which direction Adam and Eve went when they were driven from the Garden.

THE LAND OF NOD

I do not say that Cain's wife was Neanderthal. **I do say** that this Neanderthal's time of existence "fits nicely" in the time frame of "Male and Female" in Gen 1:27 to where we are now in Scripture. Science says that the Neanderthal genus came out of **nowhere**, was capable of learning, limitedly skilled in tools, and had a family life; He

168

was fully developed as found, and evolved from nothing, and then unexplainably vanished from the genetic chain.

Cain knew his wife and she conceived and bears a son called Enoch. I see some questions here:

First: How many countries were there at this time? We only know how many were watered by the same river that flowed from the garden, and **Nod** was not one of them.

Second: Where and what was the country, Nod?

Thirdly: Who was the woman?

Fourth: The time: How many days, years, centuries passed between 'male, female,' of Gen 1 and the forming of Adam then Eve; then the birth of the twin boys, Cain and Able?

Fifth: If the only inhabitants in the land of Nod are you, your wife and your only boy, <u>why would you build a city</u>?

Sixth: Who ruled Nod before Cain got there?

I can say right up front; <u>I do not know the answer to any of the six</u>. That; However, has not stopped me so far and I do not know why it should now. I will give my thoughts, but first I want to introduce what I have found on another being called **Cro-Magnon**, who suddenly appeared, then suddenly vanished.

CRO-MAGNON

The first thing to be understood about Cro-Magnon, is when he appears in history, there is an advance in knowledge and skills that are off the Richter scale in comparison to anything afore known. The Cro-Magnon man came upon the scene, according to science, at the time that the Neanderthal man began to fade from existence. It is most important for us to know that <u>there have been skeletal remains which show a combined</u> **Neanderthal-Cro-Magnon characteristic**.

Cro-Magnon came as Neanderthal fades and they are silent about evidence which shows that Mr. Cro-Magnon was here at the same time as Adam and Eve.

The first thing we know of the Cro-Magnon's life is that the <u>Cro-Magnon people lived in tent</u>s and other **man-made shelters** which is a departure from just finding a cave. Archeologists have discovered what appear to be houses erected from logs, which are attributed to this race. Further evidence shows they lived in groups of several families; not roving bands as were the Neanderthal. The Cro-Magnons were nomadic "hunter gatherers."

Why a hunter and gatherer? If this is a descendant of Cain, the LORD God told Cain that the earth would <u>not</u> yield its strength to him, but he still was <u>not</u> given permission to eat meat. This is again a deviation of what man was told, vs. **what he did.**

We must note the Cro-Magnon had many other talents which are beyond scientist's ability to explain, some are:

1. They had elaborate rituals for hunting.

2. They had rituals for births.

3. They had formal burials upon death. Multiple burials become more common. From 35 to 10 tya there was no statistical trend in differentiation by sex or age in burials. They included special grave goods, as opposed to everyday, utilitarian objects, suggesting a very increased <u>reutilization of death and burial</u>. Symbolic representation by personal adornment in burial becomes more common.

4. <u>They were the first confirmed to have domesticated animals,</u> starting by about 15 tya.

5. <u>They were the first to leave extensive works of art</u>, such as cave paintings and carved figures of animals and pregnant women.

I love science, read the following deductions and smile as I do. Huge caves, lavishly decorated with murals depicting animals of the time **were at first rejected** as fake for being <u>too sophisticated</u>. Then **they were dismissed** as <u>being primitive</u>, categorized as hunting, fertility or other types of sympathetic magic. **Re-evaluations have put these great works of art in a more prominent place in art history.** They show evidence of motifs, of following their own stylistic tradition, of impressionist-like-style-perspective, and innovative use of the natural relief in the caves. Aside from pregnant women and other goddess worship iconography, representations of people, are very few, and never show the accuracy or detail of the other animals. Humans are represented in simple outlines without features, sometimes with "masks", often without regard to proportion, distorted and isolated.

6. They used paints: At Grottes des Enfants, France, there were four burials found with red ocher, and associated with Aurignacian tools. (Ocher is a form of iron oxide.) Ocher was found in red, yellow and brown and is supposedly thought to have been used even for **"war paint"** by this man. That find is most important: a diamond in a mud puddle if you will allow. This statement puts a plug in Scripture which undeniably defines the relationship between Adam, Neanderthal and Cro-Magnon: for now just remember **war paint** for later.

7. They had tools. Cro-Magnon's tools are described as the Aurignation technology; characterized by:

A. Bone and antler tools, such as spear tips (the first) and harpoons.

B. They also used animal traps,

C. Bow and arrow.

D. They invented hafts and handles for their knives, securing their blades with bitumen, a kind of tar:

E. Other improvements included the invention of the atlat, a large bone or piece of wood with a hooked grove used for adding distance and speed to spears.

F. They invented more sophisticated spear points, such as those that detach after striking and cause greater damage to prey.

8. <u>They began the marking of time with the lunar phases</u>, recording them with marks on a piece of bone, antler or stone. Some of these "calendars" contained a record of as many as 24 lunations.

9. <u>They dug pits into the permafrost to store meats.</u> These pits were the first cold storage lockers where fruits and vegetables were stored, and what appears to have also preserved meat.

10. They began considering the new concepts of time reckoning practiced by abstract representations of the passage of time, such as spring plants in bloom, or pregnant bison that might represent summer.

In the relatively recent past, tool industries diversified. The Gravettian industry (25 to 15 tya), characterized by ivory tools such as backed blades, is associated with mammoth hunters. One type of brief industry was Solutrean, occurring from 18 to 15 tya and limited to Southwest France and Spain. It is characterized by unique and finely crafted "laurel leaf" blades, made with a pressure technique requiring great **skill**. The industry is associated with horse hunters.

The Magdalenian Culture (15 to 10 tya) produced the widest variety of tools; bone needles, harpoons, microliths (small blades 1-3 cm.). This was a culture of reindeer hunting. When the **glaciers reseeded**, the culture and the industry dissipated.

I want to emphasize that all of these findings are based upon just that; Findings. How many other more certificated findings one could find is impossible to estimate. **I do not like the dates given.**

The Layman

I have gathered the above information from several public domains, and have retained the estimated (tya) only to allow the reader to assess the information from two sides. I also wanted to emphasize how science skirts the Neanderthal, Cro-Magnon, Modern Man handshake timeline.

WHAT DOES THAT HAVE TO DO WITH CAIN

Now ignoring the dates, and I think that is the best thing to do today. I would like to put forward that when Cain went from the face of the LORD, he went to this country called Nod, and there was a race which within the timeframe of our writing could have been the male and female, or as science calls them, "Neanderthal." There is a vast gap in knowledge here. I mean the "Neanderthal" had come a long way up the learning curve, but they were far from a genius.

I must emphasize here with all my heart, whatever existed on this planet was made by our God. That goes from eternity past, before the Phase I and Phase II creations, the Restoration and the present, or eternity future. Nothing came from anywhere **except from the creative hands of our loving God.**

At the latter period of existence of the "Neanderthal", there appeared another race which no one can explain their origin. That doesn't stop science from hypothesizing though. Anyway, when the "Cro-Magnon" man came on the scene there is an unbelievable advance of knowledge in all fronts. When we take away the skill of the "Cro-Magnon" man, the Neanderthal has remarkable similarities in characteristics, which we have already pointed our, but little if any in physical statue: by that, I mean that "Neanderthal" was short, and "Cro-Magnon" was straight and taller. That should not be a surprise in the two different methods of creation of "male/female," verses Cain.

I do not call Cain a "Cro-Magnon", only that Cain's going to a land called Nod, fits an important time sequence. Allow me to explain that Cain **could not** have been the Cro-Magnon man. However, **I feel <u>Cain's offspring was the reason for them.</u>**

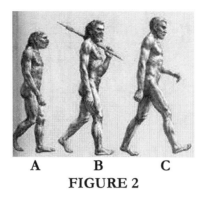

A   B   C
FIGURE 2

In Figure 2 I have tried to depict three different geniuses. Follow my thinking here. If Cain, "C" was driven from the presence of the LORD, and went to a land called Nod and there took a wife, "A" who was not of the Adam and Eve race but of the male and female race (This would coincide with what science calls the Neanderthal, the race living on the earth at that time.)

If Neanderthal "A" was the male and female race of Gen 1, they would <u>not</u> look like the Adam and Eve race"; however, Adam and Eve's son, Cain, <u>would</u> look as the one labeled "C". Now if Cain, who resembled "C", were to intermarry with "A" then their offspring would look like "B" <u>and this race would suddenly appear without anyone knowing where they came from,</u> and would be labeled by science as Cro-Magnon man, "B".

Stay with me here. I know very well the argument that DNA was so perfect at the time of Adam, that Cain could have taken his sister for a wife with absolutely no repercussions: on that point I agree. I have said in this work that DNA started perfect and has been degrading ever since; not mutating, but becoming less pure with each generation. There are those who say that if Cain had married another race that the DNA from Cain would become evident within that race: on this point **I do not agree, and will develop this point later.**

CAIN'S WIFE

I think the Neanderthal man was here when Adam was formed from the dust of the earth. <u>The world was not called Eden.</u> Eden was a land that LORD God chose on the earth, and **in that land** he planted

173

a garden and it has been referred to, ever since, as "The garden of Eden," without realizing that there was more of Eden than the garden, and much, much more of the world than the land of Eden. Perhaps it was a part of what science has called Pangaea.

At one time it is suspected that the earth was a solid mass of land, surrounded by water which some have given the termed Pangaea. We will discuss Pangaea later on, but I again caution the reader to turn to scripture <u>for their own understanding</u>. Satan can use me as well as anyone else. It is My Father who has the truth; we only search for it. The term "Pangaea" and the term Neanderthal, and Cro-Magnon are terms that fit sequences and science has labeled them as they choose when, in fact they each may encompass vast periods of time, and events.

I have read, as I am well assured many others have also, accounts of Cain taking one of his sisters for a wife, and moving to Nod. There are works that aver that Adam and Eve had thirty or more children during their lives; however, the Lord is completely silent here: Know why? If He told us where Cain got his wife, then He would have to tell us a whole lot more about her, like where she came from. That is not the saving purpose for the book of Genesis, or the whole Bible for that matter.

I do not believe that Cain took his sister for a wife. If he did, I honestly think Scripture would have told us that. Did Scripture hide the fact that Abraham was married to his half-sister: did it hide the incestuous relation of Lot's daughters; did it hide the fact that Judah had sex and impregnated his daughter in law; did it hide the rape of Bathsheba by David, or did it hide the incestuous act of David's son with his own sister? Why pull the wool over our eyes here?

Look at the following:

1. If she were his sister, then why doesn't Scripture at the very least say, "Cain <u>took</u> his wife and they journeyed to the land called Nod?"

2. Or why not say that Cain <u>took</u> a wife, and he then journeyed to the land called Nod?

3. I think Cain's wife was an offspring of the "male and female" of Gen 1, who God told to replenish the earth; to tell us anything more would open too many doors.

Using the sequence of that which has been found today, it would be the "Neanderthal" who was Cain's wife. I must make it clear that I again use the name "Neanderthal" <u>as one in a sequence and not an absolute</u>. I do not know what the offspring of the "male, female" of Gen 1 were called. I do think that this union was the start of another "tribe", and that tribe is what science calls Cro-Magnon. There are other reasons for that as well.

4. <u>It is never mentioned that Adam and Eve had any contact with Cain</u> from that day forward. That in itself is not that final. When a man gets married, he usually has little contact with his family, but when a girl gets married, she seldom looses contact with her family. Remember the old saw, "*A son is a son until he finds him a wife, but a daughter is a daughter for the rest of her life?*" We need to remember part of Cain's punishment was: Ge 4:12 "*When thou tillest the ground, it shall not henceforth yield unto thee her strength; a fugitive and a vagabond shalt thou be in the earth.*" I do not think anyone from the loins of Adam had anything, ever, to do with Cain. Remember that **Cain feared for his life** even with the protective mark the LORD God placed upon him.

5. The next reason is, **Cain's wife does not have a name.** Cain had a name, and later when Cain's son **Enoch**, takes a wife, **she has no name.** Enoch has a son, Lamech, who takes two wives, **they both have names.** Gen 4:19 "*And Lamech took unto him two wives: the name of the one was* **Adah** *(ornament, beauty), and the name of the other* **Zillah** *(shadow, protection).*" (Emphasis is mine.)

Now I am aware that the men were recorded in Scripture, and that women were seldom listed. **That is not what is being enforced here.**

Homo-sapiens of Gen 1:2 (Neanderthal/Male/Female, **A** of Figure 2), **did not use or record names for anything**. I suppose one was "grunt" and the other was "grunt-grunt."

Homo sapiens of Gen 2:4: That is to say modern man; Adam/Woman/Able or Cain (**C** of Figure 2), **used names**, and we know that because we are given those names.

When Cain married the Neanderthal (**A** of Figure 2), **she had no name.**

When Enoch, which now would be a Cro-Magnon, because of the intermarriage, (**B** of Figure 2), also married a Neanderthal, (A of Figure 2); we see **she had no name.**

When Lamech, who was now identified as Cro-Magnon, (**B** of Figure 2), married his <u>sisters</u>, who were probably one of the offspring of Enoch and now pure Cro-Magnon, **they were named** because they

175

were now a descendant of Cain, **who used names to identify their families.**

Now re-read this to see what I am saying because it is a plug that fills a hole. This sequence of events supports that Cain <u>did not marry his sister</u>, but, rather, married a female from Nod.

6. The next thing. Gen 4:20 *"And Adah bare Jabal: he was the father of such as dwell in* **tents,** *and of such as have* **cattle.***"* Gen 4:21 *"And his brother's name was Jubal: he was the father of all such as handle the* **harp** *and* **organ.***"* (Emphasis is mine)

Even though the LORD originally made Cain a tiller of the soil, his offspring must have started eating flesh. Why? Because the Lord God told Cain the earth would not yield to him its strength; there is no record of Cain's family ever giving an offering to the LORD, so, if they were not using them as lawn mowers, we must assume they were eating them. I am not trying to be comical here, it is just plain logic. I can not fix the time for musical instruments, but the tent and cattle statement sure rings a bell when studying the Cro-Magnon Man.

See something else in this verse that seems to be deliberately left out? In Gen 4:22, it tells us of another woman, the **sister** of Tubalcain was **Naamah** (sweetness, pleasantness). The <u>Bible tells us of three women in a row,</u> but leaves out the name of their grandmother. If Scripture told us who Cain's or Enoch's wives were, it would have to tell us who her parents were. Perhaps that would open a door that I am now peeping into.

Does it matter that Cain took his sister, or if Cain found a woman of a preexisting group called "Neanderthal?" To me it does, for if it is not that way, then there is a hole in Scripture's account of creation between Gen 1 and Gen 2 as I understand it, which this work cannot, and no one else can plug up: but we will, let's go on.

WAR

Gen 4:23 *"And Lamech said unto his wives, Adah and Zillah, Hear my voice; ye wives of Lamech, hearken unto my speech: for I have* **slain a man to my wounding,** *and a young man to my hurt."* (Emphasis is mine)

Gen 4:24 *"<u>If Cain shall be avenged sevenfold, truly Lamech seventy and sevenfold.</u>"* (Emphasis is mine) This verse tells us of the first recorded death by war. It seems to tell us of Lamech's death in that he is recounting the Lord's command concerning the penalty for causing the death of Cain, and that he has been wounded by battle with another.

176

Scripture does not tell us of any war, or conflict between Adam's offspring, and Cain's, yet Scripture tells us plainly that war is between Lamech and those around him, then where did these enemies originate from. If Adam was in war with anyone, Scripture would not delete it. Remember earlier I wanted us to remember "**war paint**"?

Science has said the extinction of the Neanderthal is believed, in part, to have occurred as a result of the **Cro-Magnon man warring against the Neanderthal.**

GENETIC LINE NOT OF ADAM

I know that there are those who say that if Cain had married a Neanderthal woman, and their offspring were known as Cro-Magnon, then there would be a genetic trail back to Adam by the DNA: **that is not true!** Remember that it is **the woman, not the man** who carries the genetic code of MtDNA that is passed on to the **female** offspring. When Cain intermarried, it makes a convincing argument that the resulting genetic code would show a different biological race (Cro-Magnon) which would appear from nowhere, and no one could determine where they came from because their MtDNA would not match modern man.

The MtDNA from the female is transferred from mother to daughter. The X-Y chromosome of the male is used **only** to determine the sex and physical characteristics of the offspring, and is not used to determine genetic family trees. This parallels what science says in their finds: The Cro-Magnon man's DNA **closely resembles that of modern man**, and deviates from it in only a very few places. Remember that they haven't found the bones of Cain, but the intermarried offspring of the Cro-Magnon, and the genetic code would more closely match that of the Neanderthal. One must remember that if a female were found and the MtDNA was used, the **MtDNA would track back to the Male and Female (Neanderthal), not to Cain,** and conversely, certainly not to Adam.

Now, let's put on our thinking caps here: if Cain had married his sister, the Cro-Magnon's MtDNA would have tracked back to Eve, who would show the Cro-Magnon man as modern man, and it does not. Remember that science found **Cro-Magnon and Neanderthal characteristics,** and had no other explanation other than inner marriage. **The puzzle has its pieces, and my precious, they fit.**

The Layman

The plug that is now present proves that Adam, Noah; his wife; Ham; Sham; Japheth, and their wives were not descendents of Cro-Magnon. Therefore, the genetic MtDNA trace of Cain and both the Neanderthal, and Cro-Magnon were lost forever because of the flood.

Is this all that important, one might ask.
It is critically important, because:
1. Upon the understanding of this union lies the harmony of Gen 1 and Gen 2.
2. It gives scientists and theologians, the bridge to gap chasms between these three races of individuals that have separated us in understanding in the past.
3. Without this understanding, neither all the greatest scientists who give facts of finding, nor all the pious preachers ever to stand in a thousand pulpits can bring Genesis 1 and Genesis 2 into harmony, nor explain where these three races came from.

My brethren, there is harmony throughout Scripture if only one will search it out. All we have to do is consider it with an open mind.

ANOTHER SON

Gen 4:*25 "And Adam knew his wife again; and* **she** *bare a son, and called his name* **Seth***: For God, said* **she***, hath appointed me* **another seed** *instead of Abel, whom Cain slew."*
Gen 4:26 *"And to Seth, to him also there was born a son; and he called his name Enos: then began men to call upon the name of the LORD."* (Emphasis is mine)

This also can be interpreted as "they began to call themselves by the name of the LORD (Jehovah)."

Why would they do that; because there were eight classes of man at this time? I say that because I believe that, but others may not and that is all right. I will cover what I believe are those classes later on.

Now don't loose sight that Scripture is not the same as man's division. Chapter 4 should end at verse 24. The next chapter is 25-26 and chapter 5 goes from 1-5. I deliberately threw that in to make the readers mind "buzz." I just want us never to lose sight that our divisions of Scripture are not aligned with the Holy Writ in all cases. Keep looking at those (¶).

Now for the blessing of Adam (Mankind) in Gen 5: Gen 5:1, 2.
"(1) *This is the book of the* **generations** *of* **Adam***.* **In the day** *that* **God**

***created man**, in the likeness of God made he him; **(2)**. **Male and female** created he them; and blessed them, and **called their name Adam**, in the day when they were created.*" (Emphasis is mine)

Here again, as we saw in Gen 2 where the LORD God covered, in summary, **all** the creative events, **up to that point** in Scripture. Here in Gen 5 we are in summary: **God** is now covering **all** the creative events **up to this point** in Scripture.

This summary is necessary to explain the genealogy of our Lord as covered in the book of Luke, and quite honestly abruptly omits all Adams sons' up to Seth.

There are subtle changes here: I must, once more remind all, that this usage of the term day is not a 24 hour day, but a summary of creative events **covering years**. It is to be noted that the Godhead is not divided here, but is collectively referred to as God.

This is **the book of the generations:**

1. This is interesting. The term, "The book of" is used in Scripture 99 times.

2. The term, "Generations", is used 114 times.

3. The term, "The book of the generations of" is used nowhere else in Scripture. Don't get confused with, Matthew 1:1 *"The book of the generation of Jesus Christ, the son of David, the son of Abraham."* which uses the <u>singular</u> "generation."

This is a recompilation by God of the events from Gen 1:2 all the way to Gen 5:2, up to Noah. I have studied these verses, and quite honestly I can find no one who even tries to amplify them any further than I have just related.

The term "generations of Adam" is the only way that all of creation up to this point could be explained, without explaining it.

The term Adam means "man". Jamieson-Faussit-Brown says *"Adam-used here either as the name of the first man, **or of the human race generally**."*(Emphasis is mine)

Without dissecting this, allow me to give my opinion, and I stress strongly that it is my opinion.

We have one group of man in Gen 1, we have another group in Gen 2, we have another group in Gen 4, and we have another group in Gen 5.

1. Genesis 1: Tells us of male and female, who I have termed in sequence, Neanderthal:

179

The Layman

　　2. Genesis 2: Tells us of the "forming of Adam; the planting of the garden; the "forming" of the animals, and the cloning of Woman.

　　3. Genesis 3 tells us of Adam and Eve, with twins, and one kills the other, and leaves;

　　4. Genesis 4: Tells us of Cain in Nod and another genealogy of man, who in sequence I have termed the offspring of Cain: Cro-Magnon.

　　5. Genesis 5: tells us of all creative acts to include: male and female: Adam; Seth, and omits Cain.

This is the book of the generations **of Adam.** Now the **word Adam,** as we have quoted **James-Faucet-Brown,** could equally stand for all mankind as a whole, and I think this is the proper meaning we should use.

　　In the day: In the beginning God creates with the 'lets', then the office changes to the LORD God, and He '**forms**', now we have the 'book of the generations of Adam: the office changes to God. **The key is the use of the term "in the day."**

　　If this is not an all encompassing statement from Gen 1 to Gen 5, then one must ask why Scripture says that God created Adam, when we know that **God created** male and female with the creative "Let;" and the **LORD God formed** Adam. Now don't get pious on me and point out that the three are one, because we covered that before in our explanation in Gen 1; however, knowing that the three are one **we can readily see this as an all encompassing statement, and they as one, are incorporated here in this Scripture.** In using the term "*Generations*", He is telling us of all the generations of man up to this point in time.

　　When Scripture changes something, there is a reason for that change. This is one change we need to take note of. We know from previous discussion that God is the supreme designer of everything, and that the Lord is the builder of everything. We have seen that when **judgment, laws and punishment** is to happen, Scripture always changes the office to God; conversely, **when mercy and grace is to be present,** Scripture changes the one to Lord. We are approaching dire corrective punishment of the inhabitants of the earth, and it is for that reason Scripture now identifies the one here as God.

　　The next thing which I would point out is that there is a **sudden deletion, or gap,** in the generation story. Lets look at the next verse, Gen 5:3 *"And Adam lived an hundred and thirty years, and **begat a***

180

son in his own likeness, after his image; and called his name Seth:"
Now what happened to Cain and Abel? The term "generation" is from
a man's birth, <u>until he has a son; the first or oldest son</u>. Then it would
follow that generations should be even more inclusive; yet both Cain
and Able are left out.

Are we then to believe that the generation of Adam was not
established until the birth of Seth? **That is what Scripture is telling
us** whether we agree with it or not. In Luke we read Lu 3:37, 38. 37
*"Which was the son of Mathusala, which was the son of Enoch, which was the son
of Jared, which was the son of Maleleel, which was the son of Cainan, (38) Which
was the son of Enos, which was the **son of Seth, which was the son of
Adam, which was the son of God.**"* (Emphasis is mine). This seems
like a deviation from God's plan of designating generation; however,
may I say that it is not at all.

Reason with me here: **if Cain has deceased** as a result of war
with the Neanderthal or something else over the 130 years, then Seth
would be the sole surviving son, and therefore, the rightful heir.

This is a pivotal point in God's plan. This is a recapitulation of
everything up to this point. **This now starts the genetic tree from
which salvation will bloom.** Our Father has so woven Salvation in
every verse of the Word: we must never loose sight that it is becoming
our "Tree of Life." What our Father is telling us here is that this is now
the genealogy of Adam.

Since Adam did not age until after the original sin, we do not
know how long he existed when Cain and Abel were born. We do
know that some time passed before the fall, and then some more time
passed before the two boys came upon the scene, and then they had to
grow up. What part of that is included or left out of the following I do
not know; we need to take note of it, however.

Gen 5:3 *"And Adam lived an hundred and thirty years, and **begat a
son in his own likeness, after his image**; and called his name **Seth** I
think that someday we will more fully understand the relationship
between God's Christ, and Satan as well as the relationship between
Cain and Abel, and Adam and his son Seth.

I do know that God does not mention blessing our
Grandparents until the fifth chapter when one is born in Adam's
likeness, **after his (Adam's) own image: Seth**. Cain and Abel were
not said to be born after the image of Adam, nor in his likeness; Why?
I don't know. I do think that all creative events had our Fathers
blessings; it is we who have caused blessings to be withheld.

The Layman

Here is another **"logo"** in scripture that is in support of God's creation. It does not say that Seth was in Adam's image. Note that it says "in his <u>likeness</u>, **after his own image.**" The Triune God is perfect, Adam and Eve are now dying. When the LORD God created Adam, he was in His image; therefore, Adam's DNA was perfect, and the same can be said about Woman who was cloned from Adam. However, when Adam sinned, Ro 5:12 "*Wherefore, as by one man sin entered into the world, and death by sin; and so death passed upon all men, for that all have sinned.*" Seth could not be in Adam's image because <u>DNA has now began to deteriorate:</u> He could only be **after** his image.

My Bible is again so wonderfully simply complicated, and complicatedly simple: it is wonderful. Who would dare to modify one space between thoughts and think they had not changed something most wonderful.

From Adam to Noah is **not** covered in a saving grace, hope, or looking towards that hope, in that the LORD God said "*in the day that thou eatest thereof <u>thou shalt surely die.</u>*" We know that the Lord will not leave the innocent without hope, because when Christ died on the cross, He went to <u>this group</u> and preached to them. 1Pe 3:18-20.18 "*For Christ also hath once suffered for sins, the just for the unjust, **that he might bring us to God**, being put to death in the flesh, but quickened by the Spirit:*" 19 "***By which also he went and preached unto the spirits in prison,***" 20 "*<u>Which sometime were disobedient</u>, when once the longsuffering of God waited in the **days of Noah**, while the ark was a preparing, wherein few, that is, eight souls were saved by water.*" (Emphasis is mine)

The ultimate purpose of every creative event was and is to bring salvation to the ones who <u>try</u> and follow Him.

I want to emphasize this; <u>I know</u> some brethren are of the opinion that these souls we have just addressed here were the fallen "Sons of God" that committed adultery with Seth's offspring; however, **that is <u>not</u> the case.** These, who our Lord spoke to, were peoples who lived during the time just before the flood, not the adulterous fallen ones. Whether these pre-delugean disobedient ones had any dealings with those fallen angels or not, I am not prepared to discuss; they were obviously both there at the same time. Let's ask ourselves, should our Lord preach to the damned? **They were reserved in chains forever, unto judgment.**

When the Judge damn's you, you are damned.

Some might state, "It is hard for me to understand: when there is no law, how can one break the law." Well I know our LORD God is just: I am wondering if that is not one of the reasons Jesus went and explained all things to those that were here before the flood. Wouldn't I love to have heard that sermon?

The reason I feel the LORD God went to them is since there **was no covenant** given until after the flood to Noah: then again to Abraham; at the time of Moses, and finally the Gospel given to us, I feel it is for that reason those spoken of were introduced to the Son of Man who preached to them and explained grace to them. I will leave it there since I do not have anything further to go on. I caution all not to get the disobedient ones confused with the fallen "Sons of God", remember they were bound forever in chains: Jude 1:6 "*And the angels which kept not their first estate, but left their own habitation, he hath reserved in everlasting chains under* **darkness unto the judgment of the great day.**" (Emphasis is mine) so **they were not a part of that group.**
This gives us:

1. Book of the generations of Adam.
2. The covenant God made with Noah.
3. The "bosom of Abraham."
4. The commandments given Moses.
5. The Gospel for those who would be saved by the Blood of Christ.

One may ask, "Well what happened to poor old Abel?" I don't know, I really do not know, but I do know who does, and **He called Abel 'righteous.'** I can not comment on male and female as to whether they had a "living soul" or not. Scripture makes a definitive point that Adam did, and since it is left out of the discussion of the male and female, one may, with some certainty say that they must not have; however, I know in my heart there is righteousness from God all the way from the portals of heaven down to every puff of air exhaled by a hungry flea on a dog's back.

I appreciate that I have raised a lot of questions that may never be answered here, but to just skip over it and, and then just pick up on something that supports my theory, would not be the right thing to do.

The generations of Adam, started at Adam to Seth because that was the way for God to record the generations so we would understand it without opening doors which would also lead to Cain's wife, where she came from, and then to the entire "Void and Without Form" explanation. It is up to the reader to pray through, but there is a Master plan at work here.

MULTIPLE OFFICES OF GOD

Having said that I will point out that reading Genesis, chapters 1– 8, it is important to note the following, in chapter 1 the identity of the One is "**God:**" In chapter 2 the identity of the One is "**LORD God;**" In chapter 3 the identity of the One is "**LORD God;**" And in chapter 4 the identity of the One is "**LORD;**" In chapter 5 the One is "**God;**" In chapter 6 the One is sometimes "**God**," sometimes "**LORD God;**" In Chapter 7 the One is "**LORD**," And in chapter 8 the One is "**God**," and also "**LORD God.**"

How many noticed that there were times the chapter actually had one or more "¶" in it? Did we notice that sometimes that changed the usage between "LORD God, and God, and sometimes it didn't? I will not attempt to define the reasons here, but to say that there is a definite reason and we should not overlook it if we are to understand His Word. God has designed this old book so deep that as Dr. Ironside once said *"I have plummeted its depths a good part of my life, ever diving deeper, deeper only to find myself but slightly beneath its surface after all."* We need to stop being spoon fed and reach out for the Bread of Life and the meat of Scripture for ourselves.

I want to explain why the offices of the Godhead are changing between these first chapters of the Bible:

1. In Gen 1, the identity is God who is restoring a world out of judgment.

2. In Gen 2 the identity changes to the LORD God who is laying the foundation of Salvation in its infancy.

3. In Gen 5 the identity changes once more back to God who is preparing to put the world back under judgment once more.

4. Remember; God in law and judgment

5. Remember the LORD in mercy and grace.

The man, who has no hope, has none.

What starts out as a wonderful movement, ends in tragedy: Flavius Josephus' **Antiquities of the Jews**, Chapter III states, *"Now this posterity of Seth continued to esteem God as the Lord of the universe, and to have an entire regard to virtue, for seven generations; but in process of time they were perverted, and forsook the practices of their forefathers, and did neither pay those honors to God which were appointed them, nor had they any concern to do justice towards men. But for what degree of zeal they had formerly shewn for virtue, they now shewed by their actions a double degree of wickedness, whereby they made God their enemy; for many angels of God accompanied with women and begat sons that proved unjust, and despisers of all that was good... these men did what resembled the acts of those whom the Grecians call giants."*

AN UGLY STORY

It is beyond me to understand, how a being can look into the face of God the Father, God the Son, and God the Holy Spirit, and walk away. I know nothing of heaven, and even less of Hell. I do not get delight in thinking of streets of gold, and gates of pearl. I do not get fear from lakes of fire, and brimstone. I just want to see my Trinity and get a hug: My friend that is heaven to me. The worst hell that I can imagine would be to have the vision of my LORD God and not be able to be in His presence. Everyone can have streets of gold, give me a green meadow that I can romp barefoot through and never get a chigger, or better still give me a moment to see a smile from Jehovah God as He looks my way: everyone else can have the rest. But, Alas! This is not what we now face.

Well the story goes on with Satan winning a few battles, or so he thinks, and loosing the war. Forgive me for not covering all the in betweens, but I want to get to the period just before Noah.

Now the die is cast. Satan thinks that he has won. He has destroyed the first earth either through his direct action or by divine action as a result of the Holy Judgment of God because of sin, yet our loving God will not give up our souls so easily. Satan now must be really smug in his thoughts. The new start has fallen at his whim already. He now thinks that man will not be eternal. He doesn't know that this was known by God before the world began. Now to add a *coup de grâce* to the whole thing, Satan is going to tempt the weaker angels of heaven and he thinks this will cause the destruction of the world again.

The corruption of earth: Gen 6:1 "*¶And it came to pass, when men began to multiply on the face of the earth, and daughters were born unto them,*"

Gen 6:2 "*That the **sons of God** saw the **daughters of men** that they were fair; and they took them wives of all which they chose.*"

Gen 6:3 "*¶And the LORD said, My spirit shall not always strive with man, for that he also is flesh: yet his days shall be an hundred and twenty years.*"

Gen 6:4 "*¶There were giants in the earth in those days; and also after that, when **the sons of God** came in unto the daughters of men, and they bare children to them, the same **became mighty men which were of old, men of renown.**"

Gen 6:5 "*And GOD saw that the wickedness of man was great in the earth, and that every imagination of the thoughts of his heart was only evil continually.*"(Emphasis is mine)

There were, according to Enoch, well over two hundred such angels, which he named that were a part in this intrusion. **This is not** to be confused with those angels who originally fell with Satan; these are in addition to those who originally fell.

I think these angels were a host of heaven **who stayed for a while** and then temptation overcame them and what we are now faced with is a sight most ugly. In **heaven they were angels**, on **earth they were as gods** and had absolute power, in comparison to man.

As Lord Action has said, "***Absolute power corrupts absolutely.***"

The sons of God were sinning, but judgment waited and observed. Then God declared a fixed time for this to go on, and waited. Scripture then tells us of the decrepit state of affairs, and yet He waited before the flood: Why? Remember this verse? 1Pe 3:20 "*Which sometime were disobedient, when once the longsuffering of God waited in the days of Noah, while the ark was a preparing, wherein few, that is, eight souls were saved by water.*"(Emphasis is mine) Another Scripture that parallels this one is given in Romans.

Ro 9:22 "*[What] if God, willing to shew [his] wrath, and to make his power known, endured with much longsuffering the vessels of wrath fitted to destruction:*

Ro 9:23 *"And that he might make known the riches of his glory on the vessels of mercy, which he had afore prepared unto glory,"*

One verse covers this time, the other a later time, and my friend these verses, Ro 2:3 *"And thinkest thou this, O man, that judgest them which do such things, and doest the same, that thou shalt escape the judgment of God?*

Ro 2:4 *"Or despisest thou the riches of his goodness and forbearance and longsuffering; not knowing that the goodness of God leadeth thee to repentance?"* This aptly applies to our world today.

No matter how decrepit the case may be, our Father always delays long enough to allow His mercy to be accepted or rejected.

Recognize the original divisions of Scripture: Now before we go on, let me point out that there is one of those" ¶ " at the first of Gen 6:1,2 and another at Gen 6:3 and another at Gen 6:4,5 and still another at Gen 6:6, 6:8 and so on.

We really need to pay attention to these divisions because there is a thought division for each. There is also a <u>time lapse</u> between them which need to be remembered when studying this, or any part of Scripture. I am so sorry that some translations have left them out.

WHO WERE THOSE ANGELS

I know several romanticizing remarks which follow these passages. I have heard orators try to explain that the sons of God were actually the offspring of Seth and were not angelic beings at all. I guess that will set well with the heathen and not drive them from the churches, or embarrass them. **What they were really doing was watering it down <u>so they</u> could believe it**

Reason with me here: if Seth's boys were the sons of God then why wouldn't Seth's girls, be the **daughters of God**? `That sounds pretty good to me. Let's think here, if all this transpired with the descendants of Seth and the daughters of Cain, Scripture would point this out, <u>and it does not</u>. I just can't swallow that Seth's boys went to Cain's girls and the results were <u>great men of renown</u>.

Follow this reasoning: it seems to me if this were the case, and Seth's boys were to marry Seth's girls, whom they were doing already, then why wouldn't those girls give birth to **"fantastic" men of renown**.

187

The Layman

If Seth's boys **downgraded** themselves for the daughters of Cain, what would cause the offspring to suddenly become "men of great renown?"

I feel we all need to stop, and put things in their **proper perspective**. It seems that some try so hard to water things down to be accepted by those who will never understand it all anyway, and I am afraid these orators cannot believe it themselves, so they change it to suit their thinking: We used to call that "**Stinking-Thinking**."

I didn't write the Bible, and I am not prepared to change it to make it "believable" to the politically correct crowd. The book of Enoch says that these offspring were so large that they consumes all the food that mankind grew, and then turned to eating flesh and drinking the blood thereof. They revealed hidden secrets to mankind (really that isn't what Enoch said at all. I am following the politically correct crowd: I apologize.) What he said was that the angels **taught the women the hidden arts**,) all the dark arts of astrology, the moon, the sun, and <u>known</u> secrets of God's creation.

Our present world is not far behind when we take political correctness and apply it to the Bible. God knows His creatures, and so too does Satan know Gods creatures. Why was it the Woman whom the serpent approached in the garden? Why did the LORD God command the Woman to be subject to her husband, and that she was to submit to his rule over her? Why did these fallen angels tell the women the secrets and not the men? **1 Peter 3:7** *"Likewise, ye husbands, dwell with them according to knowledge, giving honour unto the wife, as unto the **weaker vessel, and as being heirs together** of the grace of life; that your prayers be not hindered."* (Emphasis is mine) Why it is Paul and Peter both defined the wife's roll in relation to marriage, and within the Church? I have heard "religious leaders" in the Church say that they thought Peter and Paul "had a bad hair day when they wrote such?"

One would aver "You are just a woman basher." Oh! My precious if you knew me you would know different. <u>I did not write the Bible</u>, and if anyone thinks mankind's wisdom is what formed salvation in its covers, they are a very unintelligent Christian. When a man has seen the third level of Heaven and says something, <u>I listen</u>. They can do as they please, but the same man wrote in the book, Eph 2:8 *"For by grace are ye saved through faith; and that not of yourselves: it is the gift of God."* **If they want to take some Scriptures out, that he wrote, they have to take them all out.**

188

It is equally important to note this same man of God wrote, Php 4:3 *"And I intreat thee also, true yokefellow, help those* **women** *which* **labored** **with** **me** *in the gospel, with* **Clement** *also, and with other* **my** **fellow** **labourers,** *whose names are in the book of life."*(Emphasis is mine) Paul followed Scripture, he was not a woman basher; **he was a God lover**.

Let me add a remark: Woman's name was changed to Eve, Gen 3:20; Jacob was renamed to Israel, Gen 32:28; Abram was renamed to Abraham (Gen 17:5), and Sari was renamed to Sarah (Gen 17:15). God does not put woman under foot. He just knows his creation. He also loves His creation. To my knowledge, that is the only place in the Scriptures where a woman's name was changed for those purposes. Praise God, He will change **all** our names up there.

Those fallen angels did not know the deep secrets of our Father. I would imagine that these beings, taught all that they knew, but God still knew in advance that this was going to happen, and I don't believe the fallen angels knew then, nor do they know now the real secrets of God. Remember that Christ, himself, said about the second coming; Mr 13:32 *"But of that day and that hour knoweth no man, no, not the angels which are in heaven, neither the Son, but the Father."* I know our Father just does not tell-all-to-all.

I must take note of the phrase, Gen 6:4 *"There were* **giants** *in the earth in those days; and also after that, when* **the sons of God** *came in unto the daughters of men, and they bare children to them, the same* **became mighty men which were of old, men of renown."** (Emphasis is mine) I cannot bring myself to imagine what a being would look like when procreation occurred between angel and human. There are things in this world that cannot be explained when it comes to these mysteries. That these mysteries still exist, we need not forget, Col 2:18 *"Let no man beguile you of your reward in a voluntary humility and* worshipping of angels, intruding into *those* things which he hath not seen, *vainly puffed up by his* fleshly mind,"* (Emphasis is mine)

There was a warning to the Israeli's, years ago about this: Isa 8:19 *"And when they shall say unto you, Seek unto them that have familiar spirits, and unto wizards that peep, and that mutter: should not a people seek unto their God? for the living to the dead?"*

I am personally convinced these fallen ones taught the black arts which may well have existed beyond the "Void and Without Form." They had to know their punishment for doing this, but delighting for the moments of devilry, damming their souls for a fleeting sensuous moment, trading existing bliss for eternal damnation:

how sad. Yet is it only they who do such things, and not we today? We need not forget, Ro 1:32 *"Who knowing the judgment of God, that they which commit such things are worthy of death, <u>not only do the same, but have pleasure in them that do them.</u>"* (Emphasis is mine)

Dr. Scofield's interpretation on the sons of God:
    I know of Scofield's comments on "sons of God" and the neuter of Angels; However, I disagree with this great man of Biblical wisdom.
    Scofield: **First: Upon the sons of God**, Scofield gives *"Isaiah 43:6 when God is talking to Jacob whom He named Israel. The name Israel means "Having power with God, or God's fighter." Jacobs children would then be spoken of as sons and daughters much as we are as Gentiles; the adopted. It was Jesus who said in, Joh 10:34 Jesus answered them, Is it not written in your law,* **I said, Ye are gods?**"* (Emphasis is mine)
    My Answer: I think those spoken of before the flood as "sons of God," who cohabitated with the daughters of man, were:
    1. <u>before the faith of Abraham</u>, and the promise of the Lord,
    2. And were Angels who fell through their own temptation and lust of the world.
The term "sons of god" is used 11 times in Scripture. The first **two** references are to this place, **three** times in the book of Job when speaking of them shouting with joy in the first creation, and **six** times in the New Testament, where there, they are referred to being the sons of God through faith in the delivered Gospel.

    It was with Jacob Gen 32:28 *"And he said, Thy name shall be called no more Jacob,* **but Israel: for as a prince** *hast thou power with God and with men, and hast prevailed."*, that we see the LORD God renaming man. Jacob was the father of the twelve tribes, and the LORD God caused him to be renamed by the "man" that wrestled with him, and thereby by covenant, owned him. This "sons of God" does not seem to be the thrust of Scripture at this point, but well valid in the New Testament. (Emphasis was mine)

    Scofield: Second: That Angels have no sex identity: Dr. Scofield states that *"Angels are neither male of female"* in his explanation. Dr. Scofield gives, *"Mt 22:30 For in the resurrection they <u>neither marry, nor are given in marriage,</u> but* **are as the angels of God in heaven.**" for his findings. (Emphasis is mine)

My Answer:

1. As to the Angels: I take this passage (Mt. 22.30) to be interpreted *"are as the angels of God in heaven,"* and <u>if they are still in heaven, then they did not fall</u> and so the **ones who fell were, and <u>are</u> different,** because they denied their celibacy, and took on the form of man.

2. I find that <u>there is</u> a sex identity for angels. I respect this learned gentleman and his interpretation of Scripture; I do not know why he would say that angels are neither male nor female. When we read Da 9:21, *"Yea, whiles I was speaking in prayer,* **even the <u>man</u> Gabriel,** *whom I had seen in the vision at the beginning, being caused to fly swiftly, touched me about the time of the evening oblation."* (Emphasis is mine)

Whether we will be men and women in heaven is not clear to me. What is clear is that when Scripture talks of the angelic beings, they are, **he,** or **him.** We will not marry, which makes sense, for if my love is for my LORD God, I will have no more to divide to another. (Emphasis is mine)

Let's look at another amplification of this thought in **"*Rightly Dividing the Word,* by** Clarence Larkin, 1920**"**

"The outcome of that brilliant but godless civilization was to promote the rapid increase of population. Then men began to multiply on the face of the earth." Ge 6:1. In the midst of this "Godless Civilization" a startling event occurred. "The 'Sons of GOD' saw the 'Daughters of MEN' that they were fair; and they took them WIVES of all which they chose." Ge 6:2.

This polygamous relation was not between the "Sons of SETH," and the "Daughters of CAIN," a union of the godly and wicked people of that day, as some suppose, but it has a far deeper meaning. The expression "Daughters of MEN" includes the daughters of Seth as well as the daughters of Cain, hence the expression "Sons of GOD" must mean beings different from the HUMAN RACE."

Again: the title "Sons of God" does not have the same meaning in the Old Testament that it has in the New. In the New Testament it applies to those who have become the "Sons of God" by the New Birth through the gospel.

We must not forget that Angels can assume the form of MEN and eat and drink as is told us in (Ge 18:1-8). The whole difficulty vanishes when we see that it was AS MEN that the "Sons of God" (Angels) took the "Daughters of Men."

We have only to turn to the Epistles of Peter and Jude for confirmation of this. In 2Pe 2:4-9 we are told of the "Angels that SINNED," and in Jude 1:6-7 of the <u>Angels</u> that "KEPT NOT THEIR FIRST ESTATE," but "LEFT

THEIR OWN HABITATION," and are now "RESERVED IN EVERLASTING CHAINS UNDER DARKNESS" unto the "Judgment of the Great Day," the "Great White Throne Judgment." (Emphasis is mine)

These Angels are **not** the **original angels** that fell with Satan, for his angels are not reserved in chains, but are free, within allowable limits given by God. They must therefore be a "special class" of angels who have been imprisoned for some particular sin, and we are told what that sin was, it was fornication and going after strange flesh.

ANGELIC BEINGS WITH HUMAN MATES

What a catastrophe. **No wonder the Romans had so many gods**. They knew of these beings back then. The Titan was not anything impossible; the Pegasus was within realm of thought. Angels have power unimaginable. Pan was but another of their toys of creation. We of today are headed the same way when we speak of cloning humans. Where will the end be, when once we unlock but another of God's fundamental truths? Da 12:4 *"But thou, O Daniel, shut up the words, and seal the book, [even] to the time of the end: many shall run to and fro, and knowledge shall be increased."*

MEN OF GREAT RENOWN

What chaos the world must have been in. I cannot start to imagine what the offspring of this union must have been. I quoted Enoch before as saying they were so large that they ate up all the food. These are procreated beings with angelic fathers. What power they possessed, one can only imagine. **They gave up eternity for a moment of lustful pleasure.** Then again, do we not fall to such, ourselves?

"Well now!" One would say, "I don't believe that." Well then I bet they don't believe that three men walked through the fire of a furnace and came out without a hair singed on their bodies. I bet they don't believe Daniel was cat food for the lions all night. I bet they don't believe a man was swallowed hole by a fish and stayed there for three days until he got his sermon worked out to preach to Nineveh. I bet they don't believe all man; animals and fowl were in a large boat for a year. I bet they don't believe there is a Hell with real fire. I bet they don't believe that Jesus Christ walked on water. What I cannot envision, I believe by faith and let the LORD God work the rest out by Himself.

This liberal preacher was walking past a grassy area next to a fundamental institute in Dallas, Texas. He was taken back by this young man, sitting under a tree reading the Bible. The young man kept shouting, "Praise God what a wonder, what a miracle."

Curious the preacher approached and asked, "What has brought you to this level of excitement sir?"

The young man then read the Scripture where it said Ex 14:16 "*But lift thou up thy rod, and stretch out thine hand over the sea, and divide it: and the children of Israel shall go on dry [ground] through the midst of the sea.*" Then continued shouting, "Praise God what a miracle."

With this the liberal preacher said, "Now calm down young man. If you studied the lay of the land there, you would see that the children actually crossed the sea where it is only a couple of inches deep, and the winds just blew the water aside." With that, and satisfied that he had straightened the young man out, he continued on, only to halt when he once again heard the young man exclaiming.

"Praise God what a wonder, what a miracle"

Returning to the spot, the preacher asked, "Now what are you shouting about?"

With that the young man read, Ex 14:28 "*And the waters returned, and covered the chariots, and the horsemen, [and] all the host of Pharaoh that came into the sea after them; there remained not so much as one of them.*"

"What a miracle," said the young man. "**God drowned a whole army in three inches of water.**"

EXPLAINING THE CLASSES

I have developed classes of those on earth after the Phase II Creation. These are sequences of populations which I feel were here and fall in a certain order. This characterization is, for the most part, only my opinion.

1. We have the "Neanderthal" man who falls in sequence only with the male and female, and were, in my opinion, created in Gen 1:2 to Gen 2:3. I am not sure that the "Neanderthal" man made it very long before becoming extinct because of the war between them and the Cro-Magnon, or through crossbreeding they may well have lost their identity. That agreeably is a question to be answered someday. If the man of Gen 1 was not what we call the "Neanderthal," then we don't know what he was, but if he was on this earth, **and he was, then, my God made him.**

2. We have Adam then Eve who were created in Gen 2 and Gen 3.

3. We have Cain, who after his curse, Went to a land call Nod and took a wife, who I think was what science calls "Neanderthal," and as a result of that union their offspring were what I believe science calls "Cro-Magnon." Please don't get hung up on the scientific names of these. I don't know, and none of us will, until we get on the other side. They just fall in sequence and that is all. If I came from Georgia, one would call me a Georgia boy, but I would still be a God created person.

4. We have Seth that is after the likeness of Adam. This is **the blood line to our Savior, Jesus Christ.** Though Seth kept his belief in God, it seems that some part of his descendants began to stray.

5. We have the fallen angels who left their first estate and have come to earth and took what they wanted.

6. That the statement, "from Seth that men began to call upon the name of the Lord," is very plain to me, remember, Gen 5:24 "*And Enoch walked with God: and he was not; for God took him.*" It is plain that they did not just call themselves **by** names of the LORD, but called **upon** His name. Enoch was and is quite a unique person.

7. We then see even those who called on the name of the Lord falling from truth and blending into a perverse society.

8. Then there are those who have not failed: Noah, his wife, their three boys with each of their wives.

The Classes that are listed are far from a detailed account, but rather a summary of topics thus far covered. There is such a wealth of information which could be added, and the most difficult part is for me to keep from chasing squirrels as I have done from time to time.

I do not ask anyone to believe what I have written; why? Because I can prove only what is in Scripture, but with my heart I believe it. I have presented this information, and what follows only to give a glimpse into what might have been, by reading between the lines.

For someone to say that dinosaurs did not exist is foolish. I have stood at the right leg of a creature so large, I was sure glad the cables which suspended it were reliable. **The Smithsonian Institute** has many such displays. In another section of this fine institute I have viewed the flesh from, a once, frozen Wooly Mammoth from the past.

Is there anybody on the face of the earth who does not fully recognize, that what science calls the Cave Man, (Even though good science identifies them as chimps) existed? Is there anyone who truly denies that a collection of animals beyond description existed at one time on this earth, which I lump into the term dinosaur?

Is there anyone on this earth that really believes that this earth is only six thousand years old?

I fully believe what I have thus far written. I have seen the bony skeletal remains of some of these creatures, and I have my underlying faith that my God knows what He did, what He is doing, and what He is going to do to inspire me. After all, salvation is what we really seek and all we are examining here is only for us to better appreciate Him.

It is most important that we make it clear to everyone there was **a world before Ge 1:2; that world did exist**. Have anyone ever walked into the intermediate's classroom at Church and see a little one with a coloring book that they are busily coloring a picture in? And what are they coloring; a "**Dino" Dinosaur**. We make a mockery out of ourselves, and leave our youth unarmed when we teach things that do not hold water. We leave the floodgate wide open for the evolutionist and the attention getting professors to poison their minds.

When I hear some pastor stand in the pulpit and aver that the world was made in seven 24 hour days, I want to throw a song book at him. There are pastors who have glossed over Ge:1, and Ge:2 for so long that I honestly feel they would leave the ministry before admitting that what we have presented, in essence, is true. When he makes the 24/7 statement, **he should stop, look over the audience and see total unbelief in what he has just said.** I take the position, as the old saints have said: *"I do not know what happened, and I don't know when it happened, but I know who made it all happen, and God knows all about it. Amen!"*

I heard my daughter try to explain that Noah probably took dinosaur eggs on the Ark, because if they were grown, they would be too big to fit in. If everyone could have seen the crushed look on her little face when everyone laughed her to shame. She and others that we teach **want** to believe what we teach them. **They want to hang their souls on faith; however, how can they when we teach that the original earth was created in seven days and bipeds and dinosaurs of another time were not real?** "Well" Someone says, "I never said that dinosaurs never lived." I will kindly have to ask them, who made them, when did they live, where are they now?

Would I want this book taught? No! I am wise enough to say it is only my THEORY! I can, however, objectively aver that there was a world here before the Phase II Creation, that is most evident, and the evidence of it surrounds me daily.

Our little country Church is built of limestone, and almost every piece of that limestone contains fossils: Little critters known only to God, and locked in time.

I have and am sure most have heard of a book that is titled "Harmony of the Gospel's," but **never** one titled "Harmony of Genesis. If I haven't said this before, I will now; I have never heard anyone who was able to, or has even attempted, to stitch, or bring any event found in Gen 1, to match anything in Gen 2.

We have all heard pastors read in Gen 1 and then when they get to male and female of Gen 1:26, they then jump to the forming of Adam in Gen 2:7, but again, with absolutely no continuity because as they have presented the subject, there is none: sadly they should know that..

NOW ANOTHER EVENT

Here again we are in the office of the LORD; in grace to man.

Gen 6:6 *"And it repented the LORD that he had made man on the earth, and it grieved him at his heart."* I do not think that there are enough libraries on earth to hold the volumes it would take to explain, that one part of this verse: "It grieved Him at His heart."

I read a reference while studying for this book. The man who wrote it is very sound in most of his work, and I respect him highly, but not here. In his explanation of this word "Repented" he says, *"That the LORD was sorry that He ever made man."* **OH! Pooh**! My precious brethren if anyone were to think that, they just do not understand the love and wisdom of my Trinity. We must never forget that our Father knows the end before the beginning. He already knew this was going to happen. If one should doubt that, then perhaps they can explain that Christ was and is the lamb slain **from the foundation of the world.**

I could not follow a god who is ignorant of what he is doing, nor could I follow one who does not know the end as well as the beginning. How could we trust a god who was just playing it by ear, and making it up as he went along? If that were true, then eternity would only be a pipe dream that he will work on when he gets there.

My Father knew, before He made the first world, every thing that was going to take place all the way to eternity future. God put our names in the Book of Life long before we were even born. He chose the apostles long before they were born. How anyone could ever say that the LORD was sorry for what ever He did, is to say that He is ignorant of what is around Him, and brethren if anyone is of that opinion, they need to start over from scratch because they are following the wrong god. My Father and my LORD do not make it up as they go along.

This word "repented" also means, (if I can turn linguist), **to exhale with great sorrow**. If you are a parent you know the feeling. It was like you felt when one of your children just kept on testing you. I can remember when the moment came for correction. It was like I had failed. Repented would mean the same if one tested you until you had to take drastic action, in hope of correcting them and with a deep sigh and exhale of regret, you took on the task of correction. It is then you would feel the hurt.

When I told my children a certain law for the family, **I knew** which one was most likely to disobey that law. To say that my LORD didn't know all this would imply that I would be smarter than He is. May my LORD forgive me for even using such an example: I am totally agog at His wonders?

When that child violated my law, I was <u>not</u> surprised. I would see it coming, and tell them that I saw it coming and tried to steer them away from trouble. When, at last that failed, I had to take corrective action. I would hurt inside, and would take a deep breath, sigh in sorrow for what was going to take place.

One who looks at the Trinity with worldly eyes needs to back off and rethink who they are talking about.

I know my mother would say, before she got the switch out, "This always hurts me more than it hurts you." I always doubted that until the day came when I had to do the same with my precious children, and they doubted it until they had their children. **It does hurt** the parent more, it surely does, **or they don't need to be a parent** because something is wrong with them. I used to spank my kids, then draw them to me and hug them and tell them I loved them. I did, I do, and will love them through eternity.

197

The Layman

Someone I love very much once told me in anger "Love and hate are very close together, and right now I hate you." One thing should be understood: **Love never dies**. Love stops growing, **but love does not die or turn to hate**. You may hate what I am doing, or what I have become, you may lose all the respect you ever had for me, but you cannot hate what you once loved, or you never loved in the first place.

Well then why does the LORD God put people in Hell if He loves them? My friend, I believe that the LORD God loves His creation. I believe that the LORD God will love every person He puts in Hell and He would hope that they would have accepted His mercy. I disciplined my children, and sometimes severely, but I still loved them, and love them still. I have heard parents standing outside the execution chamber in Huntsville, Texas where their child, a guilty murder, lay strapped to a gurney. With tearful eyes and a broken heart they mouthed, "I love you," and then audibly sang "Amazing Grace," as life slipped away.

We need not limit the love of our LORD my friend. **That exhale of His repentance must have hurt deeply**. He knew it was coming before He even started the first world. I knew that I was going to have to correct my child before I told them the requirement, but that did not ease the pain for me, I knew it was coming even before I told them not to do the very thing I knew they would, and did do, yet it hurt: How could I even fathom that pain my Lord felt at that moment, or question that He did not know this was coming from the very beginning. The Lord still loved each soul there, but hated what they were doing. I have said this before, but it need be said again; I thoroughly believe that the Lord God Jehovah will still love every soul that He has to put into everlasting hell: For God Is Love.

I remember a movie titled "Old Yeller," whose theme was the companionship of a farm boy and his big lop-eared dog. I will not try and discuss the whole movie, only to say it brought everyone in contact with their love and affection, one for the other.

The dog contracted Rabies and had to be destroyed. The climax was that the boy was the one who had to shoot Ole Yeller, which was a long and drawn out scene. I remember, even as a lad, tears filling my eyes when the theatre rang out with a thunderous shot. The bullet struck that snarling, foaming at the mouth beast. Then, the scenes which followed were of the boy and his friend piling large rocks

198

on top of the grave of his old companion.

That lad did not form Ole Yeller in the womb. Our LORD God **did form us,** and don't tell me He did not feel pain at that moment.

The LORD God may hate what we are doing, what we have become, but precious believer, He will always love us. We can run away from Him; He will not chase us any more than the father of the prodigal son chased after him; however, if that boy had a cell phone and called him and asked if he could come home, that father would have gone and brought him out of that sin and put a new robe upon his back and a ring on his finger: So will our Father and His precious Son, our Savior. I know; been there: He did!

To further show that our Father doesn't leave a possible hole in His efforts to save, and that He considers everything; we have discussed this Scripture before.

Ro 2:14 *for when the Gentiles, which have not the law, do by nature the things contained in the law, <u>these, having not the law, are a law unto themselves:</u>* (Emphasis is mine)

Our Father is doing all within His allowable limits to save our miserable hides, and He does not regret His plan, only the pain of carrying it out from time to time.

HOW SATAN MUST HAVE CHUCKLED

God is going to have to do it all over again, and He must have thought "<u>fourth time charms</u>." He caused the destruction of the first earth: He caused male and female to violate; He caused our parents to violate; He caused the elder, Cain, to murder his twin brother, and now, even though there is Seth descendants, Satan thinks he has corrupted the entire earth and God will have to destroy it again. But wait! What is it that the LORD sees? He sees this separated group who identify themselves with Him.

I am not going to go into this very deep, but I need to note here the <u>change of office</u>, and the constant appearance of the paragraph <u>sign</u>¶. I do not know what time frame is between each of the paragraphs, but I do feel there was a considerable amount of it.

Gen 6:8 ¶ *"But Noah found grace in the eyes of the LORD."*

Gen 6:9 ¶ *"These are the generations of Noah: Noah was a just man and perfect in his generations, and **Noah walked with the LORD.**"*(Emphasis is

The Layman

mine)

Gen 6:10 ¶ *"And Noah begat three sons, Shem, Ham, and Japheth."*

The LORD sees a man called Noah who was a just man and perfect in his generations.

"Noah walked with the LORD." Love always supplants pain, but brings a pain of its own.

Again quoting Josephus' **Antiquities of the Jews**, Chapter III, *"But Noah was very uneasy at what they did; and, being displeased at their conduct, persuaded them to change their dispositions and their acts for the better; but, seeing that the* (they) *did not yield to him, but were slaves to their wicked pleasures, he was afraid they would kill him, together with his wife and children, and those they had married; so he departed out of that land."*(Addition and Emphasis is mine)

We have a world that has gone amuck, if you will excuse the phrase. Gen 6:12 *"And **God** looked upon the earth, and, behold, it was corrupt; for all flesh had corrupted his way upon the earth."*(Emphasis is mine)

This is beautiful: Read this part of scripture and we will see the office of salvation and correctional action. In Gen 6:13, **God** told Noah that the end of all flesh had come before Him: Then in Gen 6:14, **God** told Noah to build an Ark; but it was **the LORD in Gen 7:1** who told Noah to enter the Ark; in Gen 7:16 **the LORD shut him in**; In Gen 8:1, **God** remembered Noah and stopped the flood; in Gen 8:16, **God** told Noah to leave the Ark; in Gen 8:20 Noah built an alter to the **LORD;** in Gen 9:1, **God** blessed Noah, and **God** established the rainbow covenant with Noah.
Look at the change of office:

The Godhead is acting here in the same unity as it did during the restoration of the "Void and Without Form".
1. **God** told Noah that the end of all flesh had come. Gen 6:13
2. **God** told Noah to build an Ark, Gen.6:14
3 The **LORD** told Noah to enter the Ark. Gen7:1
4. The **LORD** shut him in. Gen 7:12
5. **God** remembered Noah and stopped the flood. Gen 8:1
6. Noah built an altar to the **LORD**. Gen 8:20
7. **God** blessed Noah. Gen 9:1
8. **God** established the rainbow covenant with Noah. Gen 9:14

See His change of office? **God is in the offices of the**

200

lawgiver/corrector, and controls the universe and its happenings. **The Lord and Lord God are in the offices of God in mercy, protection, and saving grace**.

God is going to have Noah start a one hundred and twenty year evangelistic program. I want to say that there is a lot of discussion about the one hundred and twenty years referenced here. Gen 6:3 *And the LORD said, My spirit shall not always strive with man, for that he also is flesh: yet **his days shall be an hundred and twenty years**.* (Emphasis is mine)

There are four popular meanings for this verse.

First: God is going to destroy man in one hundred and twenty years.

Second: Noah was to try for one hundred and twenty years before the flood, to persuade men to repent.

Third: It took Noah that long to build the Ark.

Fourth: There will no longer be nine hundred year old men. Man will be limited to just one hundred and twenty years to live upon the earth.

I think all four are right. The longer man stays on earth, the greater the possibility he will lose most of his treasures or rewards in Heaven. I did not say salvation, I said treasures or rewards. Consider: James, 5:20 *"Let him know, that he which converteth the sinner from the error of his way shall save a soul from death, **and shall hide a multitude of sins**."* How about, Co 3:12, 15. *"12, **Now if any man build upon this foundation gold, silver, precious stones, wood, hay, stubble;** 13. Every man's work shall be made manifest: for the day shall declare it, because it shall be revealed by fire; and the fire shall try every man's work of what sort it is. 14. If any man's work abide which he hath built thereupon, he shall receive a reward. 15. If any man's work shall be burned, **he shall suffer loss**: but **he himself shall be saved**; yet so as by fire."* (Emphasis is mine) When I read this, I always seem to smell smoke. I often feel that I am loosing ground. I hope you are gaining my friend, I truly do.

The LORD is going to have Noah, his wife, and the three boys with their wives enter the ark. There is going to be animals of all species in the ark; by two of the unclean, and by sevens of the clean. We missed something else. Consider the love of our LORD; did we not realize that He also saved the serpents?

They are all going to be in that ark for one year and ten days. Scripture is so exact that we know that by Gen 7, Noah was six hundred and one year, one month, and twenty seven days old at that

201

time.

Do not miss this, and buzz right over it. I will tell everyone that I didn't, but will leave them dangling, because I do not know the answer either. Why does God tell us to the day, how old Noah was? I mean at first, one might say, "Who cares." Well I care, and know there is a divine reason for it, or God would not waste printer ink by mentioning it. Just put it away for later, maybe a midnight snack sometime. I love this old Book, it is so exacting. There is something which to most would not mean much, but to me and my mind it is significant. Scripture tells us the age of Noah. Our Father knows we are prone to worship the created, rather than the creator. Note, not the years or months, but note the number of days. If Scripture said it was 28 days, we would say it was in February; if Scripture said it was 29 days we would pin it down to leap year; if Scripture said 30 days we would say it was one of four months, and finally if it said 31, we would pin it down to the remaining seven

Boy can anyone imagine the aroma of that ark? Knowing that the ark was seventy five feet wide, forty five feet tall, and four hundred fifty feet long, does not, will not, and has not, explained how Noah was able to get all those animals into the ark, even though I feel they were all calves, lambs, cubs chicks…etc. I am **not** talking about space. Can we imagine the hunting party it took, or imagine the effort it took to get them to cooperate and go inside?

I have cattle: I had one bull and there were times that I was tempted to take a gun and blow his brains out, drag him to the packers and thoroughly enjoy to the fullest the resulting steaks. If I sold that bull for five dollars a pound, and he was approaching two thousand pounds, I would not come out ahead. If Noah had to load that bull on his own power, he would still be there; however, I really do not think that Noah had to form a hunting party at all. Within all reason, even though it is not told us in Scripture, the Lord had a hand in all that. All Noah had to do is just say come here, and get in there.

I THINK MAN COULD TALK TO ANIMALS

Ok! You can stop laughing now. I really have not lost my mind. At this point I well imagine some are rolling their eyes to the ceiling and thinking all my credibility has gone out the window.

Well let me ask a question. How does one explain, Gen 3:1, 2? "**1**. *Now the* **serpent** *was more subtil than any* **beast** *of the field which the*

202

LORD *God had made. And he **SAID** <u>unto the</u> **Woman**, Yea, hath God said, Ye shall not eat of every tree of the garden?* **2.** *And the Woman **SAID** <u>unto the</u> <u>**serpent**</u>, We may eat of the fruit of the trees of the garden :"*(Emphasis is mine)

I am still waiting. The **serpent was a beast, and talked** to the Woman, and the **Woman** (human) **talked** to the serpent. That is the way I read the Bible

Noah told the animals, "Get your hides into the boat." That is all that I make of it because later we read that when the ark is parked in this mysterious place that mankind cannot find today, God says, Gen 9:2 *"And the **fear of you and the dread of you** shall be upon every beast of the earth, and upon every fowl of the air, upon all that moveth upon the earth, and upon all the fishes of the sea; **into your hand are they delivered**."*(Emphasis is mine) Animals are now afraid of man, and I think the ability to communicate between them was lost.

I am glad that animals are afraid of man. That bull of mine could have stomped me into dust should he not be afraid. All I had to do is walk towards him and he took off like I had some magical power: Know what? I do. It is a God given fear and dread, and that is pure magic.

Another quick example, if I may. Nu 22:28-31. *"**(28)**. And the LORD opened the mouth of **the ass**, and she **said** unto Balaam, What have I done unto thee, that thou hast smitten me these three times?* **(29)**. *And Balaam **said** unto the **ass**, Because thou hast mocked me: I would there were a sword in mine hand, for now would I kill thee.* **(30)**. *And the **ass said** unto Balaam, Am not I thine ass, upon which thou hast ridden ever since I was thine unto this day? was I ever wont to do so unto thee? And **he said**,* Nay. **(31)**. *Then the LORD opened the eyes of Balaam, and he saw the angel of the LORD standing in the way, and **his** sword drawn in **his** hand: and he bowed down his head, and fell flat on his face."*(Emphasis is mine)

There are many things in God's Word which we pass over because in our minds they are but "Fairy Tales." We are so prone to say, "Well a lot of things happened, WAY BACK THEN." Friend read the Word and in faith accept it. If we have ever dealt with animals we all will have to admit that they know more about us than we know of them. I would have all to notice that the <u>gender of the Angel</u> is again called out as "**his.**"

I find it fitting to reemphasize this again: Gen 9:1 *"And **God** blessed Noah and his sons, and said unto them, Be <u>fruitful</u>, and <u>multiply</u>, and <u>**replenish the earth**</u>."*(Emphasis is mine) It is <u>never told</u> to Adam by the LORD God that he is to replenish the earth. In fact it is <u>never told</u> <u>that Adam</u> is to fill the earth. It is told to the fish to fill the waters and fowl to multiply in the earth, <u>but</u> none of this is told <u>to Adam</u>. It is told to male and female of Gen 1, that they are to **replenish the earth,** <u>but</u> <u>not to Adam.</u>

After the flood there is a new Replenishment of man and a new replenishment of the earth. There is a "genetic squeeze" that has taken place. Genetic science, using MtDNA to backtrack man's existence, found during the attempt to attest that all population derived from a single ancestor in Africa, **found clear evidence that a population squeeze had to occur about five thousand years ago.** Isn't science wonderful? <u>**Good science that is.**</u>

Now there are those in research that will say that the existence of man is much older than ten thousand years. Remember the "squeeze" which was discussed? Well "genetic science," to support their time line, do not allow for four families at the time of the flood. The reason is that if they did, they would see that modern man could not have been here over **ten thousand years**; However, by saying that the "squeeze" occurred with a population of thousands, they can then justify the 500,000 to 600,000 years.

REBELLION

Now at this time mankind starts out to supplant the God of Heaven. It seems the big problem was that every one spoke the same tongue. I am not sure we are not again becoming of one language and one speech. Our language is the dollar, and since the English (well Americans anyway) are too lazy to learn other languages, the world little by little is turning to the English, and the language of the dollar; however, this I feel is about to change to a world currency.

Our loving LORD God looked down and saw that mankind was once again going astray. He noted the tower which mankind was building to make a name for all the peoples.

Now there are some that feel that his tower was built in case another flood came. If that were true, they sure had an air head for an architect. No one could build a tower 29,028 feet tall. It is felt by some the tower was for stellar worship. But let's look at the Scripture account here.

Gen 11: 1-4. "**(1)**. *And the whole earth was of one language, and of one speech.* **(2)**. *And it came to pass, as they journeyed **from the East**, that they found* *a plain in the land of Shinar;* "*and they dwelt there.* (That would be from modern Turkey I assume, and note the mention of yet another land; Shinar.) (**3**), "*And they said one to another, Go to, let us make brick, and burn them thoroughly. And they had brick for stone, and slime had they for mortar.* (**4**), *And they said, Go to, let us build us a city and a tower,* **whose top may reach unto heaven**; *and let us make us a name, lest we be scattered abroad upon the face of the whole earth.*"(Emphasis is mine)

The city of Babylon was founded by Nimrod in Shinar where it is supposed to have been in the northern part of Mesopotamia.

It is no doubt that Noah's sons and their wives had learned, from the past population many things. These black arts were passed down from generation to generation...etc. They had the written language, and Josephus tells us that there were writings which came through the flood. There were columns with inscriptions upon them which the people used to start the evil that was present in the pre-diluvium world, all over again.

It seems evident that they were not trying to protect against a flood when they built the tower to reach into heaven. Its purpose was to try and recapture some of the dark arts which were practiced before the flood. We know that there were writings of scrolls which came through the flood because of the preservation of the book of Enoch which was written prior to the flood. It is thought by Josephus that Enoch's writings were buried beneath one such column, which undoubtedly would have bore inscriptions of the 'dark' arts, and possibly the past. How the book of Enoch survived is otherwise not known, but that it did is evident by its availability today, and was known at the time of Christ.

Jude 1:14 "*And Enoch also, the seventh from Adam, prophesied of these, saying, Behold, the Lord cometh with ten thousands of his saints*". See? Who missed that? Enoch did not say angels he said "**His saints.**" Angels are not saints. Saints are born again believers-Us! One other point some have caught. How did Enoch know of salvation? I don't know, but isn't it a wonderful puzzle?

Scripture indicates that these forbidden arts were an early practice and can be found even after the flood.

De 17:2 "*If there be found among you, within any of thy gates which the LORD thy God giveth thee, man or woman, that hath* **wrought wickedness** *in the sight of the LORD thy God, in transgressing his covenant,*"

De 17:3 "*And hath gone and* **served other gods**, *and worshipped them,*

either the sun, or moon, or any of the host of heaven, which I have not commanded;"
De 17:4 *"And it be told thee, and thou hast heard of it, and enquired diligently, and, behold, it be true, and the thing certain, that such abomination is wrought in Israel:"*
De 17:5 *"Then shalt thou bring forth that man or that woman, which have committed that wicked thing, unto thy gates, even that man or that woman, and shalt stone them with stones, till they die."* (Emphasis is mine)

This is the reason when someone wants to "give me a reading", I tell them, and not too politely either I might add, to go jump off a cliff. I had this woman who lived behind me when I was in El Paso, who would always ask me, to give her, the date and time I was born. She wanted to tell me my future. I would tell her to jump in the river or such. Finally one day I told her, "Look! I do not want any of your astrology. **I believe in the one who made the stars, not the stars.**" Know what? That didn't stop her from seeking the information? Oh that we as Christians were as fervent in spreading the Gospel. This woman did not do this to harass me; she liked me and my wife. She honestly was trying to do something that she thoroughly believed in. **Oh; that I had that fervency of witness.**

This now takes us into the final phase of God's, the LORD God's and the Holy Spirit's preparation of the earth which lays the foundation for man's ultimate salvation, or his rebellious denial and loss.

There will be some that will be hesitant to admit this kind of false god worship existed and that it flourished then, after Babel, and even today. Perhaps they should read, **"Earths Earliest Ages"** by G.H. Pember/Fleming H. Revell. Consider this: The fact that these dark arts had penetrated "religion" is factually explained in the reference previously given: **"The Two Babylons"** by Alexander Hislop/Loizeaux Brothers.

And a quote from, Donald Grey Barnhouse: **"The Invisible War"** Zonderman Publishing, should suffice here.

"There is not armistice in this invisible war. What may appear to be only a skirmish may in reality be a major engagement. The importance of a spiritual battle is not to be measured by the number of troops engaged but by the principles involved, and above all by the exhibition of another phase of the impotence of any will that is not the will of God."

A world divided:

Gen 11:5 *"And the LORD came down to see the city and the tower, which the children of men builded."*

Gen 11:6 *"And the LORD said, Behold, the people is one, and they have all one language; and this they begin to do: and now nothing will be restrained from them, which they have imagined to do."*

Gen 11:7 *"Go to, let us go down, and there confound their language, that they may not understand one another's speech."*

Gen 11:8 *"So the LORD scattered them* **abroad** *from thence upon the face of* **all** *the earth: and they left off to build the city."*

Gen 11:9 *"Therefore is the name of it called Babel; because the LORD did there confound the language of all the earth: and from thence did the LORD scatter them* **abroad** *upon the face of* **all** *the earth."* (Emphasis is mine)

We are now going to see a world divided to "The Four Corners" of the globe. I know that I cover the next chapter on "Reorganization" rather rapidly, but to do justice to it would get very deep into geology and strata formations that I would be blowing smoke if I were to try. The important point to make is that our Father is not punishing these people here, not at all; no one is destroyed here. It is for this reason that the office is changed to the saving LORD. You see, our Father is giving mankind every chance to find Him and His love. Do we think that all this is being shot from the hip? Look at this. Mt 25:34 *Then shall the King say unto them on his right hand, Come, ye blessed of my Father, inherit the kingdom* **prepared** *for you* **from the foundation of the world**: (Emphasis is mine.)

Precious ones, until we are able to visualize the Lord God as something more tangible than a "Spook," we will never be able to believe. For many, what we have just covered is more of a "Fairy-Tale" than reality. It is something that happened, sometime, to someone, and doesn't apply to me at all: not true precious, it is for **both of us** that all Scripture has been written.

"What a real spiritual awakening does
is to take Jesus Christ out of the realm of "religion"
and into the world of reality.
It makes people look at themselves honestly,
stripped of their usual protective coloring."

David Jeremiah
REORGANIZATION

I think at one time the whole world was one continent, Pangaea if you please (see Figure 3 on Pg 210). I must again break the chain of thought to interject that the term "Pangaea" is man's term. What the whole planet was called is known, and it was known by the name **"earth"** because that is what God called it in Gen 1:10 *"And God called the dry land(X04) Earth; and the gathering together of the waters called he Seas: and God saw that it was good."* I have placed the term "Pangaea" within the text, again to show, perhaps, a sequence to the work. It is not my attempt to designate the earth as such; however, I am again using man's terms so that some may use it to do further research.

There are two subjects here.

One subject everyone knows, and that is the dividing of the earth's speech, but the second one is the "mental buzz"; *"scattered them abroad upon the face of all the earth."* When God changed their speech, it is believed by some, He divided the people of course, but they believe He divided the earth at the same time: some believe the land was divided over millions of years, and finally, some believe it happened at the time of the flood. We will explore the subject from two angles.

First Speech:

Even evolutionists would be hard pressed to determine why so many languages are in the world. It is my opinion that they see their trap and are being still about it until my little professor steps forward to make a fool of himself with another wild theory, to later, become fact.

If we all came from one genius, and the world was to slowly gain understanding, then everyone became dispersed from this ignorant state, evolutionist would toot it to the highest hills because everyone would still speak the same language. That is not what has happened with our languages.

Gen 11:9 *"Therefore is the name of it called **Babel**; because the LORD did there **confound the language of all the earth...**"* (Emphasis is mine) I wish I were smart enough to even speak more than one language listed in the Ethnologue. (The Ethnologue is a catalogue of more than 6,800 languages spoken in 228 countries.) All I can say is that <u>when God does something, he does it right</u>. The amazing thing is what is again mostly overlooked. 6,800 languages divided by 228 countries, means that there is an average of over 28 languages per country. If that isn't Babel, I don't know Babel when I hear it.

Second, the Division:

Gen 11:9 *"... and from thence did the LORD <u>scatter them abroad upon the face of all the earth</u>."* (Emphasis is mine)

Today we have Continents, Islands, and the Polar regions. When God divided the tongues; He did one of two things. I want to add here, **I am presenting to the reader different views of Biblical events which parallel earthly occurrences**. The babbling of the tongues we know; however, let me give my thoughts on the division of the earth.

1. When the flood was coming upon the earth, God opened the fountains of the deep. Gen 7:11 *"In the six hundredth year of Noah's life, in the second month, the seventeenth day of the month, the same day were all the fountains of the great deep broken up, and the windows of heaven were opened."*

Some feel that God could have divided the earth at the time of **the flood,** and there is good evidence that this is when, what is called the Catastrophic Platonic movement is thought by some to be predominant

2. There are those that are of the opinion that the Scriptures clearly indicate that the earth was divided both physically as well as the speech **at the time of Babel.** They support that by Gen 10:25 *"And unto Eber were born two sons: the name of one was Peleg; for **in his days was the earth divided**; and his brother's name was Joktan."* (Emphasis is mine) Based upon this Scripture, they see the earth as well as people divided then.

In theory some feel God could well have divided the physical earth at this time. He could have babbled the tongues of man, and divided the, then, earth, and man was surfboarder to where ever He wanted him.

3. There are those who theorize that the earth was **divided over millions of years,** and that continents are still moving today, which they certainly are, and God simply had man to migrate over the face of the earth at the time of Babel.

We discussed earlier about using the single term "the dry land" and noted that it could be used as noting a single mass or the term could be generic in that it could well be in reference to all the lands.

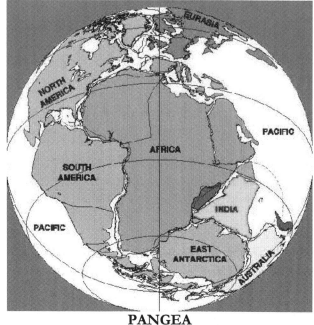

PANGEA
Figure 3

Let me present some interesting theories about what is ultimately the start of "The continental fit" theory, which first started with the **creationist**, Antonio Snider, who **in 1859** was the first to propose horizontal movement of continents, catastrophically, during the flood of Genesis.

CONTINENTAL DRIFT

Before the 1960s, it was the opinion of most geologists that the continents were stationary, and for the most part they believed that they had never moved. A handful; However, promoted the notion that the continents had moved, and hence the term continental drift was born, but they were accused by the **majority** of the scientific community, as indulging in fantasy. Today; However, that opinion has reversed, and plate tectonics incorporating **continental drift, is the ruling theory.**

Know why science tried to dismiss it as fantasy? It was because the "**creationist**," Antonio Snider, who in 1859 first proposed horizontal movement of continents and that it occurred rapidly or catastrophically during the Genesis flood. **Science is hard pressed** to follow anything a believer says, **and the clergy is just as hard pressed** to believe science. It was the statements of Ge 1:9, 10; about the gathering together of the seas in one place, which implies there was **one land mass**, which influenced Antonio Snider's thinking.

Geologists, over the years have put forward several lines of evidence that the continents were once joined together and have moved apart. This is to include **the fit of the continents, Correlation of fossil types across ocean basins,** and the **striped pattern of magnetic reversals** parallel to mid-ocean floor rifts. These patterns are found in the volcanic rock formed along the rifts, implying seafloor spreading along the rifts. And finally, the seismic observations interpreted as slabs of **former ocean floor now located inside the earth**. In other words some of the ocean flooring has been shoved down deep into the earth. This being the case, we would be hard pressed to find any **artifacts left from the other side of the "Void and Without Form" world,** to the flood.

PLATE TECTONICS

The current theory that incorporates seafloor spreading and continental drift is known as "plate tectonics." The principles of the plate tectonic **theory** may be stated as follows: *"The earth's surface consists of a jigsaw of rigid plates, each plate moving relative to adjacent plates".*

Deformation occurs at the edges of the plates, I am told, by three types of horizontal motion: **extension; transform faulting,** and **compression.**

1. Transform faulting occurs where one plate slips horizontally past another (Like sliding ones back against a wall).

2. Compression deformation occurs when one plate subducts beneath another, or when the collision causes one to push upwards while the other dives beneath. The upper plate will form landmarks such as <u>mountain ridges</u> throughout the world. Some of these get really hot and a volcano forms above it. One such example is in Central America, and the 76 volcanoes of Indonesia.

3. Extension (Seafloor spreading): Is when two plates move apart and lava extrudes beneath them. I saw one of these on a program once, and they showed where the whole area had moved apart, and there were cubic miles of lava coming up to fill the void. I have always wondered if something is coming up here where is it going down, there. I will save that for another day. One fact which I found was that there was an estimated 20 cubic Kilometers of lava filling these gaps each year.

At the time of cooling, some of the rocks' minerals are affected by the earth's magnetic field and acquire magnetism from that magnetic field. This becomes a recording of the field's direction at the time it cooled. If the seafloor were to spread in a slow and continuous "drift", the ocean floor should possess a smooth and even directional magnetic signature of each of the reversals. Indeed, the "zebra striped" (This is a term used which describes what we see when we put a piece of paper over a magnet and sprinkle iron dust on top of it.) pattern of linear smooth "magnetic anomalies" are parallel to the mid-ocean ridge crest and has been recorded in many areas.

PROBLEMS FOR A GRADUAL MOVEMENT

While the zebra-stripe pattern **has been confirmed**, drilling through the basalt adjacent to the ridges has shown that the neat pattern recorded by dragging a magnetometer above the ridge is not present when the rock is actually sampled. When a test hole is bored into the plates and a magnetometer is lowered into it, the magnetic polarity changes in patches down the holes, with no consistent pattern with depth. This condition would be expected with rapid formation of the basalt, in conjunction with rapid field reversal. If this had been a slow and gradual formation such would not be the case, the magnetometer would have recorded even magnetic forces.

The article which I read averred that a Physicist Dr. Russell Humphreys predicted, *"that if a rapid Plate Tectonics was true then evidence for rapid field reversals would be found in lava flows which were thin enough to cool in a few weeks."* He, as I am lead to believe, suggested that such rapid reversals could have happened during Noah's flood. **Such evidence for rapid reversals as he predicted,** was later found by the respected researchers Coe and Prévot. Their later work confirmed these findings and showed that the magnetic reversals were **"astonishingly rapid."**

Evidence indicates that the continents have moved apart in the past, but the real question is, if we use today's movement that I have been given, of one inch or more per year, can we extrapolate that far back in time? Using an estimated 2,500 miles of the Atlantic; it would take an estimated 1,500,000,000 years at the earliest. One might say "Well so what?" Well let's ask a question:

Have these people not heard of erosion? If it took that long to push up mountains, they would have been reduced, over the years to ant hills, before we even came upon the scene.

A Biblical View

I cannot find anywhere in the Bible where it indicates continental drift, unless of course we again consider Gen 10:25 *"And unto Eber were born two sons: the name of one was Peleg; for **in his days was the earth divided**; and his brother's name was Joktan."*(Emphasis is mine) I think this could speak of that time, but there would be another theory to understand.

Consider the passage in Genesis that we have already covered, but did not emphasize this point. It indicates that there was one land mass and one large sea. Gen 1:9 *"And God said, Let the waters under the heaven be gathered together **unto one place**, and let **the dry land** appear: and it was so. Gen 1:10 And God called the dry land Earth; and the gathering together of the waters called he Seas: and God saw that it was good."*(Emphasis is mine)

I know one will say "Yeah! It says the dry land which looks like He is saying one land all right, but what about when He uses the term seas?"

Well if we were surrounded by a sea, wouldn't we say we had a North Sea, a South Sea, an East Sea and a West Sea?

This does not mean that the earth was divided at the time of the flood, and it certainly does not mean that it was divided at the time of Babel. It does mean that there are two predominant theories:

One is that the earth slowly drifted apart.

Two is that the land catastrophically moved apart:

    1. at the flood
    2. at Babel

SEPARATION AT THE TIME OF BABEL

I have studied a couple of works which state that after the flood the earth was saturated. The fountains of the deep were still there, but if the continents were to start to drift at any time, they could actually surf across the expanse they are now separated by, and could do so within a relative short span of time. If I am not mistaken, both approaches, that is, the division occurring at the flood, and the other occurring at the time of Babel, are termed as "Catastrophic Plate Tectonics." I do know that the same science and terminology is used for both theories. When one has studied tectonics and he is convinced, that this event happened at Babel, he will use the same analogy as those who profess its happening at the time of the flood. To be perfectly honest, the continents could have separated before the Phase II Creation II, or knowing that the land was submerged until God let it appear, it would have been water logged, and could have separated then. We will examine some of the theories presented by minds greater than mine, but doing so I say that we should keep in mind that any one could, in theory, have happened at either time. I lean toward the Babel theory because of the part in Scripture which says **"in his days was the earth divided"**, plus, **Gen 11:9 "... and from thence did the LORD scatter them abroad upon the face of all the earth."** (Emphasis is mine)

When we use that term abroad today, it means someone is on the other continent. That is, "they have gone abroad." Then again to be honest, none of us knows. God could have divided the earth at the time of the flood, or before, and then picked the people up and slammed their hides down where ever He wanted to later. One thing we all agree upon, is that we must never loose sigh of the fact, that no matter what, or when it happened, it had the nod of approval from our Father.

SEPARATION AT THE TIME OF THE FLOOD

I have never met this gentleman, but would like to someday; however, Dr. John Baumgardner, working at **the Los Alamos National Laboratories (New Mexico)**, has used its supercomputers to model processes in the earth's mantle to show that **tectonic plate movement could have occurred very rapidly, and "spontaneously."** This concept is known as **Catastrophic Plate Tectonics.** As I understand it, **Dr. Baumgardner, is a creational scientist, and is acknowledged as having developed the world's best 3-D super-computer model of plate tectonics.** I have tried to represent articles found on the internet by this gentleman, and truly trust I have done him the justice he duly deserves: based upon that, the following is presented.

CATASTROPHIC PLATE TECTONICS

The model proposed by Dr. Baumgardner begins with a **pre-flood super-continent** and with the flood covering the earth, and the process, as he describes would start with, *"the cold and dense ocean floor beginning to sink into the softer, less dense mantle beneath. The friction from this sinking movement would cause enormous heat to be generated, especially around the edges, which would soften as the adjacent mantle material moved against it, making it less resistant to the sinking of the ocean floor. The edges sink would then become faster, which would drag the rest of the ocean floor along. Faster and faster movement would also create more friction and heat in the surrounding mantle. This would reduce its resistance further and so the ocean floor moves even faster. This chain reaction would continue until at its peak, thermal runaway instability would have allowed for subduction to gain speed of meters-per-second, and is called* **runaway subduction**. *Thus, crustal spreading zones would rapidly extend along cracks in the ocean floor for some 6,000 miles where the splitting was occurring. Hot material displaced by the sub ducting slabs would well up on the ocean floor, and this hot mantle material would vaporize copious amounts of ocean water, producing a linear geyser of superheated steam along the whole length of the spreading centers."* (Emphasis is mine)

"This steam would disperse, condensing in the atmosphere to fall as intense global rain ("and the flood-gates of heaven were opened" Genesis 7:11). This along with the dense cloud cover already suspended in the atmosphere, could account for the rain persisting for 40 days and 40 nights. (Genesis 7:12)."

Perhaps I should have hidden that data, in that it tears my theory apart for separation at Babel.

Dr. Baumgardner's catastrophic plate tectonics model is able to explain more geological data than the conventional plate tectonics model with its many millions of years. For example, he continues *"rapid subduction of the pre-flood ocean floor into the mantle would result in a new ocean floor that is dramatically hotter, especially in the upper 60 miles, the new ocean floor being hotter is of lower density and therefore rises 3,000 to 6,000 feet higher and caused a* **dramatic rise in global sea level**. *This higher sea level would then flood the continental surfaces and make tremendous disturbances of sedimentary deposits. The flood would then deposit large areas of sedimentary deposits on top of the normally high-standing continents. The Grand Canyon is one such area of unexplained sedimentary deposit and provides a spectacular window into the amazing layers of sediment which is the character of these sediment deposits that in many cases continue uninterrupted for more than 600 miles. Uniformitarian ("slow* *and gradual") plate tectonics simply would not account for such thick Continental sediment sequences. Gradual movement as I have indicated before does not stir up such deposits."*(Emphasis is mine)

Dr. Baumgardner's model provides a logical approach to the division of the earth, and it explains how the plates could move quickly, and in his determination, would take only a few months. The model also predicts that little or no movement would be measurable between plates today, because the movement would have come almost to a standstill when the entire pre-flood ocean floor was sub ducted. It would be as if God moved the continents, and then put a plug in between to keep them there. From this we would also expect the trenches adjacent to subduction zones today to be filled with undisturbed late-flood and post-flood sediments, just as we in fact observe. I understand that parts of the parameters of Dr. Baumgardner's mantle modeling have been independently duplicated and thus found valid by others of this discipline.

Furthermore, Dr. Baumgardner's modeling predicts, *"that because this thermal runaway subduction of cold ocean floor crystal slabs occurred relatively recently, about 5,000 or so years ago, those slabs would not have had sufficient time to be fully assimilated into the surrounding mantle."*

It is most interesting that evidence for such unassimilated relatively cold slabs has been found in seismic studies.

Water abatement from the earth: Dr. Baumgardner's model also provides a mechanism for retreat of the flood waters.

Ps 104:6 *"Thou coveredst it with the deep as with a garment: the waters stood above the mountains."*

Ps 104:7 *"At thy rebuke they fled; at the voice of thy thunder they hasted away."*

Ps 104:8 *"They go up by the mountains; they go down by the valleys unto the place which thou hast founded for them."*

Ps 104:9 *"Thou hast set a bound that they may not pass over; that they turn not again to cover the earth."*

Gen 8:3 *'And the waters returned from off the earth continually: and after the end of the hundred and fifty days the waters were abated.'*

I used both scriptures to make it clear that it really means that they went back to where they came from. They went in an orderly and continual fashion, and that they were locked in so that they could not come back and repeat the same flood.

We discussed the vast quantities of water that would be necessary to cover Mt. Everest. Considering the Platonic Theories, it may be well assumed that the mountains that we now see were not there at present heights at all. The movements of the continental shelf and **the associated subduction which would occur may allow us to postulate that ground level was more relative to the sea shore than we see today.** By relative to the sea shore, one could easily surmise that with the movement of continents, and their collisions, the geography we see today could be vastly different than they were then. There is no question if the drift occurred; the only real question still arises:

When did this occur? I believe that these gentlemen are correct in their models, and in their explanations; However, I still do not put a time on it. I cannot quote Scripture as pinpointing the time. I know Scripture says "in those days the earth was divided," but we cannot definitively state whether that means the populace and the physical earth, or just the scattering of the people.

There are questions this brings forth, and I submit them just to make all wonder, as I do. However; everyone must settle it in their minds, but considering that all mankind was scattered into cells of language, and geographically separated along with their associated animals, then the earth being scattering at Babel, answers the question of all the earth being repopulated, animal diffusions, and differing cultures being really based upon the same beliefs. Add to this the phenomenon such as the pyramids of South America and Egypt and parallel accounts of the flood on every continent on earth; one has a very strong case for a **Babel division of the people** if not the lands also at that time.

If the waters all returned to their proper place, then catastrophic Platonic's, could have happened as both explanations have said, and at any time. It is all interesting: Again, the reader must study and let the Lord God make the call. I just love providing the thread, even if we never stitch all things together. There is another phenomenon that is addressed by this drift.

ENIGMAS

Continental separation solves apparent geological enigmas. We have covered this before, but for a moment lets cover it again because it is certainly an enigma. Have we ever wondered why the pyramids were in South America and Egypt? Why the story of Atlantis is on

217

both continents and some islands? Why the similar religious rites, even though they are pagan, are found almost worldwide? Why the account of the flood is in so many languages and cultures? Have we ever wondered about the different scientific skills in observation of the heavens and why they are found on different continents? I do believe that the Indians either migrated across a land mass, or God put him along with whatever other group He wanted, on a position of land which He (God) chose.

I think He did the same with every race on the face of the earth. It is true some were evidentially dumber than others. No one can deny the intelligence of the Inca's; Not only those but also the Maya's, or the Egyptians and Ethiopian's. Others were of a slower intellect and I will be politically correct and omit further comment.

Let me relate something that started after Babel and ended about the time Cortes ravished Mexico. It is a civilization called the Maya. The Maya are probably the best-known of the classical civilizations of Mesoamerica, originating in the Yucatan around 2600 B.C., they rose to prominence around A.D. 250 in present-day southern Mexico. They were later, somewhere around the sixteenth century, attacked by Cortes who destroyed much of the Maya historical records. The Maya calendar, in its final form, probably dates from about the 1st century B.C., and may originate with the Olmec civilization. The calendar is extremely accurate, and the calculations of the Maya priests were so precise that their calendar correction is 10,000th of a day more exact than our standard calendar of today.

One of the most important roles of the calendar was not to fix dates accurately in time, but to correlate the actions of Maya rulers to historic and mythological events. The calendar was also used to mark the time of past and future happenings. Some Maya monuments, for example, record the dates of events 90 million years ago, while others predict events that will take place 3,000 years into the future. Since that calendar was designed 1,000 BC, that would covering events which should occur in this 21st century. It is that information which has caused the craze that the end of the world will come in 2012.

The Maya were able without the use of the Hubble Space Telescope, to track and predict the seasons through observation of the visible stars and planets. Their year used 20-day months, and had two calendar years: the 260-day Sacred Round, or tzolkin, and the 365-day Vague Year, or haab, was 365.242 days in length.

A most interesting thing is that the Maya was able to detect, predict, and track the wobble of the earth, which astronomers term the anomaly, a "cartioid loop." This is a wobble of the earth where the poles move in relation to our solar system, and re-occurs every 7.1 years.

When one looks at the world through the eyes of the Bible, there are wonders that fill the heart and soul. There are also wonders which one should not delve into, and star worship is one of them. The Maya had each month named for a different god. If a child was born during one of these months, they were convinced that the child's life would be directly affected the rest of their lives by, that good, that bad, or that evil god. Sounds like the Zodiac; don't we think?

I would, again, invite the reader to obtain a copy of "**The Two Babylon's**" by Hislop, published by Loizeaux Brothers. In this work are fascinating facts of indisputable evidence of religious deities, structures, and time tables which are mirror images of those found across the vast oceans?

One particular fascinating thing are other cultures account of the flood and that their world started by the procreation of his family. It does not call Noah by his Biblical name, but the facts are so plain as to be, almost, indisputable.

The separation of the one land mass is the reason that dinosaurs are found in different locals on earth and is not because there were on different continents; they were on the same continent. Just stop and think: Today alligators are not found in Alaska, Polar bears are not found in Florida. Different parts of our world support different species. So too, did the land mass of that time. As each species became extinct, because of the time table built within their DNA, a collision with a wayward object from space, Divine judgment, or whatever, they simply lay down and were covered up by the earth's own natural forces. Afterward came "Void and Without Form," and they were covered by the whole earth being inundated and remained so during the Phase II Creation II. When the flood came I suppose some rose, some sank, and some were covered by many feet of more sediment to remain there for discovery in distant future.

When the division of the earth came, and the earth was physically divided, they were moved, only to remain covered by the sedimentary layers caused by the flood, and the natural forces designed by God. It also explains the amazing similarities of sedimentary layers in the <u>Northeastern United States to those in Britain</u>. It also explains

219

the <u>absence of those same layers</u> in the intervening North Atlantic Ocean basin, as well as the <u>similarities in the geology</u> of parts of Australia with South Africa, India, and Antarctica. How else could these similarities exist without a catastrophic separation?

The catastrophic plate tectonics model includes these explanatory elements, and accounts for widespread <u>massive flooding and catastrophic geological processes on the continents</u>.

The Bible is silent about plate tectonics. It only gives us enough to maintain our weak faith. There are many creationists who believe that this concept is helpful in explaining earth's history. I have found that creationists are a different breed from evolutionist. Creationist call things outside the Bible, "Theory", and evolutionist call the entire Bible theory and all subjective data, "fact." Some creationists are still in the stage of trying to honestly prove what they have found so far, to be false: having failed to prove it false, they will then publish it as "Theory." Evolutionist will publish everything as fact with no proof.

There is admittedly much more to be gleaned from this old world. Perhaps our Father will allow us to delve a little deeper as time goes on, perhaps not. I know that someday when He shows us all, we will stand with red embarrassed faces and say "I should have seen that."

Some might say: "Well all that seems impossible. Who could ever believe all that to be true about the continents? If the continent were suddenly divided, think of the tidal wave such would cause." Assuming that it occurred after the flood, I guess they have a point. I agree if it happened during the flood there would be a tsunami, but with no land above water to break upon it would go unnoticed. Then one would say if it happened after the flood and at the time of Babel there might be a tsunami. Let's look at something that is equally puzzling.

*Jos 10:12 "Then spake Joshua to the LORD in the day when the LORD delivered up the Amorites before the children of Israel, and he said in the sight of Israel, Sun, **stand thou still** upon Gibeon; and thou, Moon, in the valley of Ajalon."*

*Jos 10:13 "**And the sun stood still**, and **the moon stayed**, until the people had avenged themselves upon their enemies. Is not this written in the book of Jasher? So the sun stood still in the midst of heaven, and hasted not to go down **about a whole day.**"*

Jos 10:14 "And there was no day like that before it or after it, that the LORD hearkened unto the voice of a man: for the LORD fought for Israel." (Emphasis is mine)

The earth would have stopped for <u>both the sun and moon to stand still</u>. What tsunami wave did that cause? Now I do not know how He got the moon to stand still because its motion is what keeps it in orbit about the earth, but He did.

I wait the day **when science will use Scripture** to guide their progress, and **our brethren will stop blinding the eye to reality. We of the faith** can not be absolutely right when we have nothing revealed in Scripture, **and science** can not be absolutely right when they have absolutely no evidence to support them.

I purely delight in what my Father has done upon this earth. I do not know "true love", but **I know of Him**, and love is what He really is. Oh! How I want to sit at His feet and have Him show me these wonders.

One assuring fact we can rest with, our Father has molded eternity for our salvation. That is the theme before the first star was ever lit, and He will not be denied His purpose.

Mt 25:21 *"His lord said unto him, Well done, [thou] good and faithful servant: thou hast been faithful over a few things, I will make thee ruler over many things: enter thou into the joy of thy lord."*

He is just so great!

"To understand the part of the Bible you don't understand,
Is to obey the part you do understand,
And before long you will begin to understand what you didn't
understand;

Understand?"

Adrian Rogers

GOD'S FOREKNOWLEDGE and MASTER PLAN

There had to be something done before the "Void and Without Form." There had to be something done before Cain and Abel. There had to be something done before Seth came upon the scene. There had to be something done before the flood. There had to be something done before Babel. There had to be something done before the patriarch Abraham. There had to be something done before the Exodus. There had to be something done before God became man. There has to be something done today.

Do I know why? No, not totally, my brethren; however, I do know that the cancer of sin has to be exposed and severely dealt with in each case. Someday we shall know all; someday we shall. We can only explore the past, we can try and figure out today, but we must place our future in His loving hands.

I am reminded of the pastor B.R. Laken who said **"*If God does not punish America for what we have become, He will owe an apology, to Sodom and Gomorra.*"** If only he were alive to see it today.

In Scripture it is told to us the proper method of purifying gold. I think God was doing that with the, "then", world as He is doing now with the one we know today. **God knew before He made the first creation, the final outcome.** This all follows a plan and purpose. Allow me to give a summarized list of our Biblical past, present, and future: forgive me for not doing the following, total justice.

1. There is a perfect heaven and apparent harmony between all present.
2. God creates the first heavens and earth.
3. There was evil in God's perfect heaven, and He heard it when one star began to sing off key.
4. There was a rebellion and Satan with his followers was kicked out.
5. The earth and its heavens are destroyed to a "Void and Without Form" condition.

6. There is a restoration with land, seas, the sky, plants, animals, and male and female with the "lets."

7. There is the personal forming of Adam, vegetation and animals. Then, the LORD God's command not to eat of the fruit, and then the cloning of Woman by the LORD God.

8. The fall of Woman and then Adam.

9. The LORD God promises salvation in the hidden phrase, "her seed."

11. Evil penetrates the first family with the murder of Abel.

13. Cain goes to Nod and parallel inhabitants begin, and they war between themselves.

14. The linage of Christ begins through Seth.

15. Angelic infiltration and subsequent adulterous sin.

16. Noah's family found to be righteous in his generation.

17. The flood and all but selected life destroyed.

18. God establishes His covenant with Noah and his sons.

19. Babel and sins return.

20. The division of the earth, and languages.

21. The establishment of God's covenant with Abraham.

22. The establishment of the covenant with Jacob (Israel).

23. The Commandments given to Moses and the children.

24. The judges, prophets and kings.

25. The linage of Christ through David, and back to Eve.

26. The coming of Jesus Christ.

27. The death of Jesus Christ.

28. The resurrection of Jesus Christ

29. The rapture of His church.

30. The tribulation.

31. The battle of Armageddon.

32. The Saints before the throne of Christ

33. The filling of Heaven and the wedding feast

34. Satan bound in prison for one thousand years

35. The Millennium reign of Christ.

36. Satan released and again deceives the nations.

37. God defeats Satan and his followers.

38. The LORD God sits on the Great White Throne and judges all not found in the Book of Life.

39. The filling of Hell.

40. A new perfect heaven and a new obedient earth.

The Layman

One has said, "What goes around comes around."

1. From the original heaven and earth, to a <u>"Void and Without Form"</u> earth (Gen 1:1).
2. To an replenished earth (Gen 1:2-Gen 6).
3. To a void earth (Gen 7).
4. To a replenished earth (Gen 9).
5. To a destroyed heaven and earth (Rev 21).
6. To a new heaven and a new earth: <u>void of what made it void</u> (Rev 22).

<u>How can someone not see God's plan in purging the impure, in order to save those who trust in Him</u>. I know it is there because the pattern is there; However, I could not fully put it in words for the entire world. Some things like the splendor of a sunset must be seen, the thrill of the first kiss on the cheek, each must be experienced, but can never be duplicated in phrases.

As he was once known, Lucifer for some unknown reason has a hate for anything pertaining to good. He was and still is instrumental in the fall of mankind. In the first earth, I am convinced that it was populated with dinosaurs, bipeds and possibly something very close to man: I, again, say that is my thoughts, supported only by what I reason.

Lucifer somehow caused the first earth to violate. I do not know if these first ones here were in sin, or if Lucifer just out of hate destroyed the then earth. It appears to me that Lucifer caused the male and female of the Phase II Creation to again violate, by becoming a **hunter/gatherer.**

When Adam and Woman came on the scene, Satan knew that our Father was going to, somehow, bring His creation back into harmony with Himself. Satan caused the serpent to tempt the weaker of the two. What relationship Satan had with, whatever the serpent was originally, is not known. The serpent causes Woman, through lustful envy, then Adam through love to violate, and God does not wipe them out. So God had to have another plan, and He had it from the beginning.

The twin boys come along, and Satan causes Cain to kill Able. Still God does not wipe Cain out, but drives him from His presence. Cain goes to the male and female group and causes them to further digress from God's wishes, because it seems <u>they start warfare</u>. Ge 4:23-24 "*And Lamech said unto his wives, Adah and Zillah, Hear my voice; ye wives of Lamech, hearken unto my speech: for I have slain a man to my wounding,*

224

and a young man to my hurt. If Cain shall be avenged sevenfold, truly Lamech seventy and sevenfold."

Adam knew his wife again, and Seth is born. Now we have Seth as the Great-Grandfather of our incarnate Lord and Savior.

From the flood to the separation of the races and languages of the people on earth, through the successes and failures of the Children of Israel, through the death, burial, and resurrection of our Savior, to the end of time as we know it, our Father has had it all planned out to the last dot and tittle.

He did it all to save us.

DR. J. V. McGee, the greatest Biblical expositor of my age, once said,

"If God were to take His hands off of me, I would turn and curse Him in five minutes, and so would you."

Take heed lest ye fall.

225

CONCLUSION

I have tried to bring to the surface what within my heart I feel is correct. Whether it is or not, only time will bear witness.

It would be my prayer that Godly men would offer proof, or Scriptural reproof, in comment to this work. There is so much I have not touched upon in this brief work; some will most likely provide further proof, some heartfelt rejection, but all to make a work for Him. It was said by Mr. Ziegler, **"silence is consent."**

The LORD God leaves open a myriad of unanswered questions about the many bony fragments found on this old world.

I do not say that the bony fragment which science calls "Cave Man" is in fact a Homo sapien. I don't know what my Father called him, I do believe in my heart that my Father called him something, and that this world was in existence for millenniums: then was catastrophically destroyed; sat in disarray for perhaps myriads of years, and God restored it to the pre-pre-Adamite state. I do not think one thing ever evolved, up or down, the "ladder" of life. There is a "pecking order" established by the LORD God, but there has never been an "evolutionary ladder."

Is the Neanderthal man the "male and female" of the restoration? I think this fits the time frame, but even though in this work I have put them in this sequence, and have used this name for sequence, I do not put a name upon Male and Female. Many discoveries have yet to be made, but we must realize that it will come only as our Father sees fit for us to find them. I do think that from what I presently know, this group of individuals falls correct in sequence with Scripture. There is one fundamental truth, **which must be understood: the Neanderthal man; the Cro-Magnon man, and Adam all existed**. No matter what the sequence, never! I repeat, NEVER lose sight of the fact that **our God made or approved everything no matter where, when, or what it may have been, or still is**. If there are answers, we cannot find them by ignoring the questions.

Was Cain really the Cro-Magnon man? No! But I believe his **procreated offspring were**. Again; I think that this genus certainly falls within the time frame of the sequence of restored events. **I do not think that Cain took his sister for a wife**, if he did, then brothers and sisters sure got along better than me and my sister ever did. Sorry about that, but if he had, I do not see why Scripture would not tell, or allude us to that.

I do think Cain started another race. Historians willingly attest to the fact that there were advances in the base of knowledge of mankind at the time of **Cro-Magnon man** which transcends explanation. Cain and his wife, then just seem to fade from history: this again, is consistent when we consider the time of flood. Our LORD God just does not tell us things, such as, where was Nod, what was the mark of Cain, and what became of the cities which were established? It would do well to note if Cain only had one son; **one does not make a city to be uninhabited**. There were people there, and they did not **all** come from the loins of Cain. The Neanderthal was not of Cain, but the Cro-Magnon was the procreated offspring of Cain and the Neanderthal. Cain got the Neanderthal out of caves and into tents, and cities.

I feel sadden in the face of evidence provided herein that it will do little in bringing the majority of **clergy** any closer to agreement than it will the majority of **evolutionary scientists** in seeing their error. This study is presented, and **backed by objective facts, with subjective analysis.**

I do think man had a period of time which was devoted to what we used to call in the military "a shake down." This is when they tested a man, an item or a unit for its worthiness. I feel the same was accomplished by our God in the original heaven and earth; However, in the case of God, He already knew what would and what would not stand the test of time. God had to allow the evil that was present within **each** created being to be revealed and be dealt with. That was consistent with the dethroning of Lucifer and his followers who wander the earth today, and for those reserved in chains, until judgment, who sinned by procreating with mankind before the flood.

The same revealing of sin can be seen with man, **he had both good and evil within him**; the actions of our parents prove that. And then the first conclusive evidence of it all came in the identities of Cain and Able.

Oh my brethren, President Roosevelt once said, *"Within every person lyeth a devil, the character of that person is what they do with him when he surfaces.*" If we do not know that, we are lying to ourselves, and are in dire need of soul searching.

After Cain is moved from the scene, "The generations of Adam" are covered as if there were no offspring preceding Seth. It is my opinion, that to cover Cain in the generations of Adam, would open a revealing door into the "male and female" of Gen 1. The world wasn't ready for all that, and perhaps it isn't now.

The flood which then gave a final purging of both the fallen angelic and mankind's dark natures is yet another period of purging and a "replenishing." Then of course there is the genetic squeeze in the occurrence of the flood. This is followed by the division of the earth and the languages, and from that point, there is the looking forward to the coming of our LORD to overcome both the rebellion of Lucifer, and mankind.

It is as if stages of culling the chaff from the wheat, is done from the very "In the beginning." In this case we can say that it started happening before time, and culling will cease only when our Precious Lord declares:

Re 10:6 "*And sware by him that liveth for ever and ever, who created heaven, and the things that therein are, and the earth, and the things that therein are, and the sea, and the things which are therein, that there should be time no longer:*"

Can I **prove** any of this? **No! I just believe it is**, but cannot tell why this work has burned a hole in my soul for years and has become so important to put forth. Do I really believe it? Would I be so foolish to mess with my Father's Word? I do not think what I have presented is anything but the honest result of soul searching of scientific data, and the Scriptures for answers. They are answers which I feel in clear conscience to be correct, or at worse, parallel to His truth.

It is for His glory, and His kingdom that we each strive to bring Him glory. God does not need any of us to help Him. As a father enjoys helping his children to overcoming the trials by his assistance, so does my Father help, if not uphold me. I Love Him and think He is just the most wonderful thing that ever happened to me, and without His constant help, I would have a very scary future.

My precious brethren, know His love, feel His love, and understand His determination to save us all. His hands are what sustain our rotten attempts at perfection.

AS I SEE IT

I know that this work is new to most. I also know of some of the books which have been published supporting the theory that each day in creation was tens-of-thousands of years long, and others who support the 24/7 approach. I have tried in as forthright a manner to present both sides of the theory. May I give but one more example, which I think will at least let everyone know where I stand on the matter? I will do this with a family, and will not name them. I will place myself within this family for continuity and so I do not have to name them.

During the Second World War, we did not have very much money, and things were rationed to the hilt. We had no radio, and of course picture shows were too costly for us as a family to attend. During most of the day, after mom fixed dad his lunch, and washed up from the breakfast meal, there was absolutely nothing to do but kick rocks in the yard.

Not as now, but back then, neighbors always looked after neighbors. They had quilting bees, they traded clothes with what would fit the kids next door, and they amused themselves as they could.

The real hit then were Jigsaw puzzles®. We would trade them with neighbors and find enjoyment piecing them together. I could only find the end and corner pieces, and that was my job.

Well one day my sister brought home two new puzzles. They looked absolutely like it would take dad to finish them if and when he got a chance to get off early enough to help.

Those of that time didn't have but one small light bulb in each room, which gave little light to do anything after dark, and dad seldom got home before way after dark.

Well mom and the girls set out turning over the pieces. It was going to be a challenge because this puzzle had 500 pieces; far more than the normal. With all the excitement that could never be understood by this generation, we set out to put all the pieces in their proper piles, set the box top in such a manner so all could see the general lay of what it was going to look like, and proceeded.

The Layman

Now if one has never done this, you first get the end and corner pieces in one spot, the sky in another, the vegetation in yet another, then look for any prominent landmarks and gather those suspected pieces in one area as well.

After spending over half of the day figuring where everything went, we were making little or no progress. Well, we had some things which matched with others, but there just wasn't any real continuity. Some of the end pieces seem to fit, but the colors just didn't quite satisfy the eye. My older sister had a little house put together, but for some reason we could not find that little house on the box top.

In frustration, mom gathered all the pieces together and put them back in the box. She then got the other puzzle down and we went through the same procedure once more of separating the pieces into their suspected grouping, putting the box top in view, then attacking the end and corners.

Again, frustration set in. It was late in the afternoon, and mom had to start preparations for supper, though she never cooked it until dad came home. Back then one didn't work 9-5 in those days: They worked light to dark.

About that moment dad came in, which was rather unusual. My sister was toying with the puzzle and murmuring about this and that. Dad crossed the room studied the puzzle pieces and asked her why she didn't get the right box top for the puzzle she was working on so she would know the total picture? Mom came hurriedly in the room and with amazement looked at the box top that was supposed to represent the puzzle, only now, to see right in the middle of the picture, a small house.

My sister looked at the puzzles at her friend's house, and they had accidentally swapped the lids. From that day forward, mom never looked at the lid to see what the puzzle would turn out like.

What is my point? Perhaps the following should have been amalgamated into the book at the fall of Woman, but I felt myself unwilling to do so from lack of editorial experience.

I made a brief parallel between the LORD/ Satan, Adam/Eve, Cain/Able...etc. I made a comparison between Adam and our Lord in that Adam was never tempted, but knew because of his love for Woman, when he took that fruit from his little wife, he would be giving his life for her, and that our Lord knew when He took the fruit of that cross, He was giving His life for His bride, the Church.

There is another, silent, between the lines story that I have never heard a single Bible expositor even hint at. A most beautiful story missed by oh so many. It was Woman, later named Eve, who brought sin into the bosom of us all. **By her rebellion**, sin was brought to all mankind.

Mary, **by her obedience**, was the one who was instrumental in bringing to us the fruit of the womb, the Christ, which would take that sin away.

Allow me to point out another thing few have seen. Christ was not 100% Hebrew: Christ was in reality, I say with joy in my heart, a **half-breed**. What we have missed is that in the genealogy of our Lord **there are four silently hidden women:** representative of every tribe on earth, who reunited the worlds MtDNA chain of **ALL** mankind, right back into the blood stream of Jesus.

Look at: Mat 1:5 And Salmon begat Booz of **Rachab**, an **Amorite**; Gen 12—26 see the incest of Judah with his daughter in law **Tamar** who was an "**Adullamite**"; Gen 4:13 we have **Ruth** of the "**Moabites**", then in 2 Sam 11: we have **Bathsheba** a "**Hittite:**" All four in the linage of, not Joseph, but of **the linage of Mary as found in the Book of Luke.**

If I were a genetic researcher, I could do this, oh so much more justice. There is a song with a line which goes something like this, **"When He was on the cross that day, I was on His mind."** Well precious, when He was on the cross that faithful day, the blood our Lord shed, carried the genetic DNA of **every race (yours and mine) on the face of the earth.** Jesus did not die only for the sins of the Hebrews, but the sins of ALL the world.

Remember the LORD God telling Adam, *"and unto dust shalt thou return?* When that Roman spear pierced our Savior's side, *"...and forthwith came there out blood and water..:"* The world's genetic blood flowed through His heart, and when it fell to the dust of the earth, the curse that was put forth on our Grandfather Adam, was, for those who accept Him, nullified, and that was our chance of deliverance; by overcoming not only the curse, but death also.

MtDNA is carried by the woman. Eve's MtDNA was passed on to her girls, who at that time married their brothers. Later those same three couples on the Ark the genetics flowed throughout the world. In Gen: 10: Sham, the Hebrews; Japheth the Gentiles of Europe and Asia Minor, and Ham of Africa, Babylon, and Nineveh.

The Layman

Satan thought he had won when the male genealogy was destroyed by the wicked king Jechonias, when in Jer 22:30 *"Thus saith the LORD, <u>Write ye this man childless,</u> a man [that] shall not prosper in his days: for* **<u>no man of his seed shall prosper, sitting upon the throne of David,</u>** *and ruling any more in Judah."*.

Satan must have sneered, "Now what was God going to do. I have made Him break His final plan." Boy has Satan been duped from the very beginning.

It was through the lustful **rebellion** of woman that sin entered into this world, and it was His plan, hidden in "**thy seed,**" that through the submissive **obedience** of a humble young girl, "Mary," that He hid so well His plan to take it out. That is what Satan missed. He was looking for the linage of our Lord to come from the men of Scripture.

You see! **That was the little hidden house of God's puzzle**. Satan had the wrong box top, and precious believer: Some **Preachers** and **Scientist, when it comes to pre-historical records,** keeps putting the wrong lid up for all of us to look at. All we have are a bunch of pieces that make up small segments of His whole picture.

The prime reason for pastors not becoming involved with what I have presented is that their calling is to save the lost, and bring them to the knowledge of the Gospel of Jesus Christ, and they fear that the congregations will feel they are siding with science.

The prime reason evolution scientist are not getting involved with what I have presented is that they have as their agenda, the motivation to prove a godless universe, and they fear that their colleagues will feel they are becoming a Christian.

Never forget: your piece may or not fit all of mine, and mine may or may not fit someone else's, but they still fit the divine lid in their order: **They all fit His puzzle; yes they do.**

You see! Only our Father knows what the lid looks like. He made the scene, cut it into pieces and gave little handfuls so we could figure it out, one piece at a time.

We may never know the whole picture, but that does not prevent, nor should it deter us from searching for that picture.

The problem with the Christian world today is that we have so many lazy eagles, and so few willing turtles.

Tell me not in mournful numbers,
Life is but an empty dream!
For the soul is dead that slumbers
And things are not what they seem.
Life is real! Life is earnest!
And the grave is not its goal;
Dust thou art; to dust returnest,
Was not spoken of the soul.

Henry Wadsworth Longfellow

God Bless

THE   LAYMAN

233

APPENDIX

SCIENTISTS PONDER:

Here is a list of unanswered questions that drive scientists forward. The first of the list are the 25 prominent ones chosen by The Science Magazine. For further information on this and many other worthwhile questions, visit www.sciencemag.org/sciext/125th.

What Is the Universe Made Of?
What is the Biological Basis of Consciousness?
Why Do Humans Have So Few Genes?
To What Extent Are Genetic Variation and Personal Health Linked?
Can the Laws of Physics Be Unified?
How Much Can Human Life Span Be Extended?
What Controls Organ Regeneration?
How Can a Skin Cell Become a Nerve Cell?
How Does a Single Somatic Cell Become a Whole Plant?
How Does Earth's Interior Work?
Are We Alone in the Universe?
How and Where Did Life on Earth Arise?
What Determines Species Diversity?
What Genetic Changes Made Us Uniquely Human?
How Are Memories Stored and Retrieved?
How Did Cooperative Behavior Evolve?
How Will Big Pictures Emerge from a Sea of Biological Data?
How Far Can We Push Chemical Self-Assembly?
What Are the Limits of Conventional Computing?
Can We Selectively Shut Off Immune Responses?
Do Deeper Principles Underlie Quantum Uncertainty and No locality?
Is an Effective HIV Vaccine Feasible?
How Hot Will the Greenhouse World Be?
What Can Replace Cheap Oil -- and When?
Will Malthus Continue to Be Wrong?